MACROECONOMICS
Truths and Myths

Brian K. Strow and
Claudia W. Strow

Kendall Hunt
publishing company

Cover image courtesy Craig White

Kendall Hunt
publishing company

www.kendallhunt.com
Send all inquiries to:
4050 Westmark Drive
Dubuque, IA 52004-1840

ISBN 978-0-7575-9730-5

Printed in the United States of America

10 9 8 7 6 5 4 3 2 1

Dedication

To Tucker, Colette, Oliver, and Thatcher

Contents

Part IV Modeling Short Term Fluctuations

Part V Fiscal Policy

Part VI Problems with Fiscal Policy

Part VII Monetary Policy

Part VIII Fiscal and Monetary Policy in an International Context

Preface

When our oldest son lost his first tooth, he was very excited. Others in his school had lost teeth and had been rewarded with money. He came to us with his tooth in hand and asked with bright eyes, "Is the Tooth Fairy real, or is it like Santa Claus?" From the very beginning we had explained to him that Santa Claus wasn't real. After asking if he really wanted to know the truth, we responded that the Tooth Fairy too was not real. His little face became totally dejected. We told him not to worry, that we would still place money under his pillow in the middle of the night. He responded, in a still very dejected manner, "Yes, but if the Tooth Fairy was real, our family would have more money. Since it isn't, our family isn't any richer; you have just taken money from you and given it to me."

Our son was only four years old at the time of that exchange, and he already knew the difference between wealth creation and income transfers. He also knew that Santa Claus, The Easter Bunny, The Tooth Fairy, and The Great Pumpkin didn't exist. Free stuff isn't just delivered to houses via sleighs and baskets. Wealth has to be created, and it can be destroyed. The purpose of this textbook is to teach students to be able to separate macroeconomic truths from myths.

Popular macroeconomic myths include, but are not limited to, the belief in macroeconomic equilibrium, infallibility of aggregate data, collective decision making, underconsumption, spending multipliers, and long run economic death. Abstractly believing in myths doesn't have to hurt anyone, but if the belief in myths causes people to take harmful actions, we have a problem.

We find Don Quixote to be so fundamentally annoying not because he has mistaken beliefs, but because he actively harms innocent people based upon his mistaken beliefs. Don Quixote's apprentices account for the vast majority of macroeconomics professors in existence. The macroeconomic textbooks they write are not only full of myths, they are actively harmful. They create a false world of macroeconomic equilibrium in order to suggest solutions that are internally logical to their model, but inherently false to reality.

The Don Quixotes love to assume that there is some type of macroeconomic equilibrium that sits around just waiting for "shocks" to knock it out of equilibrium. The world is full of shocks, and even more surprises. Every day is a shock to some economic actor. No shop keeper knows exactly how many customers she'll have the next day. No consumer knows exactly what they will buy over the next year.

The truth is that individuals make decisions based on their perceived rational self-interest. They face uncertainty about the future and hold imperfect information about the world around them today. They act, and react, to the actions of others. People are responsive beings. Disequilibrium is the norm rather than the aberration. Prices of products constantly change. People move from one job to the next. Product lines get added and deleted. The economy is in motion and will continue to stay in motion as it is constantly battered by a myriad of forces reacting against each other.

Purveyors of macroeconomic equilibrium are often one and the same as those who advocate intervention in the economy to bring it back to equilibrium. They act as if not only is there equilibrium, but that they know where it is and how to get there. No one knows exactly how many ice cream cones the US needs to produce tomorrow. No one can know the "appropriate" amount of ice cream cone production for today let alone for tomorrow. The $15 trillion US economy makes a lot more than just ice cream cones.

There is no appropriate level of consumer spending. Therefore, there can never be over or under consumption. There is no set percentage of an economy that needs to be devoted to investment. Therefore there is never any over or under investment. What can exist are bad consumption and investment decisions due to imperfect information about the future. Policies that aim to increase consumption, investment, government spending, or exports in the short run are not only based on belief in fictitious equilibriums, they do damage to long run economic growth by misallocating resources.

Calls for economic stimulus packages are often advocated by politicians with short time horizons and ulterior motives. People engage in actions that they believe to be in their rational self interest. Unless someone out there knows how many ice cream cones the economy is supposed to be making, the appropriate price to sell them at, and who gets the cones, we should leave it up to the dairy farmer to determine his milk output, the ice cream company to determine their ice cream output, and the individual ice cream consumers to determine how much ice cream is "appropriately" consumed.

We're willing to bet that individuals wouldn't put themselves into $14 trillion of debt to buy ice cream. That kind of economic damage can only be done by someone mistakenly trying to fix that which was not broken, thereby breaking it in the process. How many people must the macroeconomic Don Quixotes hurt before they are held accountable? This text intends to do just that.

The first part of this text is dedicated to the truths of long term economic growth. It attempts to explain why some countries are wealthier than others and how all economies can grow. The latter part of the book is dedicated to examining business cycles and government intervention therein. Students need to understand the Keynesian framework and its underlying assumptions to be able to assess its merit/lack thereof.

Students won't be required to believe in Santa Claus, but they need to understand that other people do. They need to be able to communicate with myth believers on their level. The inclusion in this text of myths such as macroeconomic equilibrium should in no way be misread as meaning that the authors believe in them. Rather, the boogey man is defined and exposed so that students will know not to be afraid of him in their sleep.

Finally, in this text we seek to weave the study of economic history, the history of economic thought, political economy, public finance, and public choice into the our examination of introductory macroeconomics. In this way we hope to improve students understanding of how and why government policies have affected wealth creation over time.

Chapter 1

Why Study Macroeconomics?

The world is full of choices. **Economics** is a social science that examines people's choices in a world of unlimited wants and limited resources. It assumes that people pursue their rational self-interest as they see fit. The study of economics also examines the intended and unintended consequences of these choices. **Macroeconomics** is the study of wealth creation and destruction among groups of people. In this way, macroeconomics examines the economy as a whole by exploring how people's choices work to create or destroy wealth over time within societies, countries, and all over the world.

Wealth Creation and Destruction

At any given point in time, there are only so many **resources** (natural resources, labor, human capital, capital, technology, and entrepreneurship) that can be used to create wealth. **Natural resources** are the material sources of wealth that exist in a natural state, including the land upon which production occurs. **Labor** refers to the time humans spend producing. **Capital** is a long lasting tool used for production. **Human capital** is the education, skill set, experience, and knowledge that people have. **Physical Capital** refers to forms of capital that are not human, such as a machine or factory. **Technology** specifically describes new tools used for production or electronic forms of capital. New technology is one possible product of entrepreneurship. **Entrepreneurship** refers to combining resources in a new or innovative way or risk taking. This includes inventing new products or product lines, improving the quality of existing products, increasing the efficiency of existing production and distribution, engaging in arbitrage or risk taking, and connecting sellers with buyers or connecting financiers with producers. [1]

Each of these resources is **scarce**. Scarcity exists when something is limited. If you are a college student, you may find yourself with lots of free time. On the other hand, you may be working and going to school full-time and may have very little free time. Either way, I would imagine most college students feel that time is scarce. Even if they have a lot of free time, they still would like to have more time in the day. As your time is limited, you must make decisions about how to allocate it. Will you go out tonight with friends or stay in and study? Will you study one subject in great detail or will you study for several classes in less detail? Just as you decide how to allocate your scarce time, society must make choices as to how to allocate scarce resources as it determines what to produce, how to produce it, and for whom to produce.

Who decides the answers to these questions? In a **free market economy**, individuals make decisions about what to produce, how to produce, and who gets the output. In a **command economy**, the government makes these decisions for its people. In reality, every country has some level of government intervention in their economy. **Mixed economies** occur when some economic decisions are made by individuals and others are made by governments. The US economy, then, is best described as a mixed economy.

Unlike energy, wealth can be created or destroyed. To paraphrase George Orwell, all economies are equal but some economies are more equal than others.[2] In 1651, Thomas Hobbes described the natural state of mankind as being "solitary, poor, nasty, brutish, and short."[3] For most of human history, life expectancy at

---

[1] The role of each of these resources will be discussed in further detail in Chapters 4, 5, and 6.

[2] The original quote from George Orwell's novel, *Animal Farm* reads, "All animals are equal but some animals are more equal than others."

[3] Thomas Hobbes. *The Leviathan*

birth remained under 40 years of age and most people's major economic concerns revolved around oft-rotting food, simple clothing, make-shift shelter, and herbal "remedies."

Then along came the industrial revolution, whose roots, according to Deirdre McCloskey, were in the **bourgeois revolution** which started in Holland and moved to Britain and its offshoots.[4] This cultural revolution changed people's attitudes regarding the morality of wealth creation. Life in the industrial world is no longer defined according to Hobbesian lamentation. Most of the world's wealth has been created in a relatively short period of time. This fact is easy to see thanks to Swedish statistician, Hans Rosling, who has provided a *You Tube* presentation on world economic growth for 200 countries over the last 200 years.[5]

Even more quickly than wealth can be created, it can be destroyed. Choices that result in wars, most notably civil wars, can lead to rapid wealth destruction. Choices that change the economic rules of the game also can make countries poorer. Zimbabwe was once the bread basket of Africa. Now, due largely to poor decisions made by Robert Mugabe, Zimbabwe is one of the poorest places on earth.

The year 1776 marked an important year for the study of macroeconomics in the US context. Two major things happened in that year. One was that the US declared independence from Great Britain, thereby creating a new economy. The other was that Adam Smith first published his book, *An Inquiry into the Nature and Causes of the Wealth of Nations.*[6] Smith wanted to understand why some countries become wealthier than others.

A lot has changed in the US economy since 1776. Table 1.1 illustrates that GDP per capita (average output per person) in the US increased by almost sixty

Table 1.1[7]

Year	GDP Per Capita (1990 dollars)
1700	$527
1820	$1,257
1860	$2,178
1900	$4,091
1940	$7,010
1980	$18,577
2006	$31,049

[4] Deirdre McCloskey. *Bourgeois Dignity*

[5] Hans Rosling. "200 Countries, 200 Years, 4 Minutes – The Joy of Stats – BBC Four", http://www.youtube.com/watch?v=jbkSRLYSojo

[6] Adam Smith. *An Inquiry into the Nature and Causes of The Wealth of Nations*

[7] From Angus Maddison's, *Historical Statistics of the World Economy: 1–2006 AD*

times between 1700 and 2006. Never has the US produced so much output. The US economy now produces over $15 trillion worth of goods and services per year. As Table 1.2 shows, this makes the US economy the largest economy in the world. But is it the best?

Table 1.2[8]

Rank	Country	2010 GDP in billions of US dollars	Rank	Country	2010 GDP in billions of US dollars
1	United States	$14,657,800	6	Russia	$2,222,957
2	China	$10,085,708	7	United Kingdom	$2,172,768
3	Japan	$4,309,432	8	Brazil	$2,172,058
4	India	$4,060,392	9	France	$2,145,487
5	Germany	$2,940,434	10	Italy	$1,773,547

Determining Who is "Best"

The term "best" is a normative term. Normative terms are opinions and so are value laden. **Normative economics** refers to value laden economic analysis. Like beauty, "best" is in the eye of the beholder. Still, one's determination of "best" is likely to be grounded in positive facts. **Positive economics** refers to economic analysis that is testable and fact based. If the "best" economy produces the most output per person, then the US does not have the "best" economy, Qatar does (see Table 1.3). If the "best" economy is one that produces the most wealth for the largest number of people, then the US economy, being the world's largest, is the best. The US is the only country to rank in the top ten in both output and output per person.

[8] International Monetary Fund 2010 GDP Rankings, World Economic Outlook Database, April 2011

Table 1.3[9] TOP 10 GDP PER CAPITA IN INTERNATIONAL DOLLARS

Rank	Country	2010 Per Capita GDP (PPP)	Rank	Country	2010 Per Capita GDP (PPP)
1	Qatar	$88,559	7	United States	$47,284
2	Luxembourg	$81,383	-	Hong Kong	$45,736
3	Singapore	$56,522	8	Switzerland	$41,663
4	Norway	$52,013	9	Netherlands	$40,765
5	Brunei	$48,892	10	Australia	$39,699
6	United Arab Emirates	$48,821			

Table 1.4[10] 2011 INDEX OF ECONOMIC FREEDOM WORLD RANKINGS

Rank	Country	Rank	Country
1	Hong Kong	6	Canada
2	Singapore	7	Ireland
3	Australia	8	Denmark
4	New Zealand	9	United States
5	Switzerland	10	Bahrain

Still, "best" might refer to other factors than merely production. If the "best" economy simply is the one that produces the most goods, slavery might be seen by some as "best" if it produces more output than a free society. If the "best" economy is the one that provides the most economic freedom for individuals, then Hong Kong has the "best" (most free market) economy according to the Heritage Foundation (see Table 1.4). A similar comparison can be made between US states (see Table 1.5). Does wellbeing depend solely on money or freedom? Denmark tops the list of happiest countries in the world (see Table 1.6). The government of Bhutan is so concerned with happiness that their national goal is to maximize gross national happiness rather than gross national product.

---

[9] Ibid.

[10] *2011 Heritage Foundation Index of Economic Freedom World Rankings*

Table 1.5[11] **STATE ECONOMIC FREEDOM**

Rank	State	State	(2008) Per Capita Gross State Product
1	South Dakota	Connecticut	56,272
2	New Hampshire	New Jersey	51,358
3	Colorado	Massachusetts	51,254
4	North Dakota	New York	48,753
5	Idaho	Wyoming	48,608
6	Georgia	Maryland	48,378
7	Texas	Virginia	44,224
8	Tennessee	Alaska	44,039
9	Missouri	California	43,641
10	Alabama	New Hampshire	43,623

Hong Kong

The goal of this book is not to instruct students as to which is the "best" economy in the world because the answer to which is "best" depends on the values of the readers. Rather, through use of positive facts, readers are encouraged to determine what the "best" economy looks like and learn the appropriate policies that would achieve a bettering of an economy.

Nevertheless, most people think of wealth creation as a good thing. Most people would rather have more and better food than less food or rotten food. Most people would rather live in a house than be homeless. Most people would prefer to wear clothes and have access to life enhancing and extending health care than be naked and without access to health care. Wealth cannot be consumed until it is created. As a result, the authors assume that one reason to study macroeconomics is out of a desire to understand how countries can create wealth over time to make the world a place in which increasingly more people can have a larger number of their needs and wants met.

[11] William Ruger and Jason Sorens, "Freedom in the 50 States, An Index of Personal and Economic Freedom" Mercatus Center, George Mason University, February 2009 and 2011 Statistical Abstract of the US Census

Table 1.6[12] **HAPPINESS RANKINGS**

Rank	Country	Region	% Thriving	% Struggling	% Suffering
1	Denmark	Europe	82	17	1
2	Finland	Europe	75	23	2
3	Norway	Europe	69	31	0
4	Sweden	Europe	68	30	2
4	Netherlands	Europe	68	32	1
6	Costa Rica	Americas	63	35	2
6	New Zealand	Asia	63	35	2
8	Canada	Americas	62	36	2
8	Israel	Asia	62	35	3
8	Australia	Asia	62	35	3
8	Switzerland	Europe	62	36	2

What's Ahead

The first seven chapters of this text focus on addressing the same question addressed by Adam Smith, why are some countries richer than others? This discipline in Smith's time was known as **political economy**. It was so named because government intervention in the economy, or lack thereof, has a profound impact on the growth rate of economies. For that matter, our notion of "an economy" is often that of a nation-state's economy. Since data is collected at national levels, economies tend to be defined by political borders where the subjects therein live and work within the institutional rules of the game set up by their respective government.

Governments can, and do, change over time. Politicians can be voted out of office. Monarchs can be beheaded; dictators can be overthrown. When campaigning for the US presidency in 1992, Governor Bill Clinton's famous political tagline was "It's the economy, stupid." Politics, and therefore government institutions, shape, and are shaped by, macroeconomic conditions.

Macroeconomics, as a discipline, came out of The Great Depression. People wanted to understand not just long term economic trends in an economy, but also why economic growth does not happen every year at the same pace. Throughout history, the economy has experienced **business cycles**. Periods of rapid growth and economic contraction scatter historical economic growth graphs (see Figure 1.1).

[12] Forbes Magazine, July 14, 2010 "Happiness: The World's Happiest Countries"

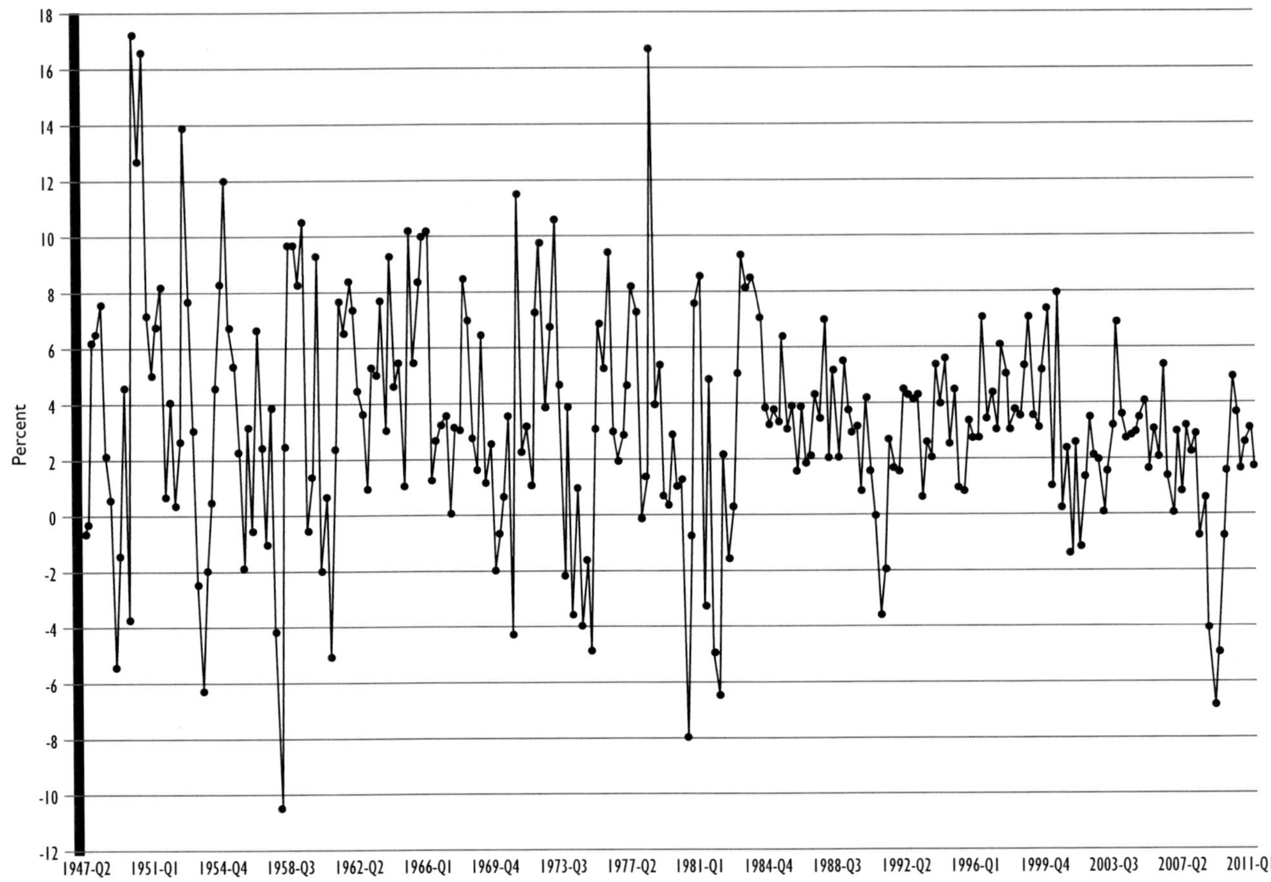

Source: U.S. Bureau of Economic Analysis

Figure 1.1 **CHANGES IN REAL GDP BY QUARTER 1947 TO 2011**
U.S. Bureau of Economic Analysis

Along with changing growth rates come the Scylla and Charybdis[13] (rock and a hard place) of price and employment instability. When average price levels increase, that is **inflation**. When they decrease, that is **deflation**. Volatile prices and **unemployment** tend to dominate short term political considerations. Unemployed workers translate into unhappy voters. People hurt by inflation (such as that of the late 1970's) and deflation (such as that of the late 1800's) often turn their anger to politicians as well. The late nineteenth century/early twentieth century politician William Jennings Bryan won the Democratic Party's presidential nomination three times on a pro-inflation platform only to lose in all three attempts to secure the US presidency.

In the 1930's John Maynard Keynes wrote, *The General Theory*[14] which focused on short term fluctuations in the economy. It is from this book that modern macroeconomics became a discipline that tried to explain, and smooth out, short term economic fluctuations. Keynes' economic analysis was confined to the short run economy because he said, "...in the long run, we are all dead."[15]

[13] A reference from Homer's *Odyssey* where Odysseus must choose to sail between two monsters

[14] John Maynard Keynes, *The General Theory of Employment, Interest, and Money*. 1936

[15] Ibid.

The two Keynesian macroeconomic tools are fiscal and monetary policy. **Fiscal policy** involves changing the level of taxes and government spending to minimize economic fluctuations. In the US, fiscal policy is largely handled by Congress and the President – though state and local governments sometimes conduct fiscal policy actions as well. **Monetary policy** involves increasing or decreasing the money supply to minimize economic fluctuations. In the US, monetary policy is handled by the central bank known as **The Federal Reserve**.

After chapter seven, the remaining chapters of the text are concerned with short term fluctuations in the economy. This portion of the test begins by defining and clarifying the economic problems of unstable growth, prices, and employment. The examination then turns to how Keynesian fiscal and monetary policies are designed to smooth out these economic conditions.

The study of macroeconomics has come a long way since the 1930's. Along the way, Keynesian policies have been critiqued to point out flaws in the theoretical and practical uses of fiscal and monetary policy. This text will include those critiques. Keynesian economic policies were all the rage until the 1980's. Nobel Prize winning economists such as Friedrich Von Hayek and Milton Friedman had been critiquing Keynesian economic policies from nearly their inception. Yet, it was only after the **stagflation** (high unemployment and high inflation rates) of the 1970's along work done by Robert Lucas that the world began to take such criticisms seriously. The PBS series, *Commanding Heights*[16], succinctly illustrates the long standing debate on government intervention in the economy.

Advanced macroeconomic theory has moved on since the days of Keynes and Hayek. Those who still prefer the use of government intervention are now known as **neo-Keynesians**, while those who prefer less government intervention are either **neo-classical economists**, or **neo-Austrian economists**. Most economists would agree that Keynes was the most influential economist of the first half of the twentieth century, while Milton Friedman who contradicted most of Keynes work was the most influential economist of the second half of the twentieth century. While the neo-Keynesian framework had successfully been critiqued, neo-Keynesian economic policy made a huge political comeback following the recession of 2008-2009.

In the end, the US economy is not an economic island. Its uses of fiscal and monetary policy impact, and are impacted by, the global economy. It is therefore important to study the US economy in an international context in order to advocate economic policies consistent with reality.

---

[16] PBS series *Commanding Heights*

Ideas matter. By studying how countries become wealthier, or poorer, over time, students can become better advocates of government policies designed to meet their objectives. By studying short term economic fluctuations, students also can learn about the pros and cons of adopting short term economic "fixes" to the economy. Why study macroeconomics? For the same reason people study anything; to better understand and improve the world.

Glossary

Bourgeois revolution—a cultural revolution that began in Holland that changed people's attitudes regarding the morality of wealth creation

Business cycles—periods of economic growth interrupted by temporary economic contractions

Capital—a long lasting tool used for production such as a machine or factory.

Command economy—an economy where governments make decisions about what to produce, how to produce, and who gets the output

Economics—a social science that examines people's choices in a world of unlimited wants and scarce resources

Deflation—a decrease in the average price level

Entrepreneurship—combining resources in a new or innovative way or risk taking

Federal Reserve—the central bank for the United States

Fiscal policy—changing the level of taxes and government spending to minimize economic fluctuations

Free market economy—an economy where individuals make decisions about what to produce, how to produce, and who gets the output

Human capital—the education, skill set, experience, and knowledge that people have

Inflation—an increase in the average price level

Labor—time humans spend producing

Macroeconomics—the study of wealth creation and destruction among groups of people

Mixed economy—an economy where both individuals and governments make decisions about what to produce, how to produce, and who gets the output

Monetary policy—increasing or decreasing the money supply to minimize economic fluctuations

Natural resources—the material sources of wealth that exist in a natural state, including the land upon which production occurs

Neo-Austrian economists—economists who focus on individual decision making who believe that fiscal and monetary policy are fundamentally counterproductive to achieving economic growth

Neo-classical economists—economists who focus on individual decision making who believe that fiscal and monetary policy have limited power in minimizing economic fluctuations

Neo-Keynesians—economists who advocate the use of fiscal policy and monetary policy to minimize economic fluctuations

Normative economics—value laden economic analysis

Political economy—the study of how government intervention in economies leads to wealth creation or wealth destruction

Positive economics—fact based economic analysis

Resources—inputs into the production process that include natural resources, labor, human capital, capital, technology, and entrepreneurship

Scarce—limited, not enough of something

Stagflation—high unemployment combined with high inflation

Technology—new tools used for production, or electronic forms of capital

Unemployment—inability of people to find a job despite actively seeking work

Questions for Review

1. What is economics? What does macroeconomics seek to study?
2. What type of economy best describes the US? Why?
3. How does normative economics differ from positive economics?
4. In your opinion, what type of economy is "best"? What values would you use to determine best?
5. Who is in charge of fiscal policy in the US? Who is in charge of monetary policy in the US?
6. What type of economists advocates government intervention into the economy to minimize economic fluctuations?
7. Name five of the world's top ten largest economies.
8. Name five of the world's top ten richest per capita economies. Name five of the top ten richest per capita US states.
9. Name five of the world's top ten happiest economies.
10. Name five of the world's top ten economically free economies. Name five of the top ten most economically free US states.
11. Which of the following statements is normative and which is positive?
    a. Capital gains taxes should be lowered to increase economic growth.
    b. If capital gains taxes are lowered, economic growth will increase.
    c. The current rate of unemployment is too high.
    d. The current rate of unemployment is 8.7%.
    e. Consumption has fallen since the US entered a recession.
    f. The US government should remove tariffs on sugar from other countries.

Chapter 2

Economic Decision Making

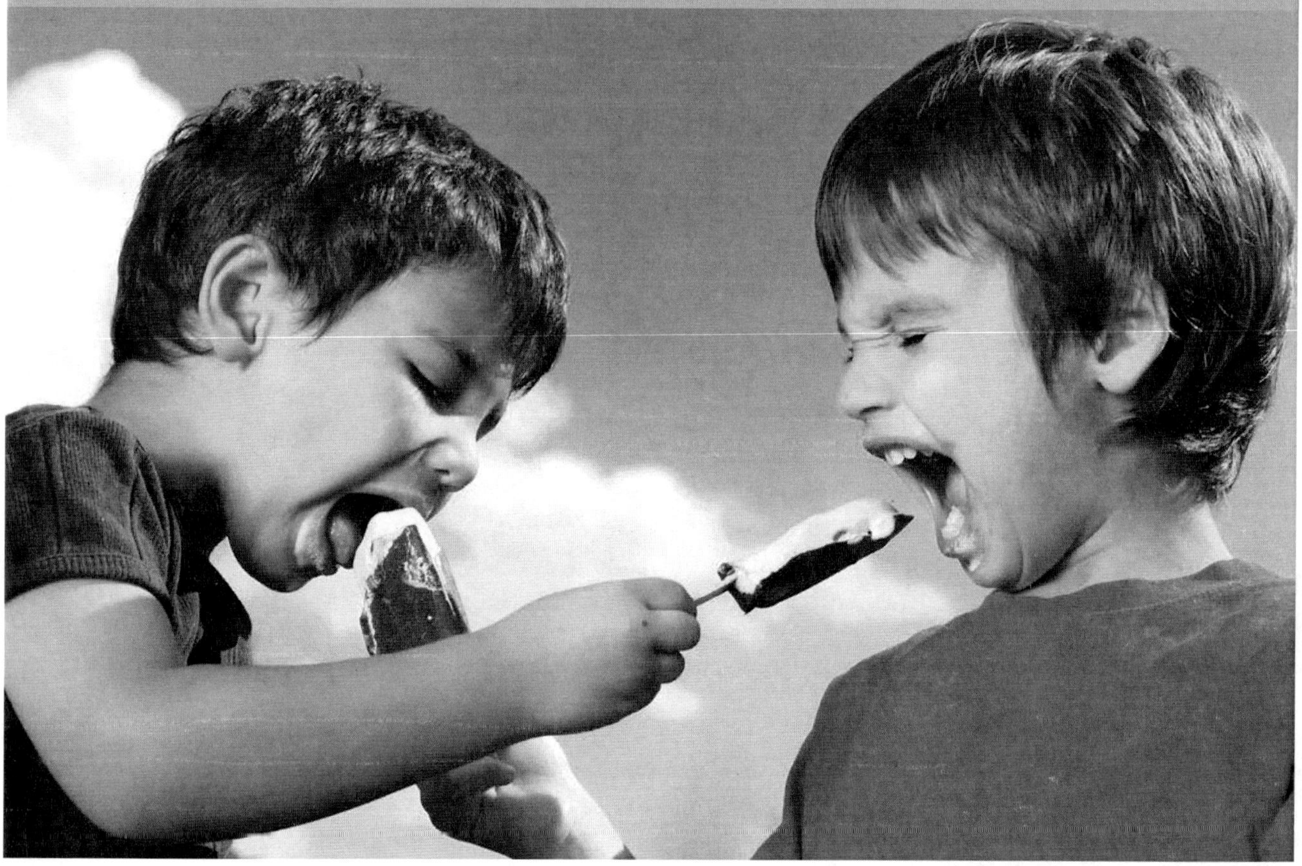

Individuals make decisions every day. College students decide what, if anything, they want for breakfast, whether or not to attend class, and which ball cap they will wear to class if they go. **Microeconomics** looks at individual decision making in a world of scarce resources and unlimited wants. Sure, most college students wants to earn an A in macroeconomics, but will they spend 168 hours a week studying for the one class? No, they won't. Studying is not free. It is not that they face a bill from their instructor every time they open up their text; it is that time is scarce. There are only so many hours in a week. This chapter examines the tradeoffs made in decision making, introduces a tool to help in the understanding of production tradeoffs, and begins the discussion of economic growth.

Opportunity Cost and Sunk Cost

So what does it cost to study an extra hour of macroeconomics? The true cost is known as opportunity cost. **Opportunity cost** is the cost of forgoing the next best alternative. It is the concept that illustrates that nothing in life is free. Everything has a cost. Because everything has a cost, people have to make choices between things that bring them pleasure relative to the costs that they impose.

"Who wants more ice cream?" The answer to that question is actually very complicated. Are you lactose intolerant? Have you already had 20 scoops of ice cream? Is the ice cream your preferred flavor? How much money does an additional scoop cost? If you weren't eating ice cream, what would you be eating or doing instead? Much like Isaac Newton's 3rd law of motion, every action has an equal and opposite reaction. In the physical universe, actions cause reactions. Choices have consequences, both intended and unintended.

In order for consumers to maximize their happiness, or business persons their profit, they must follow the **golden rule of economics**. Hint: it is not that he who has the gold rules. Rational happiness or profit maximization occurs when people engage in an action as long as the **marginal benefit** of that action is equal to or greater than the **marginal cost** of that action – including all relevant opportunity costs.

Opportunity costs occur both in the present and the future, but never in the past. That is, a decision made today has both immediate and long term consequences. However, in absence of a time machine, current decisions cannot change the past. The economic way of thinking is forward looking. Decisions that were made in the past can't be undone, and they are therefore irrelevant to the current decision making process. Costs incurred in the past that can't be undone are known as **sunk costs**. They are irrelevant to the rational decision making process.

Even reading a library book is not free.

What is the opportunity cost of continuing to read this chapter? Hint: it is not the price you paid for the book, because that is a sunk cost. Instead, the opportunity cost is whatever you are giving up in this time. Perhaps this is time sleeping, watching television, or working out. So, even if you have checked out this book for "free" at the library, reading it is certainly not free. (Nevertheless, we believe the marginal benefit of reading the book likely exceeds the marginal cost, so please continue on…).

Another example of the irrelevance of sunk cost can be found in the decision of the US federal government along with local government to bury I-95 under Boston. The project became known as "The Big Dig." They had an estimate that such a project would cost $2.5 billion dollars. Their calculations of the marginal benefits of this project were greater than that, so they went forward on construction. Information wasn't perfect and the final price tag ended up near $18 billion, much larger than the estimated marginal benefit of the project. In a world of perfect information, politicians would have had a much harder time selling the idea of the Big Dig to voters at a cost of $18 billion.

What if the estimated marginal benefit of the completed project was $7 billion? Surely, at the time of the first cost estimate, this seemed like a worthwhile project. The marginal benefit exceeded the marginal cost. When the costs hit $7 billion why didn't they stop the project? If there is no marginal benefit to a partially built highway, then the marginal benefit of finishing the project was still $7 billion. The marginal cost is only the cost going forward. The original $7 billion worth of expenses were a sunk cost. If they had stopped the project at spending $7 billion for no benefit – they would have lost $7 billion. If they believed that the marginal cost of completion was less than $7 billion, say $5 billion, then they would have spent a total of $12 billion to get $7 billion worth of benefit. Losing $5 billion isn't great, but it is better than losing $7 billion. Failure to ignore sunk costs causes people to make irrational decisions.

Macroeconomics looks at how groups of individuals make choices in a world of scarce resources and unlimited wants. Are consumers spending more and saving less? Are businesses borrowing and investing more? Do governments spend more on health care or less? Do people in foreign countries want to buy more goods from the US?

"Who wants more federal education spending?" Again, the answer is not that straightforward. How will the money be used to help education? Will it build buildings, provide texts, or pay teachers or administrators more? If the government increases education spending, what will it be replacing? Will it lower health care or defense spending? Will it reduce consumption or investment if taxes are raised to pay for the spending?

To know simply that the marginal benefit of an action is greater than zero does not provide enough information to determine if it is a good idea. It's like a one-handed clap, or a pair of one-sided scissors. Rational decisions must take the marginal cost of an action into account as well. Looking only at marginal costs in a vacuum is as equally illogical as only looking at marginal benefits. Do high speed trains have a marginal benefit to society? Yes. Do those marginal benefits exceed their marginal costs in low population density areas? Not likely.

Who Plans for Whom?

The study of macroeconomics is full of **tradeoffs** for society. Sometimes society faces tradeoffs between lower unemployment and lower inflation, between short term economic stability and long term economic growth, or between lower income inequality and economic growth. It's not enough to say that unemployment is "bad." The real question becomes what society has to give up in order to lower unemployment today. Does inflation increase as a result? Does future unemployment increase?

This is where macroeconomics runs into the problem of aggregation. What may be a good idea for one consumer or businessperson may be a bad idea for another. If there is a glut of unrented condos in Las Vegas, but a shortage of new homes in Austin, should the federal government encourage across the board construction of new residential units? Should government data crunchers be pleased when government policies increase the glut of unsold Las Vegas condos?

Individuals make decisions based not only on what they know, but also on what they think will happen in the future. Unfortunately, no one has perfect information about the future. In part that is because the future is determined not just by one individual's actions, but all of them together. If everyone else jumps off of a bridge, you still don't have to. Nevertheless, others jumping off the bridge may impact you if you are an ambulance driver, a doctor, or a performance artist in need of a flash mob.

If US consumers, as a whole, decrease their savings rate and increase their consumption rates but you do the opposite, are you helped or hurt? It depends. In a market economy their extra borrowing will give you an even greater return on your savings. If, however, the large number of borrowers turns to the government to bail them out of debt, then the government could ask the minority savers to foot the bill through higher taxes or less valuable money (by printing more).

Business people have to make choices about what to produce, how to produce it, and how to price their products. They too must work with imperfect information. Surely, yacht builders need to ponder the direction of the economy before they expand their businesses. If the economy is doing well, yacht sales should prosper. If the economy goes into recession, the demand for luxury items, like yachts, might fall.

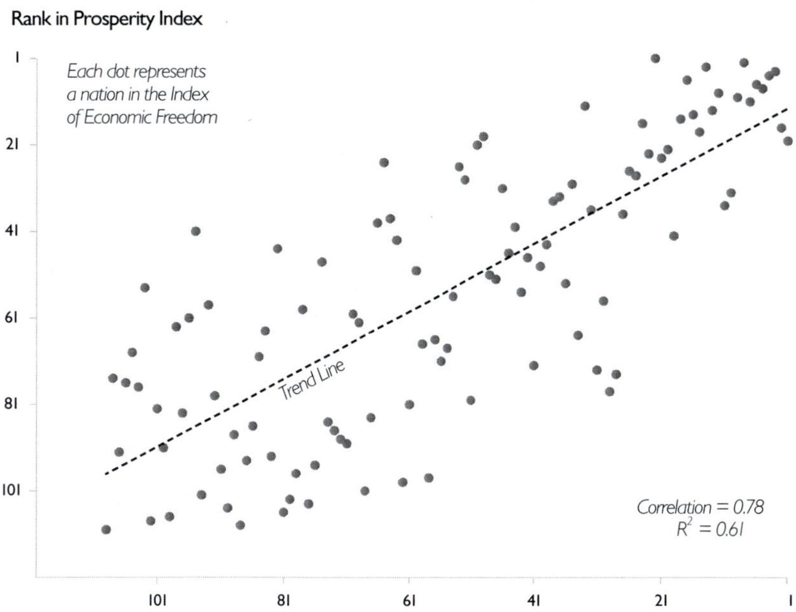

Chart 2.1 **ECONOMIC FREEDOM PROMOTES OVERALL WELL-BEING**

From 2011 Index of Economic Freedom by Heritage Foundation. Copyright © Heritage Foundation. Reprinted by permission.

It isn't always obvious how the decisions of others will impact your future decisions. As a result, people often make mistakes when planning for their future or the future of their businesses. The question is not one of whether or not dynamic planning needs to take place in an organized society. The question, as put forth by Friedrich Von Hayek becomes "who plans for whom?"

The economy doesn't grow at a steady pace. Business cycles have existed since recorded history. The sporadic nature of economic growth has implications on labor and capital markets. Unemployment and price changes (inflation/deflation) are consequences of business cycles which themselves are caused by imperfect information about the future.

One key question studied in the field of macroeconomics is what the role of government is in addressing the problems of unemployment or inflation. Because these problems are caused by a lack of perfect information, it becomes an open question as to who knows the most about the future wants and desires of people relative to the scarce amount of resources that exist both now and in the future.

The question of planning has been most distinctly addressed in the history of economic thought between Friedrich Von Hayek and Lord John Maynard Keynes. The former was of the belief that planning is best done by individuals who best knew their own tastes and preferences, while the latter believed that government experts, through the collection of macroeconomic data, could better direct the economy in such a way as to meet the goals of society. Karl Marx advocated that all of the means of production be under the control of the state while anarchists advocate that no economic decisions should be made by the state.

Chart 2.1 illustrates a clear trend between economic freedom and economic prosperity. On average, countries that allow individuals to make their own economic decisions experience greater wealth creation. Chart 2.2 shows that this is true for countries in every continent.

Who, then, is **society**? Macroeconomics, as a discipline, in generally studied in a national context, with society represented as the people living with a geographical nation state. In this way, macroeconomic study has often made very large assumptions. For instance, it assumes that the people within a society are the same. In this way, consumers can be talked about as a group of people. This may work

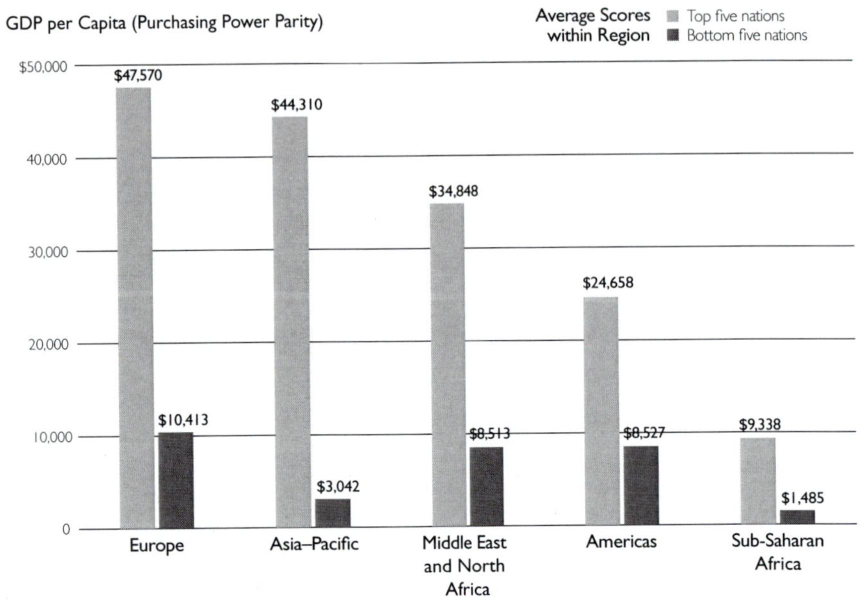

Chart 2.2 **ECONOMIC FREEDOM AND STANDARD OF LIVING**

From 2011 Index of Economic Freedom by Heritage Foundation.

for small groups of people whose social/religious traditions are the same, but it breaks down greatly as diverse people are aggregated over ever larger numbers.

To the extent that a local, state, or federal government seeks to plan economic activity, it must make assumptions as to what would be in the best interests of society. Government planning is more effective if the government guesses correctly about what it is that people want. Can a dictator or monarch predict well the wants and desires of society? How about an oligarchy or a representative democracy? What about a pure democracy? As soon as one travels down the road of government intervention in the economy, he or she not only has to ask who is planning for whom, but also why the plans are being made in this way.

Knowledge about the economy should aide individuals in a representative democracy in making voting choices that correspond to their individual values. The goal of this macroeconomic text is to make people of all ideologies better decision makers by better understanding the truths and myths behind the economy.

Production Possibilities and Economic Growth

Assume a simplified economy in the fictitious economy of Kent. Kent can produce only two goods, beer and cheese. Table 2.1 represents Kent's **production schedule**, the different production combinations available to them at a specific point in time. Also assume that all of Kent's resources are equally suited to beer and cheese production. As the country of Kent chooses (through either individual choice or government mandate) to produce more cheese, they must forgo the production of some beer. This is the opportunity cost they face for cheese production, forgone output of beer. In this case, every time that Kent increases the production of cheese by 50 blocks, they forgo the production of 200 kegs of beer. To find their opportunity cost of producing 1 block of cheese, one can set up the following ratio and solve for x:

$$\frac{50 \text{ blocks}}{200 \text{ kegs}} = \frac{1 \text{ block}}{x \text{ kegs}}.$$

The opportunity cost of 1 block of cheese is 4 kegs of beer.

Table 2.1 KENT'S PRODUCTION SCHEDULE

Beer (kegs)	Cheese (blocks)
800	0
600	50
400	100
200	150
0	200

Figure 2.3a plots the points from Kent's production schedule to form a **production possibilities frontier** (PPF for short). Kent's PPF is a graphical representation of all currently obtainable production options. The slope of Kent's PPF represents the opportunity cost of production between beer and cheese. Kent can choose to produce anywhere on or inside (to the bottom left) of the PPF. If they are producing at a point like point A, inside of the PPF, they are not currently using all of their resources for production. Perhaps some Kentians are unemployed. By employing them, Kent could increase the production of both beer and cheese.

If Kent is currently producing on its PPF, as in on points B or C, Kent is using all of its available resources for production and is said to be **productively efficient**. While points B and C are equally efficient from a production standpoint, there is nothing to say that they bring the same level of happiness to the citizens of Kent. Point D is currently outside of Kent's PPF. Point D is not currently obtainable but could be obtained in the future with the help of economic growth. See Figure 2.3b.

Economic growth, and therefore an expansion of a country's PPF, can happen for one of two reasons. Extensive economic growth occurs when more resources become available to a country. Increased immigration may increase the size of the labor force. New machines, tools, or factories could be built. New natural resources could be found. An increase in resources available for production increase the possible production bundles available to a society, but it does not guarantee that those new bundles are actually achieved.

Intensive economic growth occurs when existing resources are used to produce more output. An increase in output per unit of input represents an increase

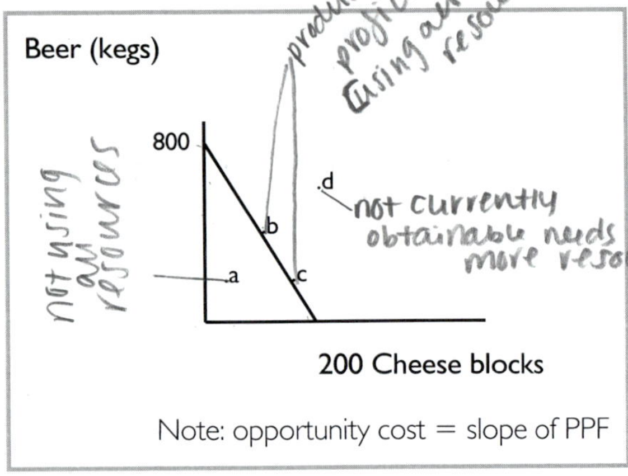

Figure 2.3a **KENT'S PRODUCTION POSSIBILITIES FRONTIER**

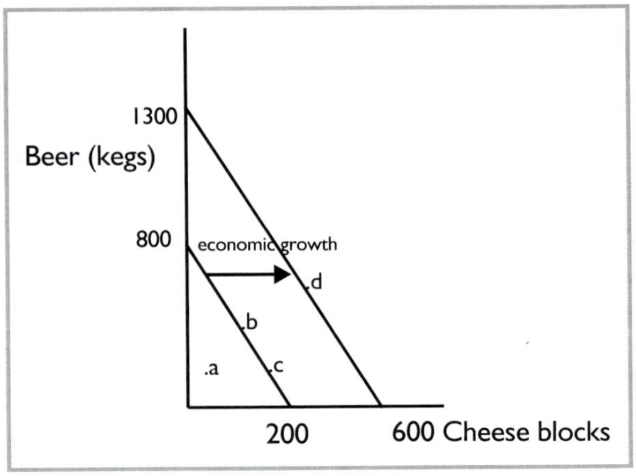

Figure 2.3b **KENT'S PRODUCTION POSSIBILITIES FRONTIER FOLLOWING ECONOMIC GROWTH**

in productivity. New technology, faster computers, and more skilled workers are just a few of the ways that productivity can be enhanced.

Notice that in Figures 2.3a and 2.3b, the PPF is a straight line and opportunity cost (represented by the slope of the PPF) is constant at -4 kegs of beer per block of cheese produced. In reality, not all resources are equally good at producing everything. Some land is more fertile than other land. Some workers, like surgeons or electricians, have specialized knowledge in their field of work. California dairy producers went so far as to claim that, "Great cheese comes from happy cows. Happy cows come from California." Can a surgeon milk a cow? They probably can. Is their opportunity cost of milking a cow higher than a trained dairy worker? Yes.

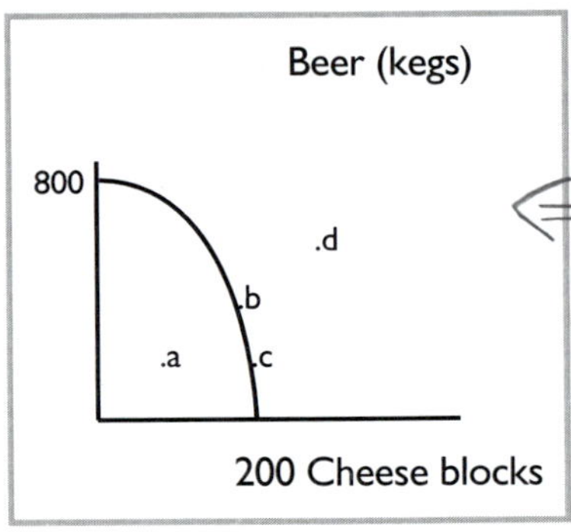

Figure 2.4 **A PRODUCTION POSSIBILITIES FRONTIER WITH SPECIALIZED RESOURCES**

Resources of all kinds are **specialized.** This means that the PPF for no country would be a straight line even if they only produced two goods. A curved PPF such as is illultrated in Figure 2.4 illustrates the **law of increasing opportunity cost** due to specialization. When resources are specialized and a country increases the production of one product, its opportunity cost of production increases. More and more resources have to be diverted from what they are good at producing to increase the production of something they are less able to produce. Specialization and trade allow a country to increase the productivity of their resources.

Chapters 3 through 7 are dedicated to understanding just how a country's PPF can expand over time. By opening up new production options, countries become better equipped at choosing the production bundles that are most to their liking.

Glossary

Golden rule of economics—rational economic action occurs when economic actors engage in actions whose marginal benefit exceed their marginal cost

Law of increasing opportunity cost—when resources are specialized, as the production of an output increases, so does its opportunity cost of production

Marginal benefit—the additional benefit incurred as the result of an action

Marginal cost—the additional cost incurred as the result of an action

Microeconomics—studies individual decision making in a world of scarce resources and unlimited wants

Opportunity cost—the cost of forgoing the next best alternative

Production possibility frontier (PPF)—a graphical representation of all currently obtainable production options

Production schedule—the different production combinations available to a country at a specific point in time

Productive efficiency—occurs when all current resources are being used in the production process. A PPF is a collection of productively efficient production options

Society—a group of people with shared interests, often used as a synonym for country in macroeconomic research

Specialized—having skills or traits that are not universally held

Sunk costs—costs incurred in the past that are irrelevant to current rational decision making

Tradeoff—relinquishment of one benefit in order to gain another

Questions for Review

1a. The country of Kent has 10 workers. Kent produces only two goods—diamond rings and alarm clocks. Suppose each worker can either make 12 rings or 4 clocks in one year (no workers are specialized). Draw the annual production possibilities frontier for Kent. Include labels and intercepts.

b. Suppose that the workers in Kent gained new clock technology such that they can now produce 8 clocks in a given year, but they can still only make 12 rings. Draw the new PPF.

2a. Given the production schedule below, what is the opportunity cost of producing 1 box?

Boxes	Rubber ducks
0	200
5	150
10	100
15	50
20	0

b. Graph the PPF for this country.

c. Does this PPF illustrate increasing opportunity costs?

3. Not So Curious George's Production Possibilities Frontier for one day:

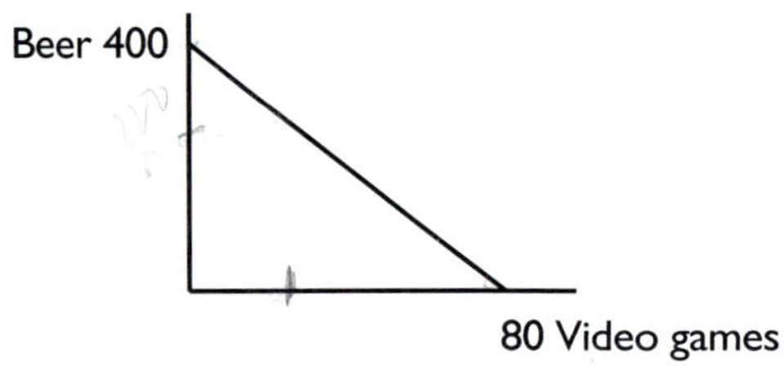

a. What is Not So Curious George's opportunity cost of producing 1 video game?

b. If Not So Curious George wanted to produce only 20 video games, how many beers could he produce in the same day?

4. Why might an economy be producing on the inside of its production possibilities frontier?

5. What leads to economic growth?

6. Why might a PPF take on a curved line instead of a straight line?

7. Why does planning need to take place in an economy?

8. Under what circumstances would you be better off if you made your own plans for your life or your business? Under what circumstances would you be better off if others made your life or business plans for you?

9. Why do tradeoffs exist?

10. What definition of society do you use? What definition should government officials use? Why?

11. What is opportunity cost? Sunk cost?

12. Suppose that Oliver has 3 choices for how to spend his afternoon and he prefers them in the order given. His first choice is to take his girlfriend to see a movie and purchase tickets for $20. His second choice is to go to the driving range and hit $20 worth of golf balls with a buddy. His third choice is to put $20 worth of gas into his motorcycle and go for a drive in the country. He only has time to do one of these choices. What is his opportunity cost of going to the movies?

Chapter 3 Gross Domestic Product

In order to survive, humans need to consume food and water, and they need shelter from the elements. In order to lengthen their life expectancy, they need to consume a diverse diet, drink clean water, use element-resisting clothing and shelter, and have access to health care. These often are called the material necessities of life. In addition to these necessities are life's conveniences. People desire to eat food that tastes good, beverages that fizzle with stimulant or relaxant effects, have shelter that provides heat in the winter and air conditioning in the summer, take cholesterol medicine to undo the effects of double-bacon cheeseburgers, and be educated and entertained by books, multi-media, and travel.

Wants for life's conveniences are unlimited. The chief economic problem is that at any given time resources are scarce. An apple, once eaten by Eve, cannot also be eaten by Adam. The challenge for the world's economy is to produce enough wealth each year to meet the needs and some of the wants of its inhabitants. With roughly seven billion people in the world, there are lots of needs and wants. It does not help that televisions do not grow on trees. Never before in world history have so many people had their needs and wants met. This is the result of wealth creation. To deny the need for wealth creation would be to deny the human race of existence.

As the world's population grows, more wealth must be created annually in order to meet the needs and wants of a larger population. Therefore, economic growth is important. An economy that produces the same amount of wealth with more people leaves each individual with fewer resources with which to meet their needs and desires. Furthermore, as people's needs and desires become increasingly met, they begin to expect even more wants to be met in the future. Unrealized expectations of future wealth do not tend to breed happiness or contentment.

Does this mean that people *ought* to make their happiness dependent upon material consumption? No, ought is a normative judgment. Money can't buy you love, but starving to death is also a drag. It turns out that people like to consume at least as much as those around them. Even as far back in time as the Ten Commandments, there were religious rules put in place that frowned upon covetousness. The desire to "keep up with the Jones's" causes people to desire ever more economic growth.

One task of macroeconomics is to determine if a country's economy is doing a better or worse job of meeting the needs and desires of the people who live in that country. It isn't a perfect science. The United States has over 300 million inhabitants and it is unrealistic that the government would be able to exactly know how much wealth was produced in any given year. In lieu of the exact answer, governments create proxy data that gives keen, but imperfect, insight into wealth creation. In this chapter, we will examine the most commonly reported measurements for production, outline imperfections with these measurements, and will examine some of the highest and lowest producing countries using these measurements.

Measuring Production

The most popular measure currently used around the globe to measure wealth creation is **Gross Domestic Product** (GDP). GDP is the total market value of all final goods and services produced within a given country in a given year. It is typically measured on a **quarterly** (3 month) basis. If GDP estimates are higher from one quarter to the next, the economy is considered to be growing. If GDP estimates are lower from one quarter to the next, the economy is considered to be contracting. A **recession** is a prolonged period of overall economic contraction.

Official dating of US recessions is handled by the **Business Cycle Dating Committee** at the National Bureau of Economic Research. According to the NBER, they define a recession as "a significant decline in economic activity spread across the economy, lasting more than a few months, normally visible in real GDP, real income, employment, industrial production, and wholesale-retail sales."[1]

GDP is a measure of production, not consumption, nor happiness. The idea is to count everything that is produced within a given quarter once and only once. If an orange is grown in Florida, shipped to Michigan, and sold at a grocery store to a consumer during one economic quarter then there are a number of productive steps that need to be accounted for. An orange farmer picked an orange, a trucker transported the orange, and the grocer housed, displayed, and advertised the orange. As a result, it is the final sales price of the orange that gets counted in GDP. That sales price takes into account all of the productive factors that went into the production of the orange. That being said, if an orange grows in a grove and nobody picks it, ships it, or markets it, GDP won't go up.

A technical problem arises when a good (such as an orange) is produced at one farm and then is transformed into a different good (orange juice) at a different plant. In this case the orange is an **intermediate good**. Intermediate goods are goods that go into the production of a final product and cannot be counted in GDP without resulting in a double counting of output. In this way, a new orange sold for direct consumption in the produce aisle has to be counted as a final product, whereas one that is used to produce a future product is not. Therefore it is not as easy as just counting oranges that come off of the farm to determine GDP.

What if the orange is produced at the end of a quarter and placed into a jar of marmalade at the beginning of the next quarter? Since GDP attempts to measure production that occurs in each quarter, the orange needs to count as having been produced in the previous quarter, and its value must be subtracted from the final sales price of the marmalade that is finished and sold in the second quarter. In this case, the orange is referred to as **inventory**. Inventory is production that has occurred, but with which no final sale, and therefore no sales receipt, has occurred.

What if the orange is grown in Mexico, but put into juice that is otherwise made in Ohio? US GDP only is supposed to count production that happens within the physical borders of the United States. Therefore, the value of the orange must be counted as it enters the US and subtracted from the final sale price of the juice to determine how much GDP went up by producing it.

[1] Public Information Office, National Bureau of Economic Research, Inc., 1050 Massachusetts Avenue, Cambridge MA 02138.

If an American juice company produces the whole juice in Mexico and sells it in Peru, US GDP won't increase at all. Conversely, if a foreign juice company produces juice in Ohio, the value of this juice is counted in US GDP. **Gross National Product** (GNP) measures the total market value of all final goods and services produced by a country's companies in a given year. GNP is not commonly used as a measure of an economy's health. A country's companies could shut down all of their domestic plants and move their jobs overseas, which may increase US GNP, but it would hurt US GDP. GDP does a better job than GDP of accounting for output derived from a country's resources.

The **Bureau of Economic Analysis** (BEA) is in charge of calculating GDP. They do so by employing the expenditure approach. They count up the demand for all final goods and services in the economy and break them into four categories: **consumption** (C), **investment** (I), **government spending** (G), and **net exports** (NX).

$$GDP = C + I + G + NX$$

© Joy Brown, 2012, under license Shutterstock, Inc.

© Ferenc Cegledi , 2012, under license Shutterstock, Inc.

If a final good or service (other than new residential construction) is purchased by a consumer, then that purchase is counted as consumption. For example, the purchase of a new car and the bill from a doctor's visit are each counted in GDP. The BEA tracks retail receipts and employment data to determine the levels of consumption in the US economy. If a consumer buys a used car for $5,000 from the used car lot, GDP does not go up by $5,000. The production of that car was counted when it was first produced. If the car dealership paid $3,000 to obtain the car and resold it for $5,000 then used car dealer services are said to have been provided and GDP would increase by $2,000.

The investment category includes the new purchase of capital, equipment, and software by businesses and governments, changes in inventory of unsold products, and the purchase of new homes by consumers. If a winery grows grapes and makes wine in a given year but places the wine bottles in their cellar to age, inventory levels increase by the cost of production, as does GDP for the year in which production took place. When the bottle is sold a year later for $40, consumption data will show an increase in GDP of $40, but investment data will show a decrease in inventory (say the $15 it took to produce the wine), and GDP on net will go up by $25 in the new year.

Government spending, for GDP purposes, is not the same as a government's budget. The only portions of the government's budget that gets counted in GDP are payments for final goods or services. If a teacher is paid by a government to teach for $40,000 a year, then GDP increases by that amount. If your grandmother is paid $24,000 a year in Social Security payments, those payments are not counted in GDP. Your grandmother, the lovely person that she may or may not be, does not produce a good or perform a service in exchange for her check, and GDP is a measure of production. Should your grandmother be paid by the USO to sing and dance for American troops, her salary would be included in GDP. Approximately two thirds of the US federal government's budget is made up of **transfer payments.** Transfer payments just take money from Peter to give it to Paul. They are not counted in GDP.

When the government pays people to provide national defense, it is considered to be a service and is counted as government spending even if the military serviceperson is physically stationed outside of the physical boundaries of the US. In such a way, US GDP was said to rise in WWII as the US government funded the war effort around the globe. In this case, while US employees and capital are being employed, the "within a country" definition is less precise. Public safety, however, is being consumed by people inside of the country.

If you buy a banana at the local grocery store, the odds are strong that that banana was not grown in the United States, yet a sales receipt for say, $1, would be generated. Consumption increases in GDP by $1. However, when that banana hit the US border, it had a value of less than a dollar (the cost of growing it and shipping it to the US), say 75 cents. This banana is an **import** and **net exports** count **exports** (X) minus imports (M). An export is something that is produced domestically but sold abroad. An import is something that is produced abroad but purchased domestically. By subtracting the 75 cents worth of production that happened overseas, net GDP only increases by the remaining 25 cents.

Reasons GDP is Not a Perfect Measurement of Wellbeing

GDP is an imperfect measure of production and an even more imperfect measure of wellbeing. As a measure of production, it fails to account for non-market activities and unreported incomes. If these are systematically repeated errors, then changes in GDP are still a reliable estimate of whether the economy is producing more or less than before.

Non market transactions are transactions that do not generate sales receipts or wage data. If you mow your own grass, you don't pay yourself for production, so GDP doesn't go up. If you hire a lawn service and pay them $25 to mow the same grass, GDP increases by $25. Hiring out household chores (that would otherwise have been done by yourself) doesn't increase production, but it does increase GDP. Likewise, if you buy a house, you do not charge yourself rent, so rental services are not counted in GDP. If you rent the same house from someone else who owns it, then the rent you pay increases GDP. Just imagine how much we could increase US GDP by moving into our neighbor's house and mowing their yard!

From babysitting to unreported server tips, economic production often goes unreported. When was the last time you held a yard sale and reported the income you earned as retail services to the IRS? International GDP estimates may be difficult to compare depending on the percentage of each economy done outside the watchful eye of government accountants.

Some producers explicitly avoid informing the federal government of their production. These producers operate in the **black market**. Drug lords and organized criminals do not tend to report their production to the government because the products they are producing are illegal. From drugs to gambling to prostitution, economic production occurs, but does not make it into GDP estimates. In this way, illegal drug producing countries' GDPs may grossly underestimate how much production is really happening in their economy.

Given that the US economy produces over $15 trillion worth of goods and services in a year, it is safe to say that not everything gets counted. In fact, quarterly GDP estimates are just that. In the month following the end of a quarter, the BEA releases its advanced estimate of quarterly GDP with the data it has collected thus far regarding economic activity in that quarter. The next month, they revise the preliminary estimate as they collect more data. The second, and last, revision comes with the final report two months after the initial estimate. Even then, the final estimate is made from survey data and not physically adding up trillions of dollars of transactions.

GDP has larger problems serving as a measure of wellbeing. In order to account more broadly for changes in wellbeing, changes in GDP would need to be considered along with changes in leisure, environmental quality, personal health, natural disasters, wars, capital depreciation, liberty, population, income inequality, and price levels.

GDP per capita measures the average output per person. As such, it is a better measurement of people's available resources.

GDP PER CAPITA = GDP ÷ POPULATION.

Yet, it too is an imperfect measurement of wellbeing. For instance, the US has a higher level of per capita GDP than France, but the French work many fewer weeks per year than their American counterparts. Output per hour worked in France is actually higher than in the US. The per capita GDP of Qatar may lead the world but it may tell us very little about how the average person in Qatar is doing if there is a high level of income inequality.

GDP and GDP per capita also fail to report the level of environmental damage being produced in a given year. A country can boost its GDP by logging all of its trees, but *The Lorax*[2] will be happy to point out why that will harm people's long term quality of life. GDP may increase by dumping toxins into rivers, but doing so will likely lower the health of those who rely on rivers and lakes for food or tourism.

Likewise, GDP does not include a measurement of liberty. For instance, GDP in the southern US fell dramatically after emancipation. Freed slaves worked fewer hours and in more pleasant working environments following emancipation. Yet, few would say that emancipation was a bad thing, despite GDP decreasing. Much like slavery, a military draft can increase GDP by forcing people to do work for which they did not volunteer. To assume that an increase in GDP during a war draft is "good" is to prefer output over liberty.

GDP also often increases due to natural disasters. If a hurricane destroys a city and the city is rebuilt, the rebuilding of the city is included in GDP, but people aren't any better off than before the flood. The broken window fallacy[3] is to assume that breaking people's windows in order to give jobs to window repairmen is a source of wealth creation. Wars often fall into this category. If GDP is to measure output by looking at the final sale prices of products, then inflation would cause GDP to increase without any new production. **Nominal GDP** is GDP in today's prices. It is the number that the federal government reports. In order to measure if the economy produced more or less output from one time period to the next, we have to control for changes in the price level. **Real GDP** controls nominal GDP for changes in prices. Therefore, when the BEA releases its economic growth numbers each quarter, they do so by reporting changes in real GDP (RGDP).

Hurricane Katrina rebuilding efforts have increased GDP, but the hurricane did not make society better off.

---

[2] Fictional character created by Dr. Seuss

[3] The fallacy noted by Frederic Bastiat in his 1850 essay "That Which is Seen and That Which is Unseen"

$$\text{REAL GDP} = \frac{\text{NOMINAL GDP}}{\text{(GDP DEFLATOR)}} \times 100,$$

Where the GDP deflator is a measure of price changes.

While GDP is not a perfect indicator of production or wellbeing, a change in real per capita GDP is the single best metric yet devised to estimate whether an economy is doing a better or worse job of producing the wealth necessary to meet the needs and desires of its citizens.

Comparisons of GDP Per Capita Across Countries

Table 3.1 compares per capita GDP between countries in 2010 international dollars. This represents the cumulative effect of past growth rates on the current production in each country. As some countries grow faster than others, their ranking in Table 3.1 continues to change on a yearly basis. Faster economic growth rates move an economy up, while slower, or negative, growth rates move a country's rank further down.

The **rule of 72** can help explain why seemingly small changes in GDP growth rates can impact people's quality of life over time. By dividing 72 by annual growth rate in GDP, we can find how many years it will take at that growth rate for GDP to double. For instance, an economy with a 3% annual growth rate will find that its GDP will double over 24 years compared to the 36 years needed by an economy with a 2% annual growth rate. This one percentage point change in growth can determine whether GDP after 72 years will have risen 8 fold (3% growth) or just 4 fold (2% growth).

When it comes to meeting the basic needs of humans, economic growth is most crucial in the world's poorest countries. The next four chapters investigate why some countries are richer than others and what can be done to improve economic growth for every country.

Table 3.1 PER CAPITA GDP[4]

Rank	Country	International $	Rank	Country	International $
1	Qatar	$88,559	158	Tanzania	$1,413
2	Luxembourg	$81,383	159	Burkina Faso	$1,360
3	Singapore	$56,522	160	Lesotho	$1,299
4	Norway	$52,013	161	Nepal	$1,271
5	Brunei	$48,892	162	Mali	$1,252
6	United Arab Emirates	$48,821	163	Burma	$1,250
7	United States	$47,284	164	Uganda	$1,241
—	Hong Kong	$45,736	165	Rwanda	$1,217
8	Switzerland	$41,663	166	Comoros	$1,202
9	Netherlands	$40,765	167	Haiti	$1,165
10	Australia	$39,699	168	Guinea-Bissau	$1,084
11	Austria	$39,634	169	Guinea	$1,046
12	Canada	$39,057	170	Ethiopia	$1,016
13	Ireland	$38,550	171	Mozambique	$1,010
14	Sweden	$38,031	172	Madagascar	$911
15	Kuwait	$37,849	173	Afghanistan	$907
16	Iceland	$36,621	174	Togo	$858
17	Denmark	$36,450	175	Malawi	$827
18	Belgium	$36,100	176	Sierra Leone	$807
19	Germany	$36,033	177	Niger	$755
20	Taiwan	$35,227	178	Central African Republic	$745
21	United Kingdom	$34,920	179	Eritrea	$681
22	Finland	$34,585	180	Zimbabwe	$434
23	France	$34,077	181	Burundi	$411
24	Japan	$33,805	182	Liberia	$392
25	Korea, South	$29,836	183	Congo, Democratic Republic of	$328

[4] International Monetary Fund 2010 GDP Rankings, World Economic Outlook Database, April 2011

Glossary

Black market—where goods and services are exchanged with the explicit intent of avoiding government recognition

Bureau of Economic Analysis—the federal government agency in charge of calculating GDP

Business Cycle Dating Committee—the committee at the National Bureau of Economic Research that officially dates recessions

Consumption—the purchase of goods or services by consumers

Export—a good or service produced domestically but sold abroad

Government spending—the purchase of goods or services by a government

Gross Domestic Product—the total market value of all final goods and services produced within a given country in a given period of time

GDP per capita—GDP ÷ population, or the average amount of production per person

Gross National Product—the total market value of all final goods and services produced by a country's companies in a given period of time

Import—a good or service produced abroad but consumed domestically

Intermediate good—goods that go into the production of a final product

Inventory—unsold, stored, production

Investment—the purchase of new capital, equipment, and software by businesses and governments, changes in inventory of unsold products, and the purchase of new homes

Net exports—exports minus imports

Nominal GDP—GDP in today's prices

Non market transactions—production that occurs but goes unreported to the government, often because the producer and consumer are one and the same

Quarter—3 month period

Real GDP—GDP controlling for changes in the price level

Recession—a prolonged period of overall economic contraction

Rule of 72—the number of years it takes for a sum to double in value can be found by dividing 72 by the annual growth rate of that sum

Transfer payments—government payments to people provided in exchange for no good or service

Questions for Review

1. What gets counted in GDP? How does it differ from GNP?
2. What are five of the ten poorest countries in the world as measured by per capita GDP?
3. Why is real per capita GDP not a perfect indicator of wellbeing?
4.

	1992	2000
Nominal GDP (in trillions)	4	6
GDP deflator	100	170

   a. By how much did Real GDP change between 1992 and 2000?

   b. Did the economy grow between 1992 and 2000 according to these numbers?

5. Why is economic growth important?
6. How many years will it take GDP to double if the GDP growth rate is 1.5%?
7. Determine which of the following would be counted in US GDP and if so, in which category (C, I, G, X, or M).

   a. the purchase of American made corn by a consumer in Canada

   b. the production of a Toyota at a plant in Kentucky

   c. the purchase of a new home in Oregon

   d. the payment of $300 to welfare recipient

8a. Why is GDP not a perfect measure of production?

   b. Give an example how one of these imperfections may affect comparisons across time or between countries.

9. Why is GDP not a measure of economic activity?
10. Why do you think GDP per capita varies so dramatically across countries?

Chapter 4

Natural Resources, Labor, and Human Capital

Have you ever wondered what goes into making a hotdog? Scary thought, isn't it? Don't worry, we do not truly want to go through an ingredient list for hot dogs, it may be close to your meal time. Instead, we want to consider the resources needed to produce hot dogs. Most obviously, one would need meat (or a meat substitute such as soy). Meat or soy in an unrefined state would be considered a natural resource because it exists in nature. Labor is necessary for grinding the meat and packaging the hot dogs, unless a form of technology is available for this job. And, if such technology exists, then labor and human capital are needed to create the technology. Ovens (capital) are needed to cook the hot dogs. Lastly, entrepreneurship plays a role in coming up with the right combination of "ingredients" to make that perfect dog. Chapters 4, 5, and 6 will examine the role each of these resources play in wealth creation along with the impact of property rights and institutions on economic growth. We now begin the discussion by looking at natural resources, labor, and human capital.

Natural Resources

A material source of wealth that exists in a natural state is a natural resource. Every country has access to some natural resources. Russia has the most land of any country. Brazil has the most tropical rainforest. Saudi Arabia has the most proven oil reserves. Natural resources are not spread equally over the globe. One source of difference in economic wealth between countries is that some countries have higher valued natural resources than others. Examples include access to deep water ports, moderate climates, scenic views, fertile land, timber, mineral deposits, and cheap energy sources (oil, natural gas, wind, solar, hydro, or tidal). However, if differences in natural resources accounted for the lion's share of the difference in wealth between countries, Nigeria would be one of the wealthiest countries in the world and Hong Kong would be one of the poorest.

Natural resources are to wealth creation as potential energy is to motion. Just because a country has vast amounts of high valued natural resources does not mean that it is wealthy. Nigeria is abundant in valuable natural resources but remains one of the poorer countries in the world. Africa, as a continent, has large quantities of oil, natural gas, diamonds, gold, and other valuable natural resources, yet many African economies remain poor. Conversely, Hong Kong has few natural resources (other than its deep water port), yet is one of the richest places in the world.

From a pro-growth policy perspective, the key is to take the potential wealth of a country's natural resource endowment and turn it into actual wealth. Natural resources can be broken down into both renewable and non-renewable resources. **Non-renewable resources**, once depleted, are forever used up. **Renewable resources**, over time, can replenish themselves and, if properly cared for, can create wealth for generations to come. The legal structure surrounding resource rights can fundamentally alter if, and when, potential wealth gets turned into actual wealth.

Growth Policies for Natural Resources

History is full of examples of peoples and countries who thought that the quickest way to get wealth was to invade other people and take their wealth. The Spartan economy was based upon conquest. Vikings invaded by the sea. And Spain sailed off with boatload after boatload of gold and silver from Latin America. Nonrenewable resources can be a key source of conflict (for example, conflict diamonds) when **property rights** to those resources are not clearly defined or enforced.

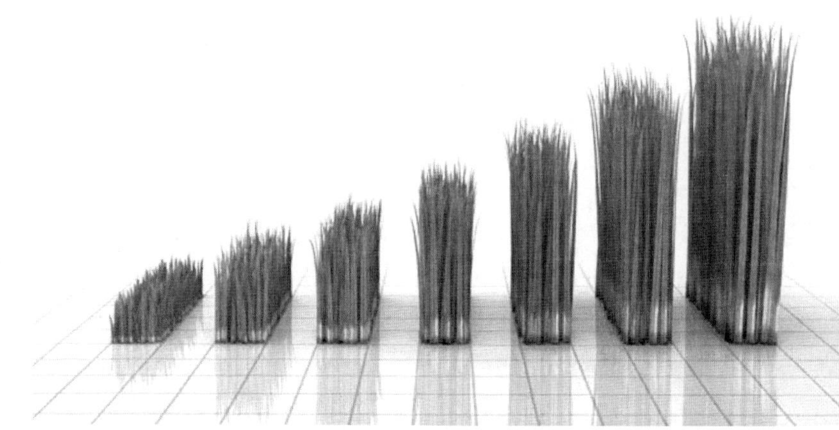

Countries where property rights are clearly defined and enforced grow faster than those with tenuous property rights. Countries that can't defend themselves from foreign invasion, or police themselves to prevent theft, will likely be poor. In absence of the rule of law, owning non-renewable resources is often more of a liability than an asset. When asked why he robbed banks, John Dillinger explained that that is where the money was.

Civil wars caused by struggles over nonrenewable resources are the chief impediment to growth in many African countries. This does not mean that the natural resources themselves are "bad." After all, diamonds are supposed to be a girl's best friend. It does mean that high levels of potential wealth are no guarantee of actual wealth. Poorly defined and enforced property rights go a long way to explaining why many poor countries remain poor.

Natural resources only become actual wealth if they are used. Knowing that oil exists in ANWAR or the Gulf of Mexico does not make the US richer if legislation is passed that prohibits drilling there for oil. The US may have fertile soil, but if the government pays farmers not to grow crops, wealth isn't created. Botswana created wealth by mining the most diamonds of any country in 2008. Perhaps the biggest controversy regarding the use of nonrenewable resources is in determining which generation has the moral right to it since once it is gone it can no longer be used by future generations. Norway creates wealth by taking oil and natural gas from the North Sea. It then takes the revenues from oil and natural gas sales and saves the money for future generations. In this way, they let future generations benefit from nonrenewable resources that are used today.

When dealing with renewable resources, property rights matter as well. If waterways are overfished, the fish supply will not regenerate. If buffalo herds are killed off, they can't reproduce. If soil fertility is exhausted, it may take years to rejuvenate it. If forests are clear cut, they take years to grow again.

When renewable resources are owned by private individuals, those individuals have an incentive to maximize their wealth creation potential over time, thereby maximizing wealth creation. Ranchers don't typically slaughter their whole cattle herd in a year. Incentives change, however, when resources are commonly owned. US bison were commonly owned in the 1800's, and the only way to profit from a bison was to kill one and skin it. There was no incentive to preserve bison and they almost went extinct. Nobel Prize winner, Elinor Ostrom, helped pioneer the field of **institutional economics** which suggests that formal and informal institutions develop to aid in wealth creation. According to Ostrom, institutions form to allocate commonly owned assets like fish or fresh water.

The value of natural resources changes over time. Middle Eastern oil wasn't highly valued two thousand years ago. The invention of the internal combustion engine changed that. Given that the future is uncertain, people don't know which resources, renewable or not, will be most valued in the future. People have much less uncertainty about what is valued today.

Political pressure or bureaucratic self-interest often influences the management of government owned renewable resources. Bureaucrats often ignore current market prices and do things like subsidize logging in national forests, or prevent sustainable logging in the same. Both errors cause a misuse of scarce resources. In 2008, a bribery scandal came to light in the Denver office of the US Department of the Interior.[1] Government workers engaged in sex and drug abuse with oil company workers and took thousands of dollars of gifts while overseeing billions of dollars worth of energy contracts. This is just one example of resource mismanagement. A look into the former Soviet Union's environment record illustrates that government command and control policies over natural resources are not likely to yield optimal resource management.

The US national park system was set up on the belief that only the federal government could protect the environment from immediate exploitation. Canada's national parks are arguably nicer than those in the US and they allowed more private investment in their parks. Incentives matter. When people have a personal incentive to take care of a renewable resource, they are more likely to do so than if they only benefit from the current exploitation of that resource.

Resources are often misused due to government regulations. Corn in the US is not turned into ethanol because it makes economic or environmental sense. Rather, it is turned into ethanol because corn farmers have lobbied Congress to mandate its use in order to drive up the price of corn. This, in turn, increases the price of food. Foods and animal feeds made from corn are more costly due to US ethanol policy. With increased profitability of corn planting, fewer other crops are grown, which drives up the cost of foods, both nationally and globally. US ethanol policy not only slows the US economy down, but it also makes it harder for poor people in foreign countries to afford food.

Thus, natural resources, both renewable and nonrenewable, are potential sources of wealth creation as long as property rights are clearly defined and enforced, resources are efficiently managed, and government policies don't incentivize their disuse or misuse. Private ownership of natural resources allows wealth-creating incentives to guide the use and care of natural resources. Where private property rights are difficult to define and enforce, institutions, both formal and informal, can be created, or allowed to evolve, to address the use and care of commonly owned resources.

[1] http://www.denverpost.com/breakingnews/ci_10428441

Growth Policies for Labor

Economic growth derived from labor can either be **extensive** or **intensive** in nature. That is, growth comes from both more and better skilled labor. An increase in the quantity of labor can either come from an increase in the population of working aged adults, or an increase in the number of hours the working aged population spends working. The former does not increase per capita output in the same way that the latter does. An increase in worker **productivity** (output per hour worked) also increases per capita output and can be brought about by an increase in the human capital of the population. Government policies can, and do, influence both the quantity and quality of the work force.

Extensive Growth: Policies Which Alter the Size of the Labor Force

Increases in the labor force come from either increasing the population, or an increase in the percentage of the existing population who take part in the labor force. An increase in the population can come from increased births (over time), increased **immigration**, decreased **emigration**, better health, and longer life expectancy.

Changing Family Size

What types of policies influence family size in the US? Most commonly, increased family size is related to policies that lower the cost of child rearing include the Family Medical Leave Act, child tax credits and deductions, and subsidized living expenses for children (food, clothing, shelter, education, and health care). Such policies all work to increase the number of children people have. In the US, families in the poorest quintile in the US have the highest average birth rate of any income quintile. Food stamps, public housing, public education, and Medicaid are all features of the US welfare state that lower the cost of child rearing to low income families. As incomes increase in the US, parents have access to less government support for child rearing and tend to have smaller average family sizes. Changing average family sizes today translate into a different potential labor force of the future.

Changes in Immigration and Emigration

Immigration and emigration are largely economic phenomenon, though war and persecution can also play key roles. An economy that has a net positive amount of immigration will see its population increase. Immigrants of working age bring some level of skills or education from their home country. In this way, the country to which they immigrate gains the advantage of their work without having had to pay for their rearing costs. Additionally, these new workers increase the domestic demand for goods and services, which stimulates other areas of the economy beyond those in which the immigrants are employed.

Regardless of the decade in study, immigrants into the US have worked more hours per year than native born workers. Government policies to restrict immigration, particularly among highly educated foreigners, have worked to slow down economic growth in the US. Policies that openly attract highly educated immigrants not only improve the quantity of the labor force, but work to increase its average skill level.

Capital and labor are opposites (complements in production), and opposites attract. Left to themselves, capital and labor will find each other and their offspring is wealth creation. If countries with large amounts of capital heavily restrict immigration into their country, capital will flow to countries that have large numbers of potential workers. In a market economy, either workers must be allowed to move to where the capital is, or capital will flow to where the workers are.

Because the demand for immigration is so much higher than the government set quota for immigration into the United States, a black market is created for immigration. Foreigners sneak across the US boarder or pay human smugglers to assist them in entering the US. Illegal immigration is not as economically valuable as legal immigration. Illegal immigrants lack the ability to use the justice system to enforce property rights. They waste valuable resources avoiding detection from immigration officials, and have an incentive to give birth to children in the US to decrease their odds of deportation. Because avoiding immigration laws makes illegal immigrants criminals, the cost of engaging in further criminal activities is lowered for said immigrants. Roughly 27% of federal prisoners are not citizens of the US. An increase in legal immigration among skilled immigrants along with the tightening of border security to prevent illegal immigration would increase both extensive and intensive economic growth in the United States.

Changing Hours Worked

Government policies also often work to lower the amount of labor people choose to supply to the labor market. Tax rates, labor laws, and social safety net programs all work to impact the amount of labor individuals supply to the labor force.

Nobel Prize winning economist Edward Prescott, in his work "Why Do Americans Work So Much More Than Europeans?"[2] illustrates the importance of marginal tax rates on labor. In the 1970's, the average worker in Germany, France, and the United Kingdom all worked more hours per year than in the US. Successive changes in marginal income tax rates (upward in Europe and downward in the US) during the 1980's resulted in US workers working more hours than workers in each of these countries by the early 1990's. When they are allowed to benefit from the fruits of their labor, workers work more hours per year. As the share of their labor that goes to the government increases, workers find less marginal benefit in an extra hour of work and decide to work less.

Child labor laws, mandatory retirement ages, and minimum wage laws all work to decrease the amount of labor provided in an economy. Minimum wage laws outlaw the employment of individuals whose marginal revenue product (the amount of revenue they can bring in for their employer) is below that level. Not only do such laws reduce the employment of low skilled workers, they prohibit such workers from gaining on the job skills.

Many governments have instituted some level of social safety net to help care for the poor and indigent. The more generous the safety net is, the less attractive an extra hour of work becomes. In many cases an extra hour of work causes such a reduction in safety net payments that work becomes unprofitable for individuals. In this way the safety net can act more like a web than a net. Welfare dependency is a symptom of poorly designed safety nets. The Welfare Reform Act of 1996 (PRWORA) increased the number of people in the labor force by limiting access to welfare and increasing work requirements for recipients. Since then, however, there has been a marked increase in disability claims.

Countries that have more generous unemployment insurance benefits have higher levels of unemployment and longer average bouts of unemployment than do societies with less generous benefits. Generous benefits result in people taking their time to find the perfect job before they head back to work. Work, by

---

2 *Federal Reserve Bank of Minneapolis Quarterly Review* Vol. 28. No. 1. July 2004, 2-13.

its nature, is often arduous. If it were always fun, it would be called play. People will avoid work in favor of play if extra work does not yield greater consumptive power.

An Example of Extensive Growth from Colonial America

Extensive economic growth may improve national security, allow a country to better take advantage of economies of scale in urbanization, or may help to increase solvency of government run pay-as-you-go pension schemes. In colonial American history, the British government favored a growing American population in order to better be able to defend the North American British colonies from French or Spanish encroachment. As America's population grew more populous, it was able to take advantage of economies of scale in transportation, urbanization, and the warehousing of goods. At the conclusion of the French and Indian War, Great Britain's incentive to increase American population lessened and they placed regulations on American colonists, seeking to prevent their westward movement.

Intensive Growth

Rather than maximizing extensive growth through a higher population, some countries show more concern about intensive growth so that there is more output per person. China went so far as to restrict the number of children people were allowed to have in order to speed up the increase in the capital to labor ratio for their economy. Other policies revolve around getting people to spend more time in the workforce or produce more output per hour worked. This can be achieved through a variety of means including better access to health care, lower incarceration rates, and higher human capital development.

Healthy workers miss fewer work days than do unhealthy workers. Better health coupled with extended life expectancy also allows workers to spend more years in the labor force if they so choose. By the end of their careers, elderly employees have amassed extensive job experience which can increase labor productivity. Public policies that improve health care or make it more affordable/accessible to workers can increase economic growth. Policies that discourage smoking (a cigarette tax), and obesity (building pedestrian infrastructure) can also lead to healthier lifestyle choices.

Conversely, extending government sponsored health care to retirees takes resources away from production. The decision for care for the elderly is one of many normative decisions people have to make when determining government policies. The role of the economist is to illustrate what tradeoffs exist. Current government health insurance programs such as Medicare and Medicaid have more to do with using resources to care for non-worker's health than they do with increasing the health of the US workforce.

The US incarcerates more people (over 7 million), and has the largest percentage of its population locked up (almost 2%), than any other industrialized country. Such a large incarceration rate hurts economic growth for two reasons. The first is that prisoners are kept from the labor market. Not only do they forgo current production, but upon their release, their ex-convict status reduces their employment prospects. The second is that the average cost of incarceration in the US is over $24,000 a year. As resources are used for prisons, they are diverted away from the private sector or from other government programs such as education.

One obvious change in government policy that might result in fewer incarcerations would be the decriminalization of illicit drugs. If rehabilitation and education replaced incarceration, economic resources could be reallocated to more productive uses.

Labor productivity, in part, is a function of human capital development. Policies that encourage, or increase, the education and skill level of the population work to increase labor productivity. This benefits both the workers who are more productive (with higher wages) and the economy generally with more output.

Intensive Growth through Greater Accumulation of Human Capital

Government policies that discourage the accumulation of human capital reduce economic growth. Highly skilled workers earn higher wages as a reflection of their enhanced productivity. Government policies, such a highly progressive income tax, that attempt to decrease income inequality reduce the marginal benefit to an individual of pursuing additional education or skills. If a high school dropout can make the same or almost the same as a medical doctor with ten years of post-high school education, then fewer people will take on the often arduous task of pursuing higher education. Income inequality is efficient if it reflects development of education or skills that bring happiness to others in terms of the goods and services they are able to produce.

The government in the US is directly involved in the operation of public schools from pre-school to post-secondary education. Policies that increase the education and skill level of students attending these schools will increase human capital levels. In 2009 an OECD study[3] of 15 year olds in 65 countries found that the US ranked 31st in math, 23rd in science, and 17th in reading among

[3] http://www.oecd.org/document/12/0,3343,en_21571361_44315115_46623628_1_1_1_1,00.html

the countries examined. Table 4.1 lists the top 10 countries in each discipline. The US was the only OECD country whose 25-34 year olds where not more likely to have graduated from high school than 55-64 year olds. Even as the US spends more money per student on education than any other country in the world, the learning outcomes fail to land in the top ten. Reform of elementary and secondary education in the US, if it increases learning outcomes, would benefit economic growth.

The US has the premier university system in the world. One major difference between elementary education and university education in the US is that students are allowed to choose which university they attend (as long as they get admitted and can pay the tuition). In many elementary school districts, students are assigned a school to attend. Competition for students among colleges and universities helps to increase the value of a college education.

College and university faculty are more likely to work for private colleges and universities than are elementary school teachers. They are also less likely to be unionized than their elementary school counterparts. While the federal government aides low income students with Pell Grants to attend the university of their choice (including private religious schools), many elementary school districts do not allow this type of voucher program. The school choice movement is a move-

Table 4.1 2009 PISA TEST SCORE RANKING

Rank	Reading	Mathematics	Science
1	China (Shanghai)	China (Shanghai)	China (Shanghai)
2	Korea	Singapore	Finland
3	Finland	Hong Kong	Hong Kong
4	Hong Kong	Korea	Singapore
5	Singapore	Chinese Taipei	Japan
6	Canada	Finland	Korea
7	New Zealand	Liechtenstein	New Zealand
8	Japan	Switzerland	Canada
9	Australia	Japan	Estonia
10	Netherlands	Canada	Australia

ment to give parents a choice of elementary and secondary schools where their children can attend without having to pay private tuition.

Still, the US ranks only 12th in its share of adults ages 25-34 with postsecondary degrees. Only 40.1 percent of young Americans hold postsecondary degrees compared to 55.8 percent of Canadian youth.[4] Low college graduation rates in the US are partly a reflection of how poorly many children are educated at the elementary and secondary education levels. Over one-third of college students in the US now must take remedial classes because their skill set was not college ready.

In an effort to make a college degree more affordable, US government policies give tax breaks for educational expenses, tax breaks for saving for college (529 savings plans), interest deductibility of student loans, and grants for low income students (Pell Grants). These incentives, however, do nothing to ensure that the education pursued with this government help actually improves a student's preparedness for the workforce.

While taking out student loans to gain a medical education often makes sense, acquiring massive student debt for an unfinished degree, or a degree in underwater basket weaving, does little to boost the worker productivity of students and becomes wasted taxpayer money. Roughly 44 percent of all students who enter a four year college in the US fail to receive a college degree.[5] This results in billions of dollars in wasted resources. Government policies that throw untargeted money at education serve to slow down economic growth by misallocating resources. Targeted educational policies, such as the use of technical training schools, can go a long way to ensure that education spending results in an increase in human capital.

Like natural resources, a country's population represents a potential source of wealth creation. Government policies can enable, or discourage, both the quantity and quality of work engaged in by a country's work force. As long as government policies discourage work and human capital development, economic growth rates will be lower than they otherwise would be. Policies that promote an increase in the quantity and quality of work help to create wealth. Still, wealth does not necessarily accrue fastest to the hardest or most educated workers. The role of capital, technology, and entrepreneurship in wealth creation are examined in the following two chapters.

---

[4] http://www.washingtonpost.com/wp-dyn/content/article/2010/07/22/AR2010072201250.html

[5] http://www.thefiscaltimes.com/Articles/2010/10/28/High-College-Dropout-Rate-Threatens-US-Growth.aspx

Glossary

Emigration—the leaving of a country to live abroad

Extensive economic growth—growth in output due to an increase in inputs

Immigration—the entrance to a country of someone who has lived abroad

Institutional economics—the study of how institutions affect the evolutionary development of the economy

Intensive economic growth—growth in output due to an increase in the productivity of existing inputs

Non-renewable resources—natural resources that once used, are depleted

Productivity—output per unit of input

Property rights—the legal right to own and use an asset

Renewable resources—natural resources that regenerate over time

Questions for Review

1. What is human capital? How is it developed?
2. What are property rights? Why are they important to the use of resources?
3. What government policies discourage human capital development? What policies encourage it?
4. What government policies discourage work? How?
5. Why do politicians often support policies that discourage work?
6. Name three of the countries who finished in the top ten in all three academic disciplines measured by the OECD educational attainment study.
7. List and explain three US government policy changes that would result in a larger US work force.
8. List and explain three US government policy changes that would result in a more skilled US work force.
9. What is the difference between potential wealth and actual wealth?
10. Is the existence of large natural resource deposits in a country helpful or harmful to economic growth? Why?
11. What role might opportunity cost play in motivating higher income families to have fewer children on average than lower income families?

Chapter 5

Physical Capital and Technology

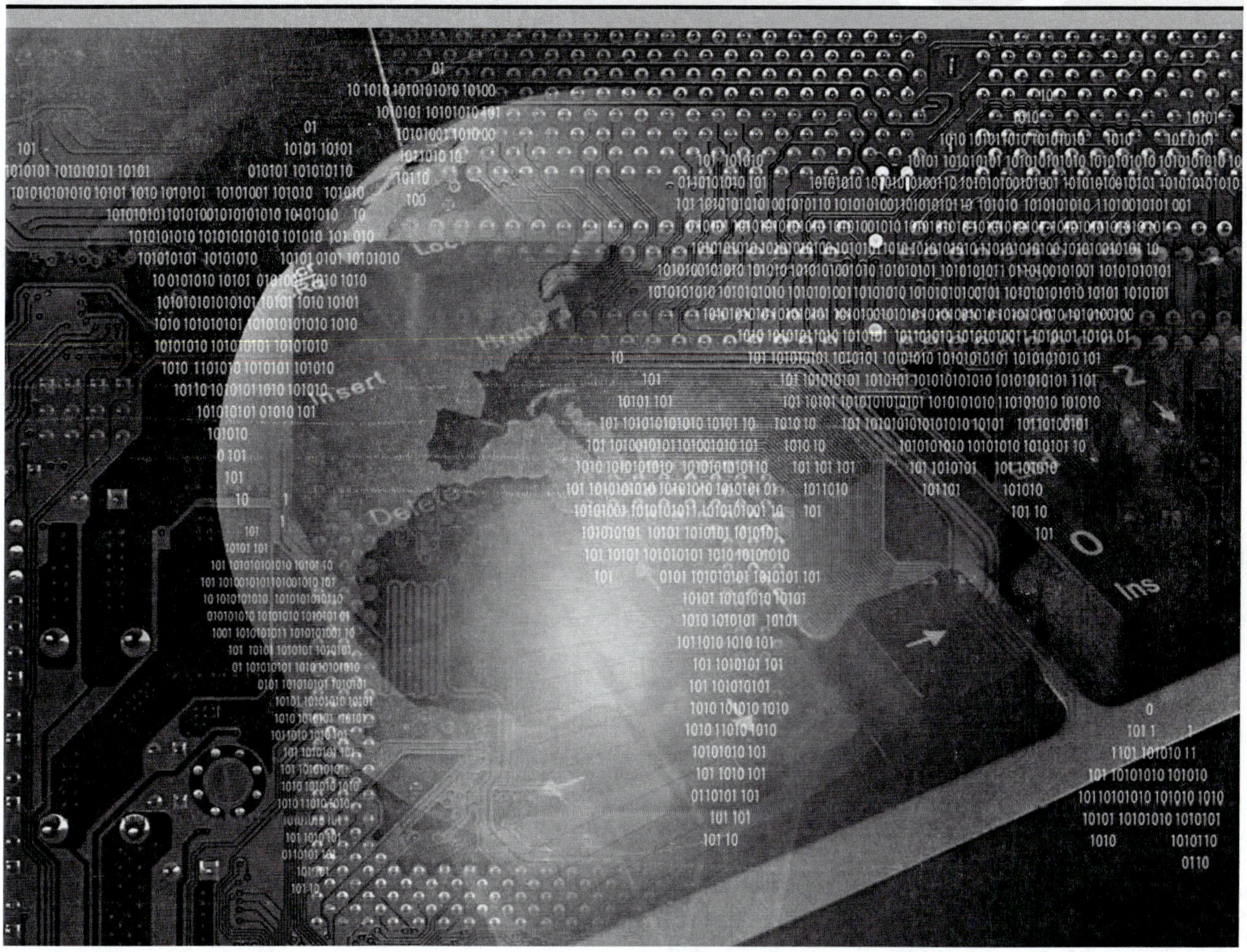

Producing wealth without the help of machines, tools, or factories is very difficult. For this reason, economic growth is highly correlated with capital investment. Societies with the highest levels of per capita output are those societies with the most capital. That is why the economic system of wealth creation is referred to as capitalism. Making stuff by hand is difficult. The production of mass quantities of goods and services is only possible with the help of capital.

Recall from chapter one that capital refers to a long lasting tool used for production. While capital can be purchased with money, money is not itself capital. About the only thing it could produce on a deserted island would be fire, and then it would not last long. Also, unlike natural resources, capital can't be found lying around under the ground. It has to be created. The creation of capital, then, represents an active decision to forgo current consumption in order to use today's resources to create capital for use tomorrow. Societies on the brink of starvation have little ability to forgo current consumption with the hope of a more prosperous future. The ability and willingness to engage in savings is a prerequisite for capital accumulation. Societies that save larger percentages of their income have faster capital accumulation rates than do societies with lower savings rates. In this chapter we examine policies that promote or restrict capital accumulation and the innovation of technology.

Policies that Promote Capital Accumulation

Governments can create an economic environment that is either friendly or hostile to the development of capital. Capital friendly policies include solid definition and protection of private property rights, low marginal taxes on capital income, low regulation of the uses of capital and sale of its output, tax policies that encourage savings, monetary policies that provide a stable currency, and the provision of complementary public infrastructure. Capital is mobile. Countries that have capital friendly environments are able to benefit from both domestic and international savings which is turned into capital formation in their country.

Property Rights

Government failure to define and protect property rights of capitalists often results in high levels of theft, the presence of civil wars, the expropriation of capital by governments themselves, competition for private capital from government owned capital, and a regulatory environment that encourages taking rather than making. Individuals and firms do not make a habit of forgoing current consumption for investment in future capital unless they are relatively certain that they will be able to benefit from the capital they create.

Capital is not attracted to high crime areas. Profits lost to theft discourage capital formation. Civil wars cause death and destruction of capital. People who don't think they will likely live very long are not apt to forgo current consumption. Firms who believe their capital is likely to get blown up aren't likely to locate in war torn areas.

Governments have often attracted private investment in major industries from foreign firms only to nationalize the capital. Typically, government officials lack the technical knowledge to operate and repair said capital so output falls as a result. At the same time, other firms then refuse to invest their capital in the country. Likewise, if private capitalists believe that a government can at any time compete with them using publicly owned capital, private capital dissipates. Government sponsored enterprises have access to the public tax revenues to cover operating losses, a benefit not typically shared by the owners of private capital.

Firms can gain wealth by producing goods people want to buy at prices they want to pay, or they can make money by lobbying governments to rig the economic playing field in their behalf. **Rent seeking** is the process of engaging in costly non-productive actions (such as lobbying) in search of profit. Rent seeking will be studied in depth in Chapter 19. When government officials pick economic winners and losers, firms redirect their resources from wealth creation to lobbying the government. This often involves reducing physical capital and employing more labor (lobbyists). Theft and rent-seeking therefore destroy wealth.

Crowding Out Verses Crowding In

By running up government debt, governments **crowd out** private investment. As consumers and firms engage in savings, their savings can be used by other consumers for consumer loans, by businesses for investment, or by governments for government loans. As governments borrow increasingly large amounts of money, less saving is left over for private capital accumulation. This is referred to as **crowding out**. Capital only can be formed once saving has occurred. The first step in increasing a national savings rate is to decrease the indebtedness of the public sector. As the US government paid down on its national debt following the US Civil War, private capital was **crowded in** and an investment boom transpired.

The Role of Taxes and Savings Incentives in Capital Accumulation

The other way to increase the national savings rate is to incentive savings. Income, capital gains, and inheritance taxes act as disincentives for consumers to postpone current consumption. Governments that replace income taxes with sales (consumption) taxes, and abolish estate taxes discourage consumption rather than savings. By allowing people to save tax free for retirement or college, individual retirement accounts and college 529 savings plans increase the rate of return to savers and thereby incentivize savings. These savings then lower the cost of borrowing for private capital accumulation. In this way, savings incentives work to encourage capital investment.

Because capital is mobile in the long run, countries that try to heavily tax income derived from capital find it more difficult to attract new capital than do countries with low marginal tax rates on capital income. Table 5.1 illustrates that the US has the second highest **corporate income tax** rate in the OECD behind Japan. Ireland, with its corporate income tax rate that is less than one-third that of the US, has attracted capital that makes it one of the richest countries in the world. Like Ireland, Canada has been luring investment from US firms seeking to lower their tax burden. These countries offer a well-trained English speaking workforce coupled with low taxes on capital, which together work to attract mass amounts of new capital investment.

Table 5.1 2011 OECD CORPORATE TAX RATES

Country	Central Gov Tax Rate	Total Gov Tax Rate	Country	Central Gov Tax Rate	Total Gov Tax Rate
Australia	30	30	Japan	30	39.54
Austria	25	25	Korea	22	24.2
Belgium	33.99	33.99	Luxembourg	22.05	28.8
Canada	16.5	27.64	Mexico	30	30
Chile	20	20	Netherlands	25	25
Czech Republic	19	19	New Zealand	28	28
Denmark	25	25	Norway	28	28
Estonia	21	21	Poland	19	19
Finland	26	26	Portugal	25	26.5
France	34.43	34.43	Slovak Republic	19	19
Germany	15.83	30.18	Slovenia	20	20
Greece	20	20	Spain	30	30
Hungary	19	19	Sweden	26.3	26.3
Iceland	20	20	Switzerland	8.5	21.17
Ireland	12.5	12.5	Turkey	20	20
Israel	24	24	United Kingdom	26	26
Italy	27.5	27.5	United States	35	39.19

The **capital gains tax** is a tax on the sale of capital that has appreciated in value. It is applied to the sale of assets ranging from factories, to houses, to shares of stock. High capital gains taxes serve as a disincentive to invest in assets that may appreciate in value. Entrepreneurs also face income taxes. High marginal tax rates on income derived from capital decrease the profitability of capital and therefore work to chase capital to lower taxed political jurisdictions.

Regulation and Infrastructure

Capital is most productive when its use is not heavily regulated and its output can be sold globally. Swiss banks for years have attracted deposits based on their low level of government regulations relating to the reporting of deposits to government authorities. Burdensome labor or environmental regulations also cause capital to seek lower regulatory environments. Firms that find it difficult to liquidate their capital due to foreign investment controls or unstable currencies will be less likely to create capital in a country. If firms find it hard to get their money back out, they won't put their money in.

Most goods can be sold anywhere in the world. As a result, the decision to locate productive capital in any given geographical location will also be a function of ease of transport in getting their products to world markets. In this way, countries that support free trade policies attract capital. Production from their capital will be able to travel to other countries without facing punitive tariffs. Firms that locate in countries with high trade barriers find it difficult to export goods due to retaliatory trade barriers placed on products from their country.

Another aspect of getting goods and services to market is the existence of needed infrastructure. This infrastructure makes capital more productive by lowering the cost of getting products to market. Roads, ports, airports, railways, energy grids, and telecommunication systems all play a supportive role in lowering the transaction costs of doing business. Different governments choose to intervene to varying degrees in the infrastructure sectors. While some governments have nationalized railways, roads, and telecommunication companies, others have privately operated roads, railways, and telecommunication companies. Infrastructure ownership and operation tends to be more efficient when controlled by the private sector rather than the public sector. Private industry is much less likely to build a bridge to nowhere than are politicians.

Policies that Encourage the Creation of New Technology

Government policies can aid or detract in the development of new technology. The most notable source of government involvement in innovation is the protection of intellectual property rights. Societies that allow inventors to reap the economic

rewards of their invention incentivize invention and innovation. The Founding Fathers of the United States thought that protection of intellectual property rights was so necessary for economic growth that they included patent protection in the US Constitution. As the economy becomes more internationalized, international protection of intellectual property rights becomes increasingly important. This topic has been a major point of negotiation in global trade talks.

Table 5.2 ranks the top ten innovating countries between 2004 and 2008. Governments can incentivize private innovation through tax credits to firms for research and development costs, or they can directly award prizes to private firms who solve a specified public problem. The British Longitude Act of 1714, under Queen Anne, offered a prize up to 20,000 British Pounds to anyone who could invent a technology to correctly determine longitude while at sea within 30 nautical miles. In this case, the British government identified a pressing national security need and incentivized the private sector to devote resources to solving the problem. An English clockmaker by the name of John Harrison invented the marine chronometer, thereby solving the problem.

Table 5.2 GLOBAL INNOVATION INDEX[1], Selected Countries, 2004–2008

Rank	Country	Rank	Country
1	Japan	6	Germany
2	Switzerland	7	Taiwan
3	Finland	8	Netherlands
4	United States	9	Israel
5	Sweden	10	Denmark

[1] Source: *The Economist* Intelligence Unit, http://www.economist.com/node/13562333

In the US, The National Science Foundation works to fund research and development through grants to researchers. Alternatively, the government could identify technological innovations they wish to see and directly employ government researchers. For instance, researchers at the National Institute of Health work on federally approved and sponsored health research. Having governments pick and fund specific research projects turns research and development into a political animal where politicians determine where innovation should occur rather than letting the market determine it. Note that government sponsored research runs the risk of appealing to special interest groups rather than the general public.

Such special interest groups can include those whose jobs are in peril as a result of the new technology. The development of ATM's, for instance, has reduced the need for bank tellers. The development of handheld computers has decreased the demand for hard cover books or printed newspapers. Governments are often approached by industries whose future prosperity is threatened by new technology to set rules against the adaption or use of the new technology. Governments that restrain from granting such regulatory or tax preferences to dying industries are able to provide a technologically friendly economic growth environment. Few would seek to prevent the creation of a cancer vaccine, even though such a vaccine could make oncologist jobs obsolete. Yet, often politicians bend to lobbyists making similar arguments concerning the preservation of jobs made obsolete by new technology. Although some individuals may lose their jobs as a result of technological innovation, such innovations increase economic growth and therefore increase the standard of living for generations to come.

© Vasily Smirnov, 2012, under license Shutterstock, Inc.

Even beyond explicit government policies toward invention and innovation, lies a society's acceptance of change. If a traditional society (such as the Amish) is resistant to technological or scientific advancement, then members of that society will be less likely to use their talents inventing new technologies or making new discoveries. Said inventions or discoveries, once made, would be very difficult to prosper from in such societies. A social ethic that embraces technological advance and educates its citizens accordingly, works to create an innovation friendly economic environment.

Thus, there are many acts that the government or society can take to encourage capital accumulation and technological innovation. Such actions lead to economic growth, but are not always politically popular despite the overwhelming evidence of their benefits to society. The next chapter looks at how job declines in one area are often a necessary consequence of innovation and entrepreneurship and how entrepreneurship is vital for economic growth.

Glossary

Capital gains tax—a tax paid upon sale of assets which have appreciated in value since their purchase

Corporate income tax—a tax paid by corporations based upon their reported profits

Rent seeking—engaging in costly non-productive actions (such as lobbying) in search of profit

Crowding in—when a decrease in government debt increases capital investment in an economy

Crowding out—when an increase in government debt lowers capital investment in an economy

Questions for Review

1. Name three of the top ten innovative countries in the world between 2004 and 2008.
2. Which country has the highest corporate income tax rate in the OECD? The lowest rate? Where does the US rank?
3. List and explain three government policy changes that would make the US more attractive to capital.
4. What factors work to determine where a pharmaceutical company chooses to locate its headquarters?
5. Why is capital important to wealth creation?
6. Why is technological innovation important to wealth creation?
7. What role do savings play in capital creation?
8. How does public debt affect private capital accumulation?
9. Suppose that a pharmaceutical company is charging such high prices for a drug that it cannot be purchased by all that need the drug. If another pharmaceutical company comes along petitioning to produce the drug for a more affordable price, should the patent be overturned? Would overturning the patent save more lives? (Note: a similar lawsuit occurred concerning the drug AZT which is used to treat AIDS. Why do you think the judge in this case upheld the patent of the original manufacturer of the drug? Did this judgment make economic and moral sense?)

Chapter 6 Entrepreneurship and Convergence

"Failure is simply the opportunity to begin again, this time more intelligently."

— *Henry Ford*

© olly, 2012, under license Shutterstock, Inc.

The economy is ever changing. Firms come and go. Jobs are gained and lost. According to the US Census Bureau, virtually all new job creation between 1977 and 2005 came from firms that are five years old or younger.[1] Older firms, on average, were net job destroyers in this time period. Joseph Schumpeter

[1] http://www.kauffman.org/newsroom/u-s-job-growth-driven-entirely-by-startups.aspx

referred to this violent churning of the economy as a process of **creative destruction**. Innovation and changing wants cause the production mix of an economy to change over time. In this chapter, we shall examine how entrepreneurship aids in the transformation of industries and will discuss convergence theory.

Changing Mix of Output in the US

Table 6.1[2] illustrates how the US economy has changed its mix of outputs since WWII. As a percentage of GDP, the agriculture and manufacturing sectors in the US have seen dramatic declines in their relative importance to US output. On the other hand, the industries which experienced the most growth were in the sectors of finance, professional services, education, and healthcare. Of these, the two biggest subcategory increases were in health care, whose percentage of GDP output went from 1.5% to 7.6% between 1947 and 2010, and finance and insurance whose percentage of GDP went from 2.4% to 8.4%.

Table 6.1 **% OF US GDP CONTRIBUTED BY SECTOR**

Sector	1947	1987	2010
Agriculture, forestry, fishing, and hunting	8.2	1.7	1.1
Mining	2.4	1.5	1.9
Utilities	1.4	2.7	1.9
Construction	3.6	4.4	3.4
Manufacturing	25.6	17.4	11.7
Wholesale trade	6.4	6	5.5
Retail trade	9.5	7.3	5.9
Transportation and warehousing	5.8	3.2	2.8
Information	2.8	4.2	4.6
Finance, insurance, real estate, rental, and leasing	10.5	18	21.1
Professional and business services	3.3	8.1	12.1
Educational services, health care, and social assistance	1.9	5.9	8.7
Arts, entertainment, recreation, accommodation, and food services	3.3	3.2	3.6
Government	12.5	13.9	13.4

[2] Source: Bureau of Labor Statistics

Table 6.2[3] lists the top ten industries which contracted the most from 2000 until 2010. The wireless revolution has aided the decline of more than one of these industries, as videos on demand, downloadable songs, online newspapers, and other technologies have decreased the demand for many products such as CD's, video rentals, and printed newspapers. Why buy CD's in a store when you can download songs online? Why rent DVD's from a store when you can stream movies online? Why buy physical newspapers when you can read them online?

ex: creative destruction

Table 6.2 **2011 TOP 10 DYING INDUSTRIES (2000-2010)**

Rank	Country
1	Wired Telecommunications Carriers
2	Mills
3	Newspaper Publishing
4	Apparel Manufacturing
5	DVD, Game & Video Rental
6	Manufactured Home Dealers
7	Video Postproduction Services
8	Record Stores
9	Photofinishing
10	Formal Wear and Costume Rental

Similarly, the creation and mass marketing of the automobile contributed to the destruction of many industries such as horse and buggy producers, blacksmiths, whip and saddle makers, stable boys, and dirt carters (manure removers). This caused many people to lose their jobs. The newly unemployed had to gain new education or skills to find a job in industries which were growing. William C. Durant, a leading buggy manufacturer left the buggy industry for the automobile industry where he later founded General Motors.

The high turnover rate among the largest firms is well illustrated through an examination of the Dow Jones Industrial Index. The **Dow Jones Industrial Index (DJIA)** is an index of the some of the largest firms publicly traded on the New York Stock Exchange. Table 6.3 illustrates how the makeup of the DJIA has changed over time. The only one of these companies continuously listed in the DJIA from 1896 until 2011 has been General Electric. For decades Woolworth's was the nation's leading retailer. Now Wal-Mart holds that position.

Markets don't make themselves. Individuals make them. Metals don't mine themselves; the George Hearsts of the world mine them. Retail goods don't sell

[3] http://blogs.wsj.com/economics/2011/03/28/top-10-dying-industries/

Table 6.3 **DOW JONES INDUSTRIAL AVERAGE COMPOSITE COMPANIES**

2011	1976	1928	1896
3M	Allied Chemical	Allied Chemical	American Cotton Oil
Alcoa	Aluminum Company of America	American Can	American Sugar
American Express	American Can	American Sugar	American Tobacco
AT&T	American Telephone & Telegraph	American Tobacco	Chicago Gas
Bank of America	American Tabacco	American Smelting	Distililllin & Cattle Feeding
Boeing	Bethlehem Steel	Atlantic Refining	General Electric
Caterpillar	Chrysler	Bethlehem Steel	Laclede Gas
Chevron Corporation	Du Pont	Chrysler	National Lead
Cisco Systems	Eastman Kodak Company	General Electric Company	North American Utility
Coca-Cola	Esmark (Swift and Co)	General Motors Corporation	Tenessee Coal & Iron
Du Pont	Exxon Corporation (Standard Oil NJ)	General Railway Signal	U.S. Leather
ExxonMobile	General Electric Company	Goodrich	U.S. Rubber
General Electric	General Foods	International Harvester	
Hewlett-Packard	General Motors Corporation	International Nickel	
The Home Depot	Goodyear	Mack Truck	
Intel	Inco (internation Nickel)	Nash Motors	
IBM	International Harvester	North American	
Johnson & Johnson	International Paper Company	Paramount Publix	
JPMorgan Chase	Johns-Manville	Posum Incorporated	
Kraft Foods	Minnesota Mining & Manufacturing	Radio Corpoaration	
McDonald's	Owens-Illions Glass	Sears Roebuck & Company	
Merck	Proctor & Gable Company	Standar Oil (NJ)	
Microsoft	Sears Roebuck & Company	Texas Company	
Pfizer	Standard Oil of Company	Texas Gulf Sulphur	
Procter & Gamble	Texaco Incorporated	Union Carbide	
Traveler's	Union Carbide	U.S. Steel	
United Technologies Corporation	United Technologies Corporation	Victor Talking Machine	
Verizon Communications	US Steel	Westinghouse Electric	
Wal-Mart	Westinghouse Electric	Woolworth	
Walt Disney	Woolworth	Wright Aeronautical	

themselves; the Sam Waltons of the world sell them. Cars don't make themselves; the Henry Fords of the world build them. Electricity doesn't generate itself; the Thomas Edisons of the world generate it. Telephones don't grow on trees; the Alexander Graham Bells of the world make them. Software doesn't write itself; the Bill Gates of the world write it. As we learned in Chapter 1, entrepreneurship refers to combining resources in a new or innovative way or risk taking. We now turn to examining entrepreneurship.

The Role of Entrepreneurship in Economic Growth

Free markets and the protection of property rights are necessary but not sufficient conditions to generate meaningful long term economic growth. Games, no matter how just the rules, need players to play and entertain. Economic growth, no matter how free the markets and just the rules, needs **entrepreneurs** to build and create.

It would take a whole textbook to list every major development in the American economy and the corresponding entrepreneur. Encyclopedic volumes would not hold all the other minor achievements entrepreneurs have made to the US economy. Economic growth doesn't happen because one big guy in Washington D.C. has a great idea. It happens because millions of people every day have ideas that they act upon. Some are big ideas, some are small ideas. Some are good ideas, and some are downright foolish.

Eighty percent of new businesses fail within the first five years. Starting a new business is a risk. Yet, a successful economy needs creative risk takers. It is no coincidence that the rapid industrialization of the US in the late nineteenth century occurred during the heyday of American capitalism. Entrepreneurs were free to improve the world and make a buck in the process. The tycoons of yesteryear were able to amass great personal fortunes, but they also improved the lot of the poor by providing electricity, better transportation, improved communication, and better products at lower prices. America would be poorer if the tycoons had not been allowed to create wealth. Unfortunately, many tycoons that brought industrialization to the US are demonized as being "Robber Barons." This pejorative term is very misleading. Robbery and wealth creation through voluntary exchanges are altogether opposites. Entrepreneurs don't amass money for themselves by forcibly taking it from other people. They offer better products or lower prices than their competitors and people freely buy their products because they believe said products will improve their lives.

Entrepreneurs wear many hats. They invent new products, innovate new product lines, improve the quality of products, increase the efficiency of existing production and distribution, engage in **arbitrage**, take risks, and connect sellers with buyers and financiers with producers. They can also see where existing products sold by existing companies in existing markets can be altered to produce more wealth.

Government Created Obstacles: Bailouts, Tax Codes, and Regulations

Government sponsored bailouts represent a complete rejection of the importance of entrepreneurs and the process of creative destruction in wealth creation. Existing firms sometimes use the political process to protect themselves from competition. They lobby for trade restrictions against foreign competition. They lobby for regulation of competing industries. They lobby for tax breaks for their existing firms to make them more competitive than other firms in their industry. They lobby for direct and indirect government subsidization of their business or industry. They lobby for regulations placed on new entrants into their industry. Existing businesses with existing employees have more political clout than hypothetical businesses that do not yet exist or that are yet to grow large.

In contrast, if a firm is allowed to fail, its assets do not disappear. They are sold off to the highest bidders, who, in turn, will put them to use in more efficient ways than they were previously employed, lest the purchasers too go out of business. Workers don't die when the firm for which they work stops production. They become potential laborers for other firms in the same or even in different industries. The sign of a healthy growing economy is not one where existing firms never shed jobs, but one in which existing firms are allowed to shed jobs to free up labor to engage in more efficient production.

The US doesn't need a vibrant horse drawn buggy industry in order to thrive. Preventing the growth of one firm or industry (via taxes, regulation, or other means) to protect another firm or industry cripples not only entrepreneurship, but also cripples economic growth by inefficiently redistributing scarce resources. Clinging tightly to existing jobs will only cause fewer new jobs to be created.

Markets are constantly evolving. By taking advantage of individual information known to Hayek's "**men on the street,**" individual entrepreneurs are able to create, innovate, and meet the needs and desires of the people around them.

Entrepreneurship is as natural to humans as breathing. It involves people trying to make the world a better place for themselves and the world around them. When Thomas Edison made and mass marketed electric lights, he not only improved his own wealth, but materially improved the lives of everyone else who could now have light after sunset without candles—except for employees of the candle industry who now needed to look elsewhere for jobs.

Governments can both foster and hinder entrepreneurship through government regulations and the tax code. Tax codes that provide low marginal tax rates applied equally to all firms benefit entrepreneurs more than tax codes with high marginal rates, but special tax breaks to politically connected firms. Since startups tend to be small politically unconnected firms, being hit with higher taxes than their larger competitors only serves to disadvantage to them.

Regulations regarding the formation of a business or regulations regarding hiring and firing of employees are particularly important to small startup firms. Table 6.4[4] shows the average number of days it takes in different parts of the world to register a new business venture. Table 6.5[5] shows the top ten best and worst countries in which to do business. The factors that went into the calculation included ease of starting a business, dealing with construction permits, registering property, getting credit, protecting investors, paying taxes, trading across borders, enforcing contracts, and ease of closing businesses.

Because entrepreneurs create wealth, it should not be surprising that the countries that are most receptive to doing business rank among the wealthiest economies in the world. Those that erect the most barriers to private industry

table 6.4.

[4] Source: Doing Business Project of the World Bank

[5] Ibid.

Table 6.4 **DAYS TO REGISTER A NEW BUSINESS**

Region	# of Days	Country	# of Days	Country	# of Days
OECD	13.8	New Zealand	1	Equitorial Guinea	136
Eastern Europe & Central Asia	16.3	Australia	2	Venezuela	141
Middle East and North Africa	20	Georgia	3	Sao Tome and Principe	144
South Africa	24.6	Macedonia	3	Republic of the Congo	160
East Asia & Pacific	39	Rwanda	3	Gunea-Bissau	216
Asub-Saharan Africa	45.2	Singapore	3	Suriname	694
Latin America & Caribbean	56.7				

Table 6.5 **BEST COUNTRIES TO DO BUSINESS IN**

Rank	Country	Rank	Country
1	Singapore	174	Timor-Leste
2	Hong Kong	175	Democratic Republic of Congo
3	New Zealand	176	Guinea-Bissau
4	UK	177	Republic of Congo
5	US	178	Sao Tome and Pricipe
6	Denmark	179	Guinea-Bissau
7	Canada	180	Eritrea
8	Norway	181	Burundi
9	Ireland	182	Central African Republic
10	Australia	183	Chad

rank amongst the poorest countries in the world. Perhaps the most important set of economic growth policies revolve around letting people improve their own lives and the lives of those around them.

Convergence

Countries in the world can be placed into one of three categories. **Industrialized countries** (the first world) have the highest levels of per capita GDP along with high levels of capital accumulation. Examples include the US, Canada, Japan, Hong Kong, Australia, New Zealand, South Korea, and most of Western Europe. **Industrializing countries** (the second world or emerging markets) have lower per capita GDP than industrialized countries but higher levels than the non-industrialized countries. Examples include, China, India, most of Eastern Europe, most of South America, much of Southeast Asia, Mexico, and Russia. **Non-industrialized countries** (the third world) are the poorest countries in the world. These countries are disproportionately located in Africa and Central America.

All things being equal, entrepreneurs will move capital and technology to where they can pair them with cheaper wage labor. Accordingly, the non-industrialized economies of the world should have the highest economic growth rates as they attract **foreign direct investment** in capital and gain access to foreign technology. Industrializing countries should have the next highest growth rate followed by the industrialized world. As countries get closer and closer to the per capita income levels of the industrialized world, their economic growth rates should slow down. Playing economic catch up should be easier for an economy than leading the economic pack. From bicycle racing to car racing, the headwind is born by the first cyclist/car and other racers are able to draft. Likewise, poorer economies can economically draft off of richer ones. This concept is called convergence theory. **Convergence theory** suggests that countries with a lower per capita GDP should grow faster than countries with a higher per capita GDP until their economies catch up. As poor countries catch up, their economic growth rates slow down causing their per capita GDP to converge with richer countries.

Does convergence theory hold? It is largely holding for the industrialized world. Table 6.6 shows 2011 growth rates in selected countries as forecast by *The*

Table 6.6 **2011 FORECAST GDP GROWTH RATES**

Industrialized Countries		Industrialized Countries	
Canada	2.9	China	9
United States	2.6	India	8.6
Euro Area	1.9	Argentina	6.9
Japan	-0.2	Vietnam	6.9

Economist magazine.[6] Emerging markets are attracting entrepreneurs, capital, and technology at faster rates than the industrialized world.

Who benefits? Should industrialized countries be concerned? Actually, this process of wealth creation benefits inhabitants both in and out of these countries. A rising level of capital and technology works to increase wages, per capita GDP, and consumption levels of citizens of the industrializing world. It benefits producers in industrialized countries who gain access to cheaper production and wider markets for their goods and services. It also benefits consumers in the industrialized world who now have access to cheaper goods and services.

Convergence, as evidenced by many non-industrialized countries, is not an economic given. Capital and technology have to be moved to third world countries by entrepreneurs, both domestic and foreign. Capital doesn't move itself. If the economic rules of the game discourage entrepreneurship in a country, then convergence won't happen, or its pace will be diminished. Many poor countries who could experience fast economic growth continue to stay poor because their cultural/political rules of the economic game are not conducive to entrepreneurial actions.

Poorly defined or enforced property rights are a leading cause of the lack of convergence amongst many of the world's poorest countries, according to work done by Hernando De Soto.[7] All risk and no reward make entrepreneurship a dull tool. If entrepreneurs are not allowed to benefit from their market innovations, they will not engage in them.

---

[6] http://www.economist.com/node/18837035?story_id=18837035

[7] *The Mystery of Capital: Why Capitalism Triumphs in the West and Fails Everywhere Else*. 2000.

Glossary

Arbitrage—moving resources whose prices vary between markets until the price of the resource is the same in all markets

Convergence theory—countries with a lower per capita GDP should grow faster than countries with a higher per capita GDP until their economies catch up

Creative destruction—economic innovation that renders existing technology, capital, human capital, or firms obsolete

Dow Jones Industrial Index—an index of 30 of the largest firms publicly traded on the New York Stock Exchange

Entrepreneurs—people who invent new products, innovate new product lines, improve the quality of products, increase the efficiency of existing production and distribution, engage in arbitrage, take risks, or connect sellers with buyers and financiers with producers

Foreign direct investment—the building of capital by foreign firms

Government sponsored bailout—the use of tax dollars to prevent a private firm from financial decline or bankruptcy

Industrialized countries—countries with the highest capital to labor ratios

Industrializing countries—countries with are quickly increasing their capital to labor ratio

Man on the street—a person who, according to Friedrich Von Hayek, possesses knowledge about himself and his direct surroundings

Non-industrialized countries—countries with the lowest capital to labor ratios

Questions for Review

↓agriculture, mining

1. What is entrepreneurship? Give examples of recent innovations. Name job sectors that may have seen declines as a result of this innovation. What is the net impact to society from the innovation? ↑health care, finance.
2. Why is entrepreneurship important to wealth creation?
3. What government policies promote or deter entrepreneurial activity?
4. Name ten famous US entrepreneurs and the industry in which they operated.
5. What is convergence theory?
6. Is convergence theory holding in reality? Who benefits from convergence?
7. What impediments to economic convergence exist?

Chapter 7 Specialization and Trade

"Anything you can do, I can do better. I can do anything better than you.... Can you bake a pie? No. Neither can I."

Source: "Anything You Can Do", *Oklahoma*

The inputs we have examined in previous chapters are not homogenous. Some land is more fertile than other land. Workers have various levels of knowledge and skill regarding the production of any number of goods and services. Even capital is specialized. One can use a stapler as a hammer, but not very well. In this chapter, we shall examine the wealth creating benefit of trade, explore the mechanisms for restricting trade, scrutinize arguments in favor of enacting such restrictions and outline their counterarguments.

Why Trade?

For a moment consider all of the items you have used today. Perhaps you brushed your teeth with toothpaste, cooked a ham and cheese omelet on a stove, dressed in a sweater and jeans and tennis shoes, drove in a car to work, etc. Imagine now if you had to produce every item you consumed today. It would not be possible for us to consume at our current standard of living if we had to produce everything ourselves, as we couldn't produce as much. Similarly, individuals who live alone on a specific piece of land and don't trade with other people live very poor existences. Firstly, their land, fixed in some particular climate, will be good at producing some things but not others. The tropical rainforest of Honduras is good for growing bananas, but not wheat. The fertile fields of Illinois are good for growing corn, but not for growing oranges. Self-sufficient farmers, therefore, lack variety in their diet. A lack of dietary variety leads to a shorter life expectancy than a diversified, balanced diet.

In temperate climates, self-sufficient farmers also face problems of food supply management as food doesn't grow in the winter. Life on the isolated American frontier of the 1800's involved canning of fruits and vegetables for winter, less variety of food than we see today, and frequent starvation. Less than 40% of homestead entries in Montana were completed in the 1800's. That is, even when the government was giving away free land, people couldn't generate enough wealth from the land to avoid starvation.

At the time of the American Revolution, roughly 80% of Americans were farmers. Now fewer than 2% of Americans are farmers. This has been the result of increased use of capital, technology, education, and trade. Without trade, all of our days would be consumed worrying about where our next meal would come from. With trade, the biggest food question for many Americans seems to be, "Where do we go out to eat tonight?" And, even as the local food movement has seen a recent growth in popularity, trade still plays an important role. Those striving to eat locally can consume more if they trade with other farmers than if they only eat what they themselves can grow.

The first argument for why we should engage in trade is that voluntary trade creates wealth. When two people voluntarily agree to an exchange of goods or services, they are doing so because each values the marginal benefit of the other's offer to be higher than the marginal cost of what they have to give up. Trade creates wealth by allowing goods and services to flow from where they have a lower marginal value to where they have a higher marginal value.

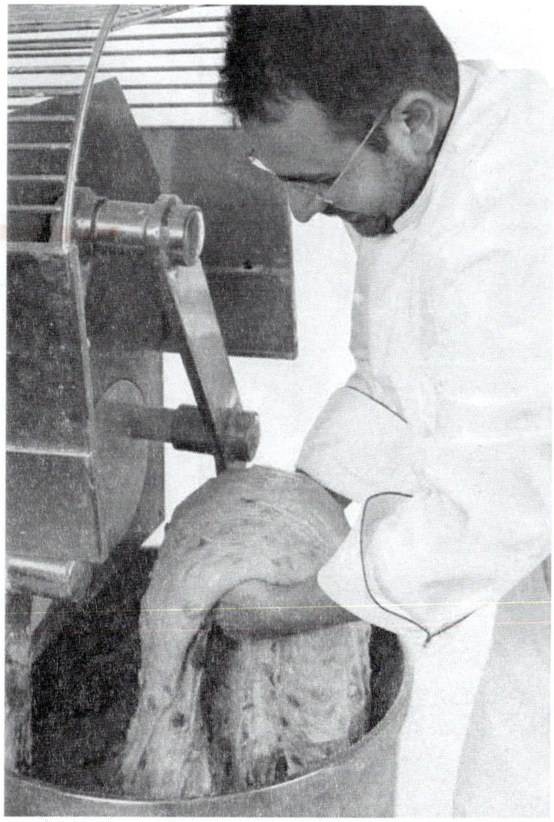

© areashot, 2012, under license Shutterstock, Inc.

A baker may like cake, but even Marie Antoinette would concede that there is only so much cake a guy can eat. Therefore, he often values the production of a new cake less than does the butcher who is cake-less. By trading meat for cake, both the butcher and the baker can improve their wellbeing by giving up something of little marginal value in exchange for something of a higher marginal value to them.

Furthermore, since the baker is specialized at baking, the ability to trade for meat frees up his time to focus on what he produces well. By focusing on his baking, the baker specializes according to his specific skills. As resources are allowed to move from areas of production where they are ill suited to areas of production where they excel, more production is allowed to occur. This **specialization** and **division of labor** was a chief source of wealth creation noted in Adam Smith's *Wealth of Nations* in 1776,

The second argument in favor of trade, then, is that different resources are specialized in the production of different goods and services. In order for a Canadian to gain access to a banana, they must trade with a country whose climate is conducive to banana production. While Canada doesn't produce bananas, they do produce oil from the Alberta oil sands. The US imports more oil from Canada than from any other country in the world.

Coffee beans grow best in high altitudes such as is found in Columbia and Kenya. Cashmere comes from silk worms in Kashmir. Diamonds often come from the Southern Horn of Africa. Utility (army) knives overwhelmingly come from Switzerland. Many oriental rugs come from Pakistan. Whether it is the unequal spatial distribution of natural resources or skill and education levels across the globe, increased trade allows people to take advantage of finding even more people whose skills or resources differ and therefore widening the access of traders to a larger diversity of products.

© Guryanov Andrey Vladimirovich, 2012, under license Shutterstock, Inc.

Some products are too large for every country to make. There are only two jumbo jet producers in the world, Boeing and Airbus. Yet, many airlines in different countries want to be able to acquire jumbo jets. The scale of production of jumbo jets precludes small economies from entering the market for their production. If Air Jamaica wants a plane they will need to trade with a country outside of the Caribbean. There are no core industries that a country must have to gain wealth. The key to wealth creation lies within every country using the unique resources and skills that exist within each country to specialize and trade with other countries.

Free trade creates wealth. Trade is not a **zero sum game**. It is **positive sum**. Since World War II, the single biggest catalyst for worldwide economic growth has been increased international trade. China used to be the richest country in the world. Then they built a great wall around themselves, isolated themselves, and became one of the poorest countries in the world. Since the early 1990's China has decided to be part of the international economy and their annual growth rate has averaged near 10%.

Transaction costs (transportation, cultural differences, government regulations, and currency exchanges) often restrict the amount of trade that is feasible. It is easy to trade with a member of your family who lives in your house. You know you can trust them, they live near you, you speak the same language, and you share the same currency. Trading with your neighbors down the street isn't much harder.

As transaction costs rise due to increased distance or cultural differences, the fewer wealth creating trades will be made. Still, ocean shipping is the cheapest form of transportation, so it is often cheaper to ship butter from New Zealand to Puerto Vallarta, Mexico than it is to ship butter there from inland neighboring Mexican states.

Trade's Wealth Creating Mathematical Certainty

To illustrate how trade is a positive sum game, envision two countries, the US and the UK in a world where the only two products produced are ginger ale and beef. Chart 7.1 reveals the output per worker per day in each country if they dedicate their entire day to the production of that good, either beef or ale. For example, a worker in the US is able to produce either 15 lbs of beef or 60 liters of ale.

Chart 7.1

An **absolute advantage** exists if one can produce more output per unit of input. The US has an absolute advantage in the production of beef over the UK because a US worker can produce more beef per day than can a UK laborer. Similarly, the UK is said to have an absolute advantage in the production of ginger ale as one worker in the UK can produce more ginger ale than a similar worker in the US. In this case, it is apparent that one country is really good at producing one product while the other is good at producing another product.

If the US and the UK in this example engage in free world trade, two things will happen. The first is that wealth will be created, and the second is that both countries will be made better off. Assume that each country has exactly two

Chart 7.1

	US	UK
Beef (lbs)	15	5
Ginger Ale (liters)	60	100

workers. In a world of no trade, if one worker in each country produced each good, then world production would look as follows:

US production	UK production	World production
15 lbs beef	5 lbs beef	20 lbs beef
60 liters ale	100 liters ale	160 liters of ale

Now assume that each country specializes in the product where they have an absolute advantage. Both US workers will produce beef while both UK workers will produce ginger ale.

US production	UK production	World production
30 lbs beef	0 lbs beef	30 lbs beef
0 liters ale	200 liters ale	200 liters of ale

By engaging in specialization and the division of labor, world wealth increased. The same inputs were used in both scenarios, but in the free world trade scenario 10 more lbs of beef and 40 more liters of ginger ale were produced. The world's production possibilities frontier expands under free trade. As long as both countries want both products, they can make more of them by using the same quantity of inputs, but allowing those inputs to specialize in what they do best. Figure 7.1 illustrates the change in the world PPF that would happened by allowing trade. Note the straight line illustrates the total production in the world without trade. As there are two countries producing, each with two workers, if both produced only beef they could produce 40 lbs of beef (15 lbs per worker in the US and 5 lbs per worker in the UK). However, if free trade is allowed, the PPF would bow outward creating more possible production options for the world economy. Note: the endpoints do not change because they are still only possible with both countries producing that single good. But, for all points in between consumption possibilities and world production possibilities increase.

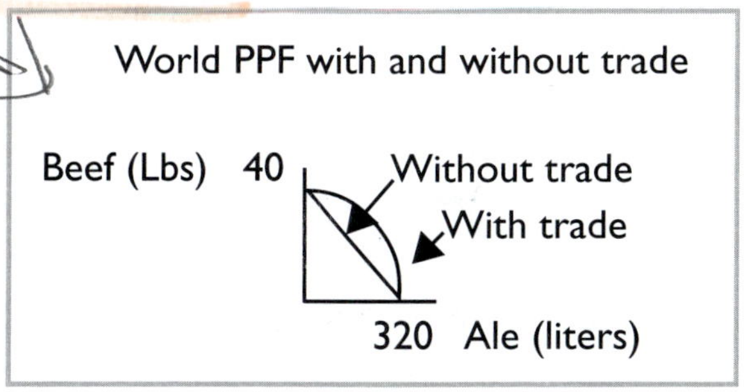

Figure 7.1 **WORLD PPF'S ASSUMING EACH COUNTRY HAS TWO WORKERS**

Sure each country could be self-sufficient in the sense that they could make both beef and ginger ale, but both countries can have more of both products if they specialize and trade. Note that every time the US produces 15 lbs of beef, they are forgoing 60 liters of ginger ale. Consequently, the opportunity cost of 1 lb of beef is 4 liters of ginger ale (this is found by dividing 60 by 15). In this case, the US should be willing to trade a pound of beef to the UK as long as they get more than 4 liters of ginger ale in return (so that they get more than their own opportunity cost of producing it). Similarly, the UK could produce beef, but when it does so, it forgoes the production of 20 liters of ginger ale (100 divided by 5). The UK would not want to offer more than 20 liters of ginger ale for one pound of beef. Both countries will end up with more output if they trade one pound of US beef for somewhere between 4 and 20 liters of ginger ale.

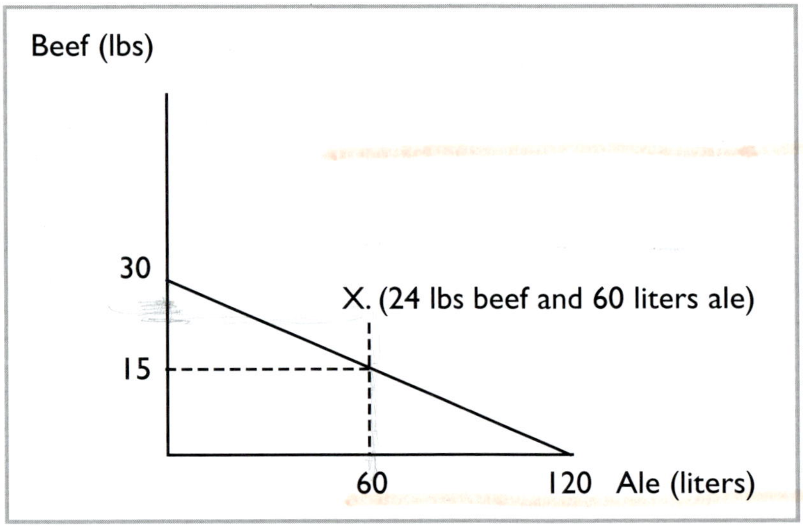

Figure 7.2 **US PPF WITH 2 WORKERS**

Suppose the countries agree on a terms of trade of 10 liters of ginger ale for one pound of beef. If the US wants to consume 60 liters of ale, then it will have to trade 6 lbs of beef. It will still have 24 lbs left to consume. Note that in absence of trade, producing 60 liters of ale required the entire time of one worker, leaving only 15 lbs of beef (the other worker's production) for consumption. This is illustrated in Figure 7.2. Point X containing 60 liters of ale and 24 lbs of beef would be off of the production possibility frontier of the US in absence of trade, and yet is possible for consumption if the countries engage in trade. Similarly, Canada benefits by being able to now consume 6 lbs of beef and 140 liters of ale, a combination they could not have consumed in absence of trade. In this way, free trade creates wealth!

What if a country has an absolute advantage in the production of everything? Would they ever benefit from trade? Again, assume a two country two good world represented by the following levels of output per worker per day.

Chart 7.2

	US	Canada
Wheat (bushels)	10	8
Potatoes (bushels)	50	32

In this case, the US has an absolute advantage in both wheat and potatoes, as one worker in the US can produce more of either good than a worker in Canada. To determine whether or not the US will benefit from trade with Canada, one must first determine which country has a **comparative advantage** in the production of each good. A country has a comparative advantage if its opportunity cost of production is lower than the other country. If each country has a comparative advantage in a different product, both countries will benefit from trade.

The opportunity cost of a worker producing one bushel of wheat in the US is 5 bushels of potatoes. In Canada, the opportunity cost of producing one bushel of wheat is only 4 bushels of potatoes. Canada gives up fewer potatoes to produce wheat than does the US, and therefore Canada has a comparative advantage in wheat production. The opportunity cost of producing one bushel of potatoes in the US is one-fifth of a bushel of wheat. In Canada, the opportunity cost of producing one bushel of potatoes is one-fourth of a bushel of wheat. By having a lower opportunity cost of production, the US has a comparative advantage in potato production.

Notice the opportunity cost of one bushel of potatoes is the reciprocal of the opportunity cost of one bushel of wheat. In this manner, every country is mathematically guaranteed to have a comparative advantage in the production of something. No matter how bad a country is at producing goods, it will be better at producing some goods than others and therein will be their comparative advantage.

In this case, as long as Canada receives between four and five bushels of potatoes for one bushel of wheat, both the US and Canada will gain from trade. Canada could grow potatoes but would have to forgo 4 bushels of potatoes to produce a bushel of wheat. Canada must at least receive four bushels of potatoes to be made better off from trade. Likewise, the US could grow wheat but would have to forgo the production of five bushels of potatoes to grow it. Instead, if they grow the five bushels of potatoes and sell less than that to Canada for a bushel of wheat, they can have more output.

Trade Agreements

In order to reduce global trade barriers following WWII, many countries got together to sign onto **Global Agreement on Tariffs and Trade (GATT)**. The **World Trade Organization (WTO)** was formed to implement GATT and now has 153 members. The reduction in global trade barriers brought about through GATT has done more to increase world trade than have **regional trade agreements**.

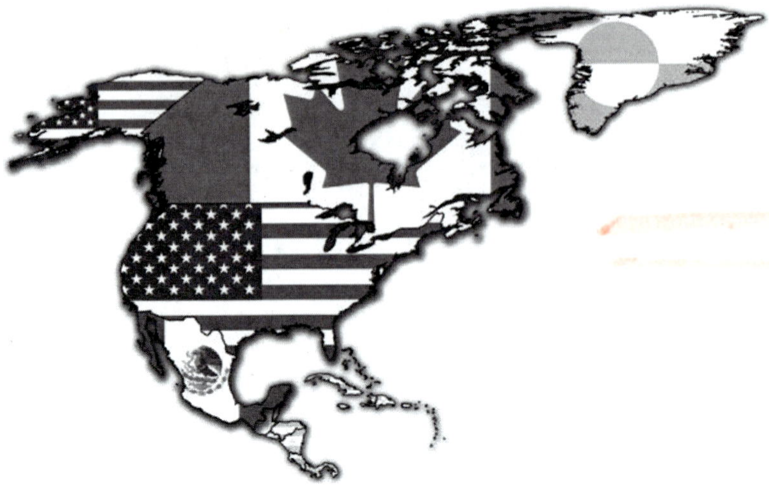

With each round of trade negotiations, the WTO seeks to lower more trade barriers. Because the agreements apply equally to all 153 countries, they all must approve of the agreements before they can take effect. Therefore, the trade agreements with the largest potential to speed economic growth are also the politically most difficult to achieve. As a result, many countries have enacted **multilateral trade deals** between smaller numbers of countries. Each round of WTO negotiations is named after the location where they begin. The current round of negotiations is the DOHA round.

The European Union has a free trade deal among its members. ***The North American Free Trade Agreement (NAFTA)***, enacted in 1994, lowered trade barriers between Canada, the US, and Mexico. This was an important deal for all three economies, as both Canada and Mexico rank among the top five biggest trading partners with the US.

NAFTA helped all three North American economies grow. Unemployment in each of the countries fell in the late 1990's following NAFTA's ratification. **The Free Trade Area of the Americas (FTAA)** was a proposal to form a free trade area for the Western Hemisphere, but formal negotiations for this treaty have been stalled since 2005. However, the US did pass the **Dominican Republic - Central American - US Free Trade Agreement (CAFTA)** in 2004.

The US also has **bilateral trade agreements** with Australia, Bahrain, Chile, Colombia, Israel, Jordan, Korea, Morocco, Oman, Panama, Peru, and Singapore. Exports to Peru doubled in the year after the Peruvian free trade agreement.

Table 7.1[1] **TOP US TRADING PARTNERS, 2010 IN BILLIONS OF US $**

1. Canada	$ 525
2. China	$ 457
3. Mexico	$ 393
4. Japan	$ 180
5. Germany	$ 131

[1] Source US Census Bureau Foreign Trade Statistics

While bilateral trade agreements don't reduce as many trade barriers as multilateral trade deals, they are easier to negotiate.

The Balance of Trade

In 1950, imports and exports made up less than 5% of the US economy. By 2009, US imports were 14% of US GDP while exports were 11% of US GDP. The US economy has become more globally integrated as a result of reduced trade barriers and lower transaction costs from technological advancements in transportation and communication.

In the 1960's and 1970's, the US ran a trade surplus with the rest of the world. Currently, the US runs a trade deficit. Table 7.2[2] illustrates the tremendous increase in both imports and exports that the US has experienced since 1960.

Some people mistakenly believe that a trade surplus is "good" while a trade deficit is "bad". The truth is that the most important trade statistic is the total dollar value of trade. The more that specialized goods and services are voluntarily traded, the more wealth gets created. If a country runs a trade deficit, they must also run a **capital account surplus**. When Americans buy goods from abroad, they must first exchange their dollars for foreign currency. When the US runs a trade deficit, someone outside of the US must be collecting US dollars.

for the products we traded w/ them

These dollars can go to one of three places. If the dollars forever remain outside of the US and are used by people in other countries to exchange goods amongst themselves, then the US has successfully traded worthless pieces of paper for real goods and services. In other words, in this scenario the US never

Table 7.2 **US BALANCE OF TRADE IN BILLIONS OF DOLLARS**

	Exports	Imports	Trade Surplus/Deficit
1960	25.9	22.4	3.5
1970	56.6	54.4	2.2
1980	272	291	-19
1990	535	616	-80
2000	1,070	1,449	-378
2010	1,289	2,330	-998

[2] Source World Bank

has to give anything of value in return for the goods it received. If the dollars return to the US in the future, then the US will run a trade surplus at that point in time as foreigners buy more US goods and services. Alternatively, the foreign owners of US dollars could store their currency in US financial institutions. This money is then made available for consumers, firms, and governments to borrow to consume, invest, and spend in the economy. A trade deficit is only natural for a country that seeks to use foreign savings for their own investment in capital.

At any point in time the **balance of trade** plus the **capital account** must equal zero. In early US history, the US faced relative capital scarcity and ran years of trade deficits as foreign savers poured money into US financial markets. As the US government now piles up trillions of dollars of debt, their need for a capital inflow to purchase this debt causes the economy to run a trade deficit. Budget deficits (spending more than is received in revenues) cause trade deficits, which is why the two are known as the **twin deficits**. Politicians who dislike the trade deficit often advocate increased trade barriers to reduce imports. Rather than lower wealth creating trade, politicians who earnestly want to reduce the trade deficit should focus their attention on lowering the budget deficit or increasing the domestic savings rate. A low amount of domestic savings relative to the domestic demand for borrowing will result in a trade deficit. If the borrowing fuels current consumption, future economic growth will be compromised. If the borrowing fuels investment in productive capital, then future economic growth will be enhanced.

Trade Barriers

There are four ways governments can restrict trade: a tariff, a quota, an embargo, or regulation. A **tariff** is a tax on imports. **Quotas** restrict the quantity of an import into a country, while **embargoes** outlaw all trade with a country. Countries can also use their regulatory powers to put foreign producers at a disadvantage in the market.

While both tariffs and quotas can be used to restrict trade, tariffs destroy less wealth than do quotas. If a tariff is placed on an imported good, then the sales price of that good will increase. Foreign producers will receive a lower price for their good while consumers pay more for the good. The difference between what the producer receives and the consumer pays is the amount of the tariff which the government collects. In addition, the prices of domestically produced versions of the good increase as demand for those goods increase. So, domestic producers have increased revenue. (In both cases, consumers of domestic and foreign goods that have a tariff must now pay more for the good).

While both foreign producers and domestic consumers are hurt by a tariff, the federal government does gain tax revenue and domestic producers of the good have increased revenue.

Under a quota, the federal government gains no tax revenue. By restricting the importation of goods, foreign producers are able to sell fewer products, but also face less competition for their products. As a result, they are able to charge higher prices to US consumers. Just as with tariffs, not only will US consumers pay more for imported goods under a quota regime, they will also pay more for domestically made goods as there will be less competition in the market to keep prices low.

Because a tariff is applied equally to all foreign producers, the most efficient (low cost) producers will still have a competitive advantage over their less efficient competition. However, under a quota, government officials pick which companies get to sell their products in the market. This type of government selection encourages bribery and corruption and means that bureaucrats rather than consumers choose the products that are for sale. There is no guarantee under a quota system that the most efficient producers will be selected to export their goods.

Embargos also increase the price of domestically produced goods. The US has an embargo on trade with Cuba since 1960. Embargos do the most damage to a country's wealth because they outlaw all wealth creating trades between two countries. Embargos not only hurt the country at which they are directed but also hurt consumers in the enforcing country by limiting access to goods and raising prices on domestically produced goods that do not have to compete with lower prices from abroad. Embargos are typically reserved for countries with which a country is at war.

Arguments for Trade Restriction

Given the wealth creating power of lower trade barriers, why do we live in a world awash in trade restrictions? The answer to this question is political rather than economic. There are many reasons used by politicians to support trade restrictions. Below are lists of the **protectionist** arguments used along with their counterarguments. A protectionist is someone who advocates trade restrictions on imports.

1. **To protect US jobs**—There is a belief that restricting the importation of goods and services will cause Americans to buy more domestically produced goods. This increase in domestic demand will then lead to the need to hire more Americans.

   Counterargument—Trade restrictions destroy more jobs than they create. As we illustrated in the earlier section on comparative advantage, forcing resources to abandon their comparative advantage will cause world production to fall. Resources in the US go from where they can create a lot of production to areas where production is more difficult. Although some politically connected jobs are saved by protectionism, in net more job creation potential exists with trade.

Example—The US restricts the importation of foreign grown sugar into the US in order to save sugar growing jobs in the US. Rather than let sugar come from the sugar cane fields of Jamaica or Brazil, politicians would rather have US citizens buy sugar from Florida sugar cane or plains state sugar beet growers. The result is that the price of sugar in the US is double what it is in the rest of the world. This does create jobs in the US sugar growing industry. However, it has destroyed even more jobs in the candy making industry as large US candy makers have moved their production facilities oversees to take advantage of cheaper sugar inputs. Additionally, sugar has been replaced in American foods and sodas with high fructose corn syrup to avoid the high cost of sugar. Coke and Pepsi only use high fructose corn syrup in the US and they do so because of government tariffs on sugar.

2. **To gain a price advantage**—If trade restrictions increase the price of foreign made goods, then more people will choose to buy American made goods.

Counterargument—If the US places a tariff on imports, other countries will retaliate with tariffs placed on goods and services exported from the US. Jobs will then be lost in export oriented industries.

Example—When the US placed a tariff on European made steel in 2002, the European Union threatened retaliation by placing tariffs on US made goods such as Harley Davidson motorcycles, Florida oranges, and cars made in Michigan. As a result, the US repealed the steel tariff rather than risk losing jobs in the motorcycle, car, and orange industries.

3. **For political reasons**—The US may wish to punish countries they consider to be part of the "axis of evil"[3]

Counterargument—Political reasons are rarely consistent.

Example—When Fidel Castro came to power in Cuba during its communist revolution, private businesses and property were nationalized. The US has placed a trade embargo on Cuba until such time as they reimburse the former owners of the nationalized property for their losses, many of whom live in Florida. In fact, during the American Revolution the American government confiscated property from loyalists and forced them to move to Canada. These loyalists have never been reimbursed for their loss of property.

When Mao Zedong came to power in China during its communist revolution, private businesses and property were nationalized. Yet, the US trades with China even as they refuse to repay those who lost property during their revolution.

[3] A term first used by President George W. Bush in his 2002 State of the Union Address

The US does trade with some communist countries; it just does not trade with ones that have a huge expatriate presence in a presidential swing state. While the US economy is hurt by not trading with Cuba, it would be hurt even more by not trading with China.

4. **For national security reasons**—It is not in the national security interests of the US to sell stealth bombers or nuclear weapons to countries that seek our destruction.

   Counterargument—Everything is not a national security issue.

   Example—In 2001, the US Army cancelled an order of black berets (hats) because of "national security interests". It was deemed not in American's national security interest to buy berets made in China[4]. Given that a beret can't actually stop a bullet anyway, it is difficult to surmise the national security interest. Nevertheless, the contract was awarded to an American company who couldn't meet the deadline and had to outsource the berets to Mexico.

5. **To prevent dumping**—If a country is allowed to sell its goods below cost, they will do so until they put domestic manufacturers out of business. Once that occurs, they can raise their prices and take advantage of consumers.

   Counterargument—Selling below cost cannot be made up by selling in volume; a company just loses more. As a result, dumping, rarely, if ever, happens. In reality, if a company sustained losses in order to force out competition, then as soon as they raise their prices, new entrants will arise to compete. Thus, dumping is not prone to be a successful strategy for foreign companies. Most likely, those businesses that claim dumping is occurring are actually just observing that their competitors are able to produce at a lower cost.

   Example—The US made the claim that Europe was **dumping** steel in the US, which kept West Virginian steel companies at a disadvantage. However, when the WTO investigated, no dumping was found to have taken place.

   If dumping were ever found to occur (say in plasma TV's) then US consumers would benefit. People in other countries would be paying for our consumption.

6. **To protect infant industries**—New industries may need time to develop without competitive pressures. Once they develop and become competitive trade barriers can be reduced.

   Counterargument—Once an industry benefits from restricted completion, it will be politically difficult to remove that protection, as existing workers would likely lose their jobs. Existing workers bear concentrated benefits to the protection, while consumers bear diffused costs. As such, existing workers will be easier to organize politically than general consumers.

---

[4] May 2, 2001 CNN.com "Army Berets won't be made in China"

Example—Alexander Hamilton advocated the **American System** of high tariffs on manufactured goods in the early 1800's. His argument was that once Americans learned how to manufacture textiles, they could then effectively compete with British firms which had already undergone the industrial revolution. As a result, by the time of the US Civil War, the US had a lower per capita income level than did Australia, whose colonies did not have high tariffs placed on British manufactured goods. So the infant industry argument most likely slowed economic growth in the US during the 1800's.

7. **To avoid exploitation of the poor**—It is not fair to hire someone and pay them $2 an hour to work.

Counterargument—Over a billion people currently live on less than $1.25 a day. To them a job that pays $2 an hour would greatly improve their ability to meet their and their families' needs and wants. By restricting trade with poor countries, protectionists increase world poverty rather than alleviate it.

Example—When firms open factories that pay higher than average wages in a country, lines often form to get job applications. While $10 a day might not sound like a good deal to a US worker, it is an eight fold increase in the per capita income of someone making $1.25 a day. So, their standard of living actually increases from such opportunities.

8. **To protect the environment**—Companies will move their plants away from countries with tight environmental standards to countries with lower standards.

Counterargument—Rising incomes are positively correlated with improved environmental conditions. When people are faced with the choice of pollute and eat or don't pollute and don't eat, they choose the former, just as the US did in its history. As countries become wealthier, one of the things they demand is a cleaner living environment. As trade creates wealth, it is works to make the environment cleaner.

Example—The US used to let manufacturers dump hazardous byproducts into rivers and lakes. As the economy became wealthier, people were more willing to allocate money towards protecting the environment, and public opinion worked to create the clean air and clean water acts.

While trade creates wealth, not everyone is made better off in the short run as result of reducing trade barriers. If a person has invested in physical or human capital that is specialized in an industry that is not competitive and is only in existence due to government protection, then the removal of that protection will cost them their investment and/or their job. However, since trade crates wealth, more jobs will be created than are destroyed by reducing trade barriers. As that provides little solace to the person currently losing their job, trade agreements often contain language to provide financial support to workers who need new training to take advantage of the new jobs created by expanded trade.

Glossary

Absolute Advantage—a country has an absolute advantage when it can produce more output per input than another country

American System—a system of high tariffs proposed by Alexander Hamilton, the first US Treasury Secretary

Balance of trade—the flow of goods and services reflected by a trade surplus or a trade deficit

Bilateral trade agreements—an agreement between two countries to lower trade barriers

Capital account—the net amount of public and private international investment

Capital account deficit—when a country invests more abroad than is invested by foreigners domestically

Capital account surplus—when a country invests less abroad than is invested by foreigners domestically

Comparative Advantage—a country has a comparative advantage if its opportunity cost of production is lower than another country

Division of labor—the specialization of people in specific jobs or tasks

Dominican Republic – Central American – US Free Trade Agreement (CAFTA)—a trade agreement between the US, the Dominican Republic and Central American Countries

Dumping—selling goods below cost

Embargo—outlawing all trade with a country

The European Union—a political union of 27 European countries

The Free Trade Area of the Americas (FTAA)—a proposed regional trade agreement for the Western Hemisphere (minus Cuba)

Global Agreement on Tariffs and Trade (GATT)—a treaty signed by countries after WWII to lower trade barriers

Infant industries—new industries that have just been created

Multilateral trade deals—a trade agreement between three or more countries

The North American Free Trade Agreement (NAFTA)—a regional trade agreement between Canada, Mexico, and the United States

Positive sum game—a game where players can engage in win-win scenarios

Protectionist—someone who advocates restrictions to trade

Quota—a limit on the quantity of an import

Regional trade agreements—a trade agreement between countries in geographical proximity

Specialization—the ability to a specific job well

Tariff—a tax on imports

Transaction costs—transportation, cultural differences, government regulations, and currency exchanges

Twin deficits—the budget deficit and the trade deficit

World Trade Organization (WTO)—an organization formed to implement GATT and now has 153 members

Zero sum game—a game where one player wins at another's expense

Questions for Review

1. Why is free trade a positive sum game?
2. Why are four arguments in favor of erecting trade barriers? What are their counterarguments?
3. Who are the top US trading partners?
4. What is NAFTA? The WTO? The Free Trade Area of the Americas? What are bilateral trade agreements?
5. What are the pros and cons of using bilateral and regional trade agreement rather than the WTO to lower trade barriers?
6. What is a trade deficit? A trade surplus? Which does the US have now? Why?
7. The numbers in the following tables illustrates how many units of a good can be produced in one day by one person in each country.

	US	China
jeans	32	12
computer chips	4	3

   a. Which country has the absolute advantage in jean production?
   b. Which country has the absolute advantage in chip production?
   c. Which country has a comparative advantage in jean production?
   d. Which country has a comparative advantage in chip production?
   e. What is the opportunity cost of 1 chip in the US? In China?
   f. What is the opportunity cost of 1 jean in the US? In China?
   g. Would these two countries be willing to trade? If so, how many jeans would be traded for one computer chip?
8. Compare and contrast a tariff, a quota, and an embargo.
9. Does every country need to produce automobiles? Why or why not?
10. Has the US economy become more or less globally interconnected since WWII? Why and to what benefit?

Chapter 8
Unemployment

Have you ever been stuck in traffic in the middle of the day? Have you ever wondered to yourself "Don't these people blocking my lane have jobs?" It turns out that in April of 2011, only 58.4% of Americans aged 16 and older had a job.[1] Including kids under age sixteen, fewer than half of Americans have a job. While this does not mean that the US unemployment rate is over 50%, it does mean that the US is not producing anywhere close to their production possibilities frontier. In this chapter, we examine what it means to be unemployed and consider policies which affect unemployment rates.

[1] Source: US Bureau of Labor Statistics

Measuring Unemployment, Employment, and Labor Force Participation

Why do so few people have a job? Everyone doesn't want a job, and some who want one have not yet found one they are willing to take. If work was completely enjoyable, it would be called play. Work serves as a means of producing income, but some individuals have other means. People who are independently wealthy do not have to work in order to consume. They can draw down on existing wealth. Young children can rely on their parents provide them with goods and services. The government even implements transfer payment schemes in order to protect groups of people (the elderly, the disabled, and the poor) from having to work.

The labor force is made up of people aged 16 years and older who have a job or who are actively looking for one.

LABOR FORCE = EMPLOYED + UNEMPLOYED

One is considered **unemployed** if he or she is actively looking for a job but not working. The official **unemployment rate** in the US is calculated by the **Bureau of Labor Statistics (BLS)**. They survey households and businesses to determine the percentage of the **labor force** who is actively looking for a job but who don't have one.

$$\text{UNEMPLOYMENT RATE} = \frac{\text{UNEMPLOYED}}{\text{LABOR FORCE}}$$

From children, to retirees, to stay at home parents, to slackers, many people choose not to actively look for a job and therefore aren't considered to be unemployed. Thus, the employment rate is a better indicator of production than the unemployment rate. The employment rate is the percentage of the population that is employed.

$$\text{LABOR FORCE PARTICIPATION RATE} = \frac{\text{LABOR FORCE}}{\text{WORKING AGE CIVILIAN NONINSTITUTIONALIZED POPULATION}}$$

The US has experienced a large increase in the **labor force participation rate** of women.[2] Between 1972 and 2008, the labor force participation rate of women grew from 43.9% to 59.5%. The overall US labor force participation rate grew from 60.4% in 66% in the same period, even as the rate for men actually fell from 78.9% to 73%. While these demographic changes have done little to the unemployment rate, they very much impact both the employment rate and the level of production in the economy.

The truth is that most people wouldn't show up for work if doing so didn't increase their ability to engage in consumption. Unemployment is considered to be undesirable because it creates both **human costs** and **economic costs**. When people want a job in order to meet the needs of themselves and their loved ones

---

[2] Ibid.

but cannot find one, people get stressed out. Human costs are costs related to the physical, psychological, and social costs incurred by the absence of wealth creation. A loss of income can translate into an inability to meet one's physical needs for food, shelter, clothing, or health care. A loss of a job may also affect one's sense of self-worth. Unemployment is positively correlated with social ills such as crime, suicide, and divorce.

From an economic perspective, unemployment represents lost production. Once a person forgoes working for a month, they can never travel back in history to work during that month again. That month will forever be a lost month of production for that individual. As multiple people who want jobs go without them, an economy loses out on their production and less wealth is created. The larger the unemployment rate, the greater the forgone production and loss of wealth production. Figure 8.1 illustrates historical unemployment rate fluctuations as related to recessionary periods.[3]

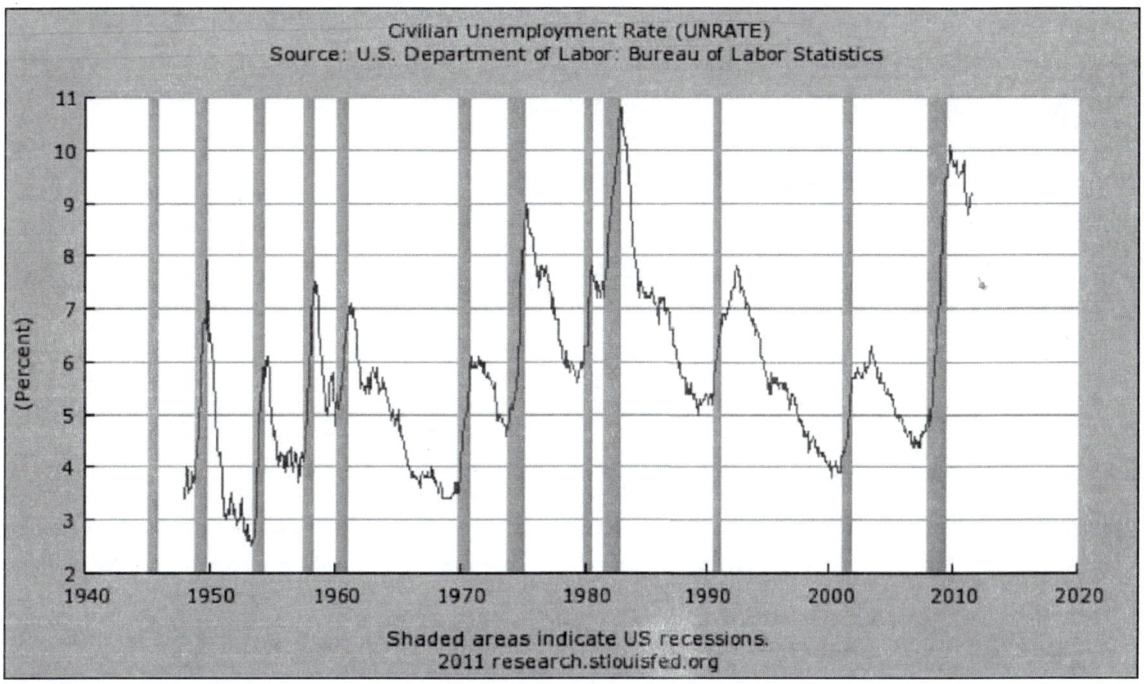

Figure 8.1 **CIVILIAN UNEMPLOYMENT RATE**

[3] Federal Reserve Bank of St. Louis

Table 8.1 APRIL 2011 UNEMPLOYMENT RATES

US	9.0%

Race or Ethnicity	
White	8.0%
Black or African American	16.1%
Hispanic or Latino	11.8%
Asian	6.4%

Age	
16–19	24.9%
20+	8.3A%

Education (age 25+)	
No high school	14.6%
High School	9.7%
Some College	7.5%
Bachelor's Degree +	4.5%
Black or African American Aged 16–19	41.6%

Gender	
Male	9.4%
Female	8.4%

Nativity	
US Born	7.7%
Foreign Born	9.3%

State	
North Dakota	3.3%
Nebraska	4.2%
South Dakota	4.9%

State	
Rhode Island	10.9%
California	11.9%
Nevada	12.5%

Who is Most Likely to Experience Unemployment?

Some groups of people are more likely to experience bouts of unemployment than others. Unskilled, blue collar workers are more likely than skilled, white collar workers to become unemployed. Less educated workers often have a much higher unemployment rate during a recession than do college graduates. Teenagers, because they have less job experience, and typically less education, have much higher unemployment rates than do older workers. Note that among African American teens, 41.6% of those wanting a job had not yet found one in April 2011. Less educated workers were particularly hard hit because of the decline in manufacturing jobs during the most recent recession and during the decades prior. This leaves fewer jobs for low skilled labor. Unemployment rates also tend to vary by race, gender, and location. Table 8.1[4] represents a snapshot of unemployment in April 2011.

[4] Ibid.

In order to properly understand unemployment and its costs, we need to understand first its causes. There are four different categories of unemployment: seasonal, frictional, structural, and cyclical unemployment.

Unemployed lifeguards in the winter represent seasonal unemployment

Seasonal Unemployment

Seasonal unemployment is caused by a change in seasons. Construction and agriculture are two industries that are weather dependent. There are fewer jobs in these industries during the winter months. When calculating the unemployment rate, the BLS reports seasonally adjusted data so that the unemployment rate that is reported already controls for a change in seasons. Seasonal unemployment is a natural part of the economy, and it is not as troubling as some other forms because it is temporary and will adjust with the seasons.

Frictional Unemployment

Frictional unemployment is caused by a natural movement of people from one job to the next. Few people stay at the same job their whole life. Frictional unemployment includes those who are changing jobs to search for better jobs as well as those just entering or reentering the labor force. New college graduates searching for jobs are frictionally unemployed. Like seasonal unemployment, frictional unemployment is a natural part of the economy. This type of unemployment is also not particularly troubling because it is also temporary and actually is beneficial for the economy as people sort into better jobs. To prevent this type of sorting would be inefficient.

Unemployed recent college graduates represent frictional unemployment

Structural Unemployment

Structural unemployment is caused when people lack the skills necessary to perform jobs currently in demand by the market. A high school dropout may really want a job, but may lack the needed skills to be able to take advantage of job openings in fields that require specific knowledge. It could be that a person has amassed quite a bit of knowledge in the study of philosophy, but philosophers may not currently be in great demand in the economy. The multiple job openings for trained nurses does little to help the philosopher find a job, unless they go to school and gain the training necessary to become a nurse.

Not all sectors of an economy expand or contract at the same rate. People remain unemployed when they lack the skills needed to fill job openings or refuse to gain skills currently in demand by the market. When an economy experiences an increase in technology or capital investment, certain skills often become unneed-

Those unemployed due to mismatched skills represent structural unemployment.

ed or replaceable. The automobile put a huge dent in the employment prospects of wagon makers and wheel wrights.

Luddites were a group of Englishmen who rebelled against the industrial revolution (and machines) mistakenly thinking that machines cause unemployment. While new technology or capital will make some jobs obsolete, they create the need for new jobs, albeit perhaps ones that require a different skill set. To say that no person should ever suffer from structural unemployment is to deprive the world of new technology and capital. To end structural unemployment, the world would have to return to one where all production was made by hand, where life was indeed solitary, nasty, brutish, and short.

Knowing that structural unemployment is part of a dynamic growing economy doesn't provide much solace to the person who just lost a job that they had the skill and training to do. A society who wants a growing economy, however, must come to grips with the fact that changes in employment are necessary components of a thriving economy. Societies that provide easy access to worker retraining will have an advantage in minimizing the human and economic costs associated with structural unemployment.

Cyclical Unemployment

Cyclical unemployment is caused by a reduction in output in the economy following downturns in the economy. As unsold inventories of goods begin increasing, producers lower production of future output until they see the demand for their goods and services increase. It takes fewer people to produce fewer goods and services, and therefore employees get laid off. This reduction in output will be permanent in some industries (and individuals unemployed in those industries will suffer from structural unemployment), while the reduction in output will be temporary in other industries as demand for their good or services rebounds with a growing economy. Cyclical unemployment, then, is caused by a mismatch of

Recessions lead to cyclical unemployment.

tion and consumption through time due to uncertainty in ever changing consumer demand.

Full Employment

The optimal amount of unemployment is not zero. A growing economy that allows the freedom of employment for workers will always have some frictional, seasonal, and structural unemployment. Government policies to outlaw these types of unemployment would result in slavery and long term retardation of economic growth rates. Economists consider **full employment** to be when cyclical unemployment is zero.

While no one knows what the unemployment rate would be if there were no cyclical unemployment, economists theorize that it would be between 5 and 5.5%. This theoretical level of zero cyclical unemployment is commonly referred to as full employment or **NAIRU** (the non-accelerating inflation rate of unemployment). When the unemployment rate falls below this level, inflation tends to increase. The shortage of skilled laborers in the marketplace, forces prospective employers to offer higher compensation to attract workers to their firms. The increased labor cost increases the cost of production of goods and services, and these cost increases are passed on to consumers in the form of higher prices. So, inflation results from unemployment falling below NAIRU. Consequences of an increase in the average price level are examined in more detail in the next chapter.

Government Policies and Unemployment

Government policies can, and do, alter both employment and unemployment rates. The provision of a social safety net (income support for the indigent), reduces the human costs associated with unemployment. If a person who loses their job can collect **unemployment insurance** payments from the government, they can continue to pay for food, clothing, and shelter as they look for a new job. Unemployment insurance payments in the US are typically paid out up to 26 weeks following job loss. However, in times of recession, the US government often increases the duration for which one is eligible for benefits. The tradeoff is that the more generous the unemployment insurance is, the longer the average bout of unemployment lasts. A sure-fire way to increase the unemployment rate is to make unemployment less undesirable.

Many European countries allow unemployed workers to collect up to 80% of their former salary for up to two years. As a result, most European countries have higher levels and longer average bouts of unemployment than the US.[5] Robert Barro found that by extending unemployment insurance benefits during the 2008-2009 recession, the American government actually increased the unemployment rate.[6]

---

[5] "Explaining European Unemployment" *NBER Reporter: Research Summary* Summer 2004

[6] "The Folly of Subsidizing Unemployment" *Wall Street Journal* August 30, 2010

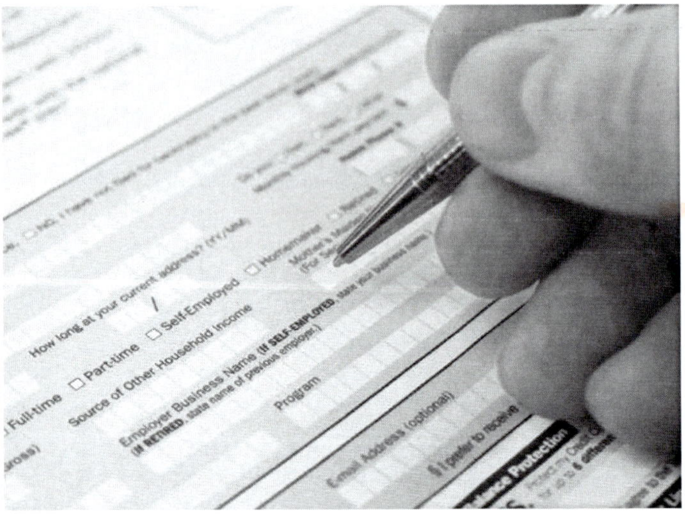

Likewise, minimum wage laws increase unemployment amongst the lowest skilled workers in the economy. Such laws outlaw all work whose net product is less that the prescribed wage. Young high school workers who can only generate $6 of new revenue from their employer will not be hired if the minimum wage rate is set at $7.25 an hour. Countries with higher minimum wage laws see higher levels of unemployment, particularly among young people. Requirements placed on employers regarding health coverage for their employees have a similar effect to minimum wage laws in discouraging employment.

Labor force rules regarding the ability to hire and fire workers also affect a country's unemployment rate. Firms that find it difficult to fire inept employees are less likely to hire new full time employees until they are certain that said employees merit hiring. The irony is that the more tightly a society clings to existing jobs, the less likely they are that new jobs get created, and consequently unemployment increases.

Employment has grown fastest in US states that have adopted **right to work laws**. These laws make **labor union** membership voluntary. Between 1993 and 2003 in right to work states, non-farm private sector jobs increased by 24% compared to a 14% growth rate for forced union states.[7] Real income grew by 37% in right to work states compared to 26% in forced dues states during the same time period.

According to the BLS, a majority of union members in the US are now government workers rather than private sector employees. Private sector union membership has been falling since WWII, while federal employees only gained the right to unionize and **collectively bargain** in the 1960's, with legislation signed by President Kennedy. While unions are often portrayed as being beneficial for workers, economic evidence indicates that unions slow economic growth and increase overall unemployment in the economy.[8]

While unemployment can be a problem for the person or family suffering from it, policies designed to reduce the human or economic costs of unemployment need to be carefully designed so that they don't end up causing more, rather than less unemployment. In theory, the government could hire more workers during a recession, but government rules make it hard to fire them later. Evidence from the Great Depression indicates that government jobs prolong unemployment.[9] While many obtained artificially created government jobs, they put off

---

[7] Source: Us Department of Labor

[8] Richard Vedder *"Right-To-Work Laws: Liberty, Prosperity, and Quality of Life" Cato Journal,* Vol. 30, No. 1 (Winter 2010)

[9] Jim Powell. *FDR's Folly, How Roosevelt and His New Deal Prolonged the Great Depression* 2003.

looking for lasting jobs and thus delayed the transition back into private sector employment.

Table 8.2[10] illustrates the US unemployment rate since 1920 in presidential election years. The US electorate has had a tendency to hold the US President accountable for the unemployment rate. Unemployed workers make for discontented voters, who tend to turn on incumbents. The two periods of post WWII American history when the US unemployment rate hit double digits were between September 1982 and June 1983 where it topped out at 10.8%, and in October 2009 when it hit 10.1%.

So, Politicians often are motivated to take actions to reduce short run unemployment, despite the fact that in the long run such actions may actually do more harm than good.

Table 8.2 HISTORIC US UNEMPLOYMENT RATES

1920	5.2%	1968	3.6%
1928	4.2%	1972	5.6%
high 1932	23.6%	1976	7.7%
1936	16.9%	1980	7.1%
1940	14.6%	1984	7.5%
1944	3.2%	1988	5.5%
1948	3.8%	1992	7.5%
low 1952	3.0%	1996	5.4%
1956	4.1%	2000	4.0%
1960	5.5%	2004	5.5%
1964	5.2%	2008	5.8%

[10] Ibid.

Glossary

Bureau of Labor Statistics (BLS)—an agency in the US Department of Labor that calculates unemployment and inflation rates

Collective bargaining—when an employer negotiates with representatives of a labor union in regard to the working condition of employees

Cyclical unemployment—unemployment caused by a reduction in output in the economy

Economic cost—forgone production

Frictional unemployment—unemployment caused by a natural movement of people from one job to the next

Full employment—when cyclical unemployment is zero

Human costs—costs related to the physical, psychological, and social costs incurred by the absence of wealth creation such as divorce, suicide, crime, depression, hunger, or thirst

Labor force—people 16 years of age and older who are either currently employed or actively looking for a job

Labor force participation rate—the percentage of people aged 16 and older in the labor force

Labor union—a group of laborers who work together to improve their working conditions

Luddites—a group of Englishmen who rebelled against the industrial revolution (and machines) believing that machines cause unemployment

NAIRU—the non-accelerating inflation rate of unemployment, also known as full employment

Right to work laws—laws that make membership in unions optional for employees

Seasonal unemployment—unemployment caused by a change in seasons

Structural unemployment—unemployment caused by people lacking the skills necessary to perform jobs currently in demand by the market

Unemployed—someone who actively looking for a job but not working

Unemployment insurance—transfer payments given to recently unemployed workers who are actively looking for a new job

Unemployment rate—the percentage of the labor force that is actively looking for a job but kind find one

Questions for Review

1. How is unemployment defined in the US? Would a stay at home parent be classified as unemployed? What about a student who is not seeking work and is not currently working?
2. Is the unemployment rate or the employment rate a better indicator of production? Why?
3. How has the labor force participation rate of women changed in the last fifty years? For men? Why do you think these changes have occurred?
4. Why do many European countries perpetually have higher unemployment rates than the US?
5. What is meant by full employment? Where is the economy relative to their PPF curve if the economy is operating below full employment?
6. List and describe four types of unemployment. Which of these types is most disconcerting to the economy and why?
7. What government policies lead to increased unemployment rates?
8. Why is unemployment considered to be harmful?
9. Suppose the Island of Yore has 40,000 non-institutionalized civilians over the age of 16. Of these individuals, 25,000 are working. 5,000 are not working but are actively seeking work. The remaining 10,000 are either stay at home parents or are retired. What is the unemployment rate, employment rate, and labor force participation rate for Yore?

Chapter 9
Inflation

Have you ever heard your grandparents talk about the good old days when a candy bar cost less than a quarter and a coca cola could be purchased for a dime? Have you noticed that as five and dime stores have shut down, dollar stores have taken their place in retail? In fact, the prices of individual goods and services change constantly. A gallon of milk is not the same price every time you go to the grocery store; nor do all grocery stores charge the same price for milk. Changes in the relative prices of goods and services reflect changes in people's ability and desire to buy a product relative to the changing costs (including opportunity costs) of producing them. Rising milk prices may reflect an increased love of dairy products by the masses, or it could reflect higher feeding costs for the dairy cows.

The prices of all products don't change at the same rate or even in the same direction. The price of an HD TV may fall, even as corn prices increase. **Inflation** is said to have occurred when there is an increase in the average price level. Likewise, **deflation** is a decrease in the average price level. This chapter will examine what is meant by the average price level, explain how average prices are measured, and explore the impact changing prices has on society and on economic growth.

Measuring Price Levels

The most common measure of average prices in the US is the **consumer price index (CPI)**. The CPI measures the collective price movements of a theoretical market basket of goods and services that the average urban consumer typically buys. The basket includes specific products that fall under one of the following categories: food and beverages, housing, apparel, transportation, medical care, recreation, education, communication, and other personal goods and services.[1]

The price of the market basket is measured every month and it is compared to the price of the market basket from the previous year. The quantities of the goods and services in the basket are assumed to be the same regardless of the change in relative prices. However, people respond to price changes. Therefore, the CPI overstates the true burden of inflation because it doesn't allow people to respond to changing relative prices. In this, and other ways, the CPI is not a perfect **cost of living index**, but it is the one used for most **cost of living adjustments (COLAs)**, including those used by the federal government.

---

[1] For more information on current CPI calculations visit http://www.bls.gov/cpi.

The CPI also overstates inflation because the quality of products tends to improve over time. TV's are in the CPI market basket, but a black and white floor model TV of the 1950's is not really the same product as an HD flat screen TV of today. Even if the price of TV's has gone up, people are getting a better product than they did before. Price changes can also cause consumers to shop at different stores (for example, discount stores). The CPI assumes that consumers will buy the same products at the same stores every month, regardless of economic circumstances.

Every now and then, the Bureau of Labor Statistics (BLS) changes the makeup of the market basket to reflect changes in consumer behavior. Cassette tape prices were replaced by CD prices, which in turn were replaced by the price of digital downloads. The BLS performs some statistical adjustments to take account of the change in the makeup of the market basket. Still, new products are often around awhile before they become standard enough to make it into the market basket. It is often the case that a new good experiences price decreases before it is included in the CPI. Collectively, these concerns may end up overstating the burden of inflation by a full percentage point.

On the other hand, for some individuals the CPI underestimates their real cost of living increase from year to year. If food, health care, and education costs increase much faster than the CPI while housing prices fall dramatically, college students who are not trying to buy a house may find that the CPI underestimates their true burden of inflation. In March of 2011, New York Federal Reserve Bank President William Dudley made a speech in Queens New York regarding the CPI. He commented that the price of an IPAD was going down even as food prices were going up. One heckler called out "I can't eat an IPAD."[2]

In order to calculate the CPI, the BLS takes the current price of the market basket, divides it by the price of the market basket in a base year (currently the base period is 1982-1984), and multiplies the result by one hundred.

$$\text{CPI} = \frac{\text{CURRENT PRICE OF MARKET BASKET}}{\text{PRICE OF MARKET BASKET IN BASE YEAR}} \times 100$$

The rate of inflation from one year to the next can be calculated using each year's CPI in the following manner:

$$\text{INFLATION RATE} = \frac{\text{CPI MOST RECENT YEAR} - \text{CPI EARLIER YEAR}}{\text{CPI EARLIER YEAR}} \times 100$$

[2] http://www.reuters.com/article/2011/03/11/us-usa-fed-dudley-ipad-idUSTRE72A4D520110311

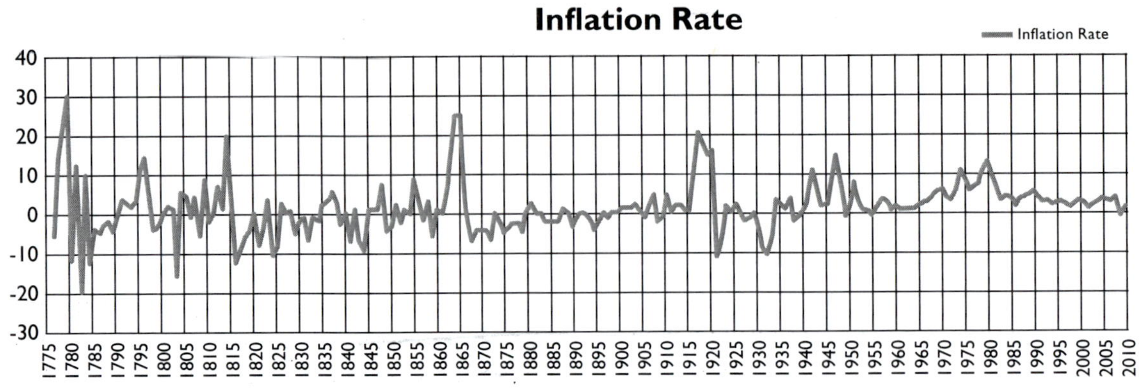

Chart 9.1 INFLATION RATE

Samuel H. Williamson, "Seven Ways to Compute the Relative Value of a U.S. Dollar Amount, 1774 to present," Measuring Worth, April 2011

Through the 1700's, 1800's and early 1900's, the US economy routinely experienced both inflation and deflation (see Graph 9.1). Inflation rates have tended to spike during major wars as governments have sought to help pay for war expenses by expanding the money supply. The only years in which the US inflation rate exceeded 20% were 1777, 1778 (American Revolution), 1813 (War of 1812), 1864, 1865 (US Civil War), and 1917 (WWI), The US went from 1955 until 2009 without a single year where there was annual deflation. This was the longest period in US history where deflation was absent.

If a change in a single product's price improves the efficiency of markets by sending signals to consumers and suppliers, then such a price change will improve the allocation of scarce resources and enable wealth creation. This does not mean that all individuals will be happy to see the price change. A baker who sees the price of cake and cookies fall due to a low carb diet fad won't be happy with the price change. However, it will act as a signal to move resources out of baking and into another industry that will better meet the needs and wants of consumers. Rising gasoline prices won't make drivers happy, but they will act as signals to move resources to oil production and gasoline refinement.

The Impact of Changing Prices

Changes in individual prices affect different people differently. So too do changes in the average price level. There are people who are helped by inflation, and there are people who are hurt by it. Likewise, some are helped while others are hurt by deflation.

Inflation can be a problem for people because it can increase consumer and business uncertainty, increase advertising costs, hurt people on fixed incomes and those who like to hold onto cash, hurt lenders who don't correctly anticipate inflation, and hurt taxpayers with bracket creep or capital gains taxes that are not indexed for inflation. These problems are discussed below.

As inflation rates rise, they also tend to be more variable. This makes long term business planning more difficult. Uncertainty with regard to prices businesses will charge or wages they will have to pay makes it difficult to agree to make long term investments or engage in long term labor contracts. Inflation, if correctly predicted, doesn't cause these problems. If a business owner knows that the inflation rate for next year will be 2% and she knows that she wants to give her employees a 1% **real wage** increase, then she will have to increase their nominal wages by 3%. A **nominal wage** is what physically appears on the labor contract, whereas real wages discount nominal wages by the amount of inflation.

NOMINAL WAGE INCREASE – INFLATION RATE = REAL WAGE INCREASE

If the employer gives her employees a 3% raise but inflation turns out to be 5%, then her employees will be taking a real pay cut, not on paper, but in terms of their ability to buy other goods and services with their pay check. They will have more physical money, but that money will be able to buy fewer goods.

Because all prices don't change at the same rate, the producers whose prices rise fastest may benefit from inflation, while the producers whose prices rise the slowest will be hurt. The opposite is true for consumers. Higher prices for the things they buy make consumers worse off, but lower prices for the things they buy make them better off.

Because prices are changing more quickly during periods of high inflation or deflation, it becomes more difficult for consumer to know if they are getting a good deal on what they are buying. This increases the **search costs** for consumers who want to make sure they aren't overpaying for products they spend a lot of their income on.

Increased Advertising Costs

As prices rapidly change, it becomes more costly for a business to advertise their prices. Restaurants usually advertise the price of the food on their menus. Often these menus are laminated. The faster prices change, the more often a restaurant will have to create and laminate new menus. During period of **hyperinflation** (over 200%) business begin advertising on chalk boards rather than on print, media, or billboards because the costs of producing, printing, or painting a new ad become too high relative to how long that new advertisement will be useful. The costs of advertising a business's prices are called **menu costs**.

People on Fixed Incomes and Those Holding onto Cash

As prices rise, the **purchasing power** of any one dollar decreases. Each dollar buys fewer goods or services. People who are on fixed incomes (the elderly on a fixed pension, or a child on a fixed allowance) are hurt by inflation because their income doesn't increase to keep pace with higher prices. Conversely, they would benefit from deflation. Social Security checks receive a COLA based upon the CPI, so social security recipients whose buying patterns mimic the average urban consumer aren't hurt by inflation. And, if inflation is overstated then recipients are actually better off.

People who save cash in coffee cans, under their mattresses, or in their wallets, or in non-interest bearing checking accounts are hurt by inflation. As prices rise, the purchasing power of this money falls. As such, in an inflationary environment, a dollar today is worth more than a dollar a year from now. When one of the textbook author's grandmothers died, a stash of money was found in coffee cans in her basement. This money had less purchasing power when it was discovered than it did when it was stashed because prices have risen considerably since then. The **present value** of a dollar is equal to its future value controlling for inflation and the opportunity cost of earning interest on the dollar.

PRESENT VALUE OF \$ = FUTURE VALUE OF \$/ (1 + THE NOMINAL INTEREST RATE)^{YEAR}

Lenders

In order to protect themselves from inflation, savers need to place their savings in financial institutions that pay them a rate of return that is equal to, or larger than, the rate of inflation. If future inflation were known, then savers could perfectly protect their money from inflation. However, future inflation is not known. Savers and lenders who underestimate future inflation can be hurt. If they place their savings in a certificate of deposit that pays a 2% rate of return, while the inflation rate turns out to be 5%, they will lose 3% of the purchasing power of their savings. Conversely, borrowers who lock in a nominal interest rate expecting low inflation would benefit from a high and rising rate of inflation as they will pay back their loans with less valuable dollars.

NOMINAL INTEREST RATE – INFLATION RATE = REAL INTEREST RATE

Bracket Creep and Capital Gains Taxes

When a business or person buys an asset, that asset appreciates in value, and if they decide to sell it, they will owe a capital gains tax. This tax is not indexed for inflation. If Bob buys one share of stock for \$10 and sells it at \$20 during a period of time with 100% inflation, then Bob will have to pay a capital gains tax on the \$10, he *made* in nominal terms even though his real wealth didn't increase at all. The higher the inflation rate, the more people end up paying taxes on inflation rather than on real gains to their wealth. Likewise, if tax brackets aren't indexed for inflation, then higher nominal incomes caused by inflation could push people into higher tax brackets, even if their real income hasn't increased.

Like inflation, deflation can cause business and consumer uncertainty while increasing menu costs. These costs are minimized with stable prices. People on fixed incomes and people who like to hold onto cash benefit from deflation. As long as one's income doesn't fall, deflation allows one to consume more with his or her income. Drug dealers, because they deal in cash to avoid detection, may prefer deflation to inflation, as long as the price of their drugs falls slower than other prices.

In the late 1800's many farmers took out loans during a period of deflation. This meant that the price of their corn and wheat fell each year as they tried to pay back their farm loans. This caused a number of farmers to lose their jobs. Unexpected deflation can harm borrowers while it helps lenders. Still, the price of corn fell less quickly than the cost of shipping the corn over railroads, so farmers benefited relative to railroad companies from the deflation.

The biggest fear of deflation is that producers won't invest in new capital to build new products if the price of their output is falling. However, during the deflation of the late 1800's the price of capital goods fell more quickly than did prices of consumer goods. Investment increased causing one of the fastest economic growth spurts in US history.

To summarize, groups of people that tend to be hurt by inflation tend to be savers (the wealthy), lenders (banks), small business owners, consumers, people on fixed incomes (generally the elderly), and taxpayers. Groups that tend to be hurt by deflation are debtors, and businesses whose prices would fall faster than others. The US government may be hurt by deflation more than inflation because they are less likely to collect as much income tax, sales tax, or capital gains tax revenue as they need to make interest payments on their large debt. Even though deflation is preferred to inflation by most consumers (voters), the **Federal Reserve** (the US central bank) has purposely tried to prevent deflation since WWII in order to protect business investment and government debt.

Deflation could also cause consumers to engage in less consumption as they believe that future prices will fall further. This could lead to excess inventories on the part of firms. Furthermore, if deflation is accompanied by unemployment, falling prices may make labor market adjustment more difficult. Workers are more likely to tolerate falling real wages if their nominal wages increase rather than decrease.

Causes of Inflation or Deflation

There are three main things that cause a change in the average price level: an overall increase in the cost of production, an overall increase in demand for goods and services, and an increase in the money supply. The first two causes account for most short term fluctuations in the average price level. The latter is the only explanation of why prices today are higher than they were a generation ago.

Almost all production involves hiring laborers (paying them wages) and using energy. As wages or energy prices increase, these costs are passed along to consumers. The double digit inflation of the late 1970's and early 1980's can in part be explained by an increase in the price of oil caused by collusion within **OPEC (Organization of Petroleum Exporting Countries)**. As their collusive agreement fell apart, the price of oil fell, and so did the inflation rate. During times of war, demand for goods and services typically increases in order to support the war effort. This causes inflation during the first part of military buildup, until people start cutting back on the purchase of consumer goods.

Nobel Prize winning economist Milton Friedman once said that, "Inflation is always and everywhere a monetary phenomenon." The oldest macroeconomic theory that is still in use is the **quantity theory of money**. It is an accounting identity that shows that long term changes in prices levels are connected to long term changes in the supply of money. Inflation is all about the relative scarcity of money vs. goods and services.

THE QUANTITY THEORY OF MONEY: MV = PY

The left hand side of the equation is how much money is spent in the course of a year. To find this, one must take the amount of money in circulation (M) and multiply it by the number of times each dollar is spent over the course of the year (V), the **velocity of money**. The right hand side of the equation is Nominal GDP. It is the average price level (P) multiplied by Real GDP (Y). As output occurs, money is used to pay for the factors of production. The dollar value of output must be equal to the amount of money being spent during the same time period.

To isolate the average price level, one can divide each side of the above equation by real GDP (Y).

$$P = \frac{MV}{Y}$$

If there is no real economic growth and the velocity of money remains unchanged, then the only way that the average price level could increase is to increase the **money supply**. Though the velocity of money is not constant from one year to the next, it remains relatively constant (though increasing due to computers and ATMs) from one generation to the next.

Put another way, If V is constant, inflation occurs when the money supply increases faster than real RGDP, and deflation occurs when the money supply goes up more slowly than real GDP. When gold was used as the source of money, inflation was caused when the supply of gold increased faster than economic growth. This is what happened in Spain circa 1600s when they brought boatloads of gold back from the Western Hemisphere.

The US has a **fiat currency** (a currency with no intrinsic value) and consequently, they can increase or decrease the supply of money any time they wish. Long run inflation or deflation occurs as a result of active government or central bank policies. Deflation did not just vanish on its own during the last half of the twentieth century; it was prevented due to central bank policies.

There is some controversy between two Noble Prize winning economists, Milton Friedman and Friedrich Von Hayek as to the cause and effect of changes in the money supply and real GDP. Between 1929 and 1933, real GDP fell by 29%, prices fell by 25%, the money supply fell by 33% and the velocity of money fell as well. Did the reduction in the left hand side of the quantity theory of money cause a decline in the right side, or the other way around? Friedman supposes the former while Hayek supposes the latter.

Milton Friedman and Anna Schwartz argue in "The Great Contraction, 1929–1933," that the decline in the supply of money caused credit markets to freeze up and caused otherwise sound banks to close do to a lack of available liquidity. These bank failures and credit shortages caused business investment to nearly vanish.

Friedrich Von Hayek argues that the reduction in the velocity and the money supply was caused by a slowdown in investment. He argues that business investment declined not because of a credit crunch but because they were already operating well under full capacity and had no need to expand. This lower demand for loans caused the supply and velocity of money to decrease. The connection between loans and the money supply will be examined further in Chapter 22.

In the 2008–2009 contraction, the central bank acted as if Friedman was correct. They provided liquidity to banks and financial institutions to keep them from failing. By increasing the money supply, the Federal Reserve attempted to boost business investment and GDP. Still, banks sat on new reserves and business borrowing did not recover. Businesses that were operating below capacity had little desire to invest in new capital. In the end, both economists provide insight into the cross causation between money supply and real GDP.

Providing short term liquidity to prevent solvent banks from closing can help to prevent an economic slowdown brought on by a collapse of the financial sector. The financial sector is needed to align lenders and borrowers. In their absence, business investment becomes very difficult. On the other hand, as the phrase goes, "you can lead a horse to water, but you can't make it drink." An increase in the money supply does not guarantee that businesses will want to invest when they are uncertain or pessimistic about the future, or they are paying down debt from previous investments. Further, if inefficient banks are kept open with bailouts despite poor lending decisions, then banks may have an incentive to continue to make risky decisions that inhibit economic growth.

Glossary

Consumer price index (CPI)—a measure of inflation that examines the price change in a basket of goods and services consumed by a hypothetical urban worker

Cost of living adjustment (COLA)—a change to wage or transfer payment to adjust for a change in the average price level

Cost of living index—a measure of how much more or less expensive it is to meet the needs and wants of consumers

Deflation—a decrease in the average price level

Federal Reserve—the US's central bank

Fiat currency—a currency whose value is based solely on confidence in the issuing government, it has no intrinsic value

Hyperinflation—an inflation rate over 200%

Inflation—an increase in the average price level

Menu costs—the added advertising cost associated with changing prices

Money supply—the amount of money in circulation

Nominal interest rate—the interest rate that appears on a financial document

Nominal wage—the wage that appears on a labor contract

OPEC—Organization of Petroleum Exporting Countries

Present value—what a future valued good or service would be worth if possessed today

Purchasing power—the quantity of goods and services a dollar is able to buy

Quantity Theory of Money—nominal GDP must equal the amount of money spend on goods and services

Real interest rate—the nominal interest rate minus inflation

Real wage—a nominal wage controlled for inflation or deflation, it represents the purchasing power of a nominal wage

Search costs—costs incurred by consumers as they try to determine if the most cost efficient consumption pattern to meet their needs and wants

Velocity of money—the number of times the average dollar changes hands in the course of a year

Questions for Review

1. Who is hurt by inflation? Why?
2. Who is helped by inflation? Why?
3. Who is hurt by deflation? Why?
4. Who is hurt by deflation? Why?
5. What is the CPI? How is it calculated?
6. Why does the CPI overstate the true burden of inflation?
7. What is the present value of $400 received five years from now if the nominal interest rate is 3%?
8. If the nominal interest rate is 8% and the inflation rate is 2%, what is the real interest rate?
9. If the inflation rate is 4% and you want to give your employees a 5% increase in their real wage, by how much would you need to increase their nominal wage?
10. What causes inflation and deflation?
11. Why has deflation largely disappeared in the US?
12. In the land of Sanders only two goods are consumed, fried chicken and coleslaw. The price of a bucket of fried chicken was $10.00 in 1990 and $14.00 in 2000. The price of a serving of coleslaw was $1 in 1990 and $2 in 2000. The typical Sanderian consumed 25 buckets of chicken and 20 servings of coleslaw a year in 1990.

    a. What is the price of the market basket in 2000?

    b. What is the CPI for 2000 using 1990 as the base year?

    c. If the CPI for 1995 is 130, with 1990 as the base year, then what was the rate of inflation between 1990 and 1995?

    d. If the CPI for 1995 is 130 and the CPI for 1996 is 133, what is the rate of inflation between 1995 and 1996?

    e. If the CPI for 1991 using 1990 as the base year is 85, state briefly what must have happened to the prices between 1990 and 1991.

Chapter 10

Circular Flow and Financial Institutions

"All the world's a stage.
And all the men and women merely players.
They have their exits and their entrances;
And one man in his time plays many parts."

—*William Shakespeare* - As You Like It

Much like a Shakespearean play, the economy is inhabited by many different actors, each of whom plays multiple roles. Any effort to model the economy must begin with an outline of who the actors are and how those actors relate to each other. In reality, individuals make economic decisions for themselves and for their dependents. Modeling individual decision making is the realm of microeconomic study.

The study of macroeconomics generally considers the actors in the economy to be groups of people, like consumers. This is not to say that all consumers are homogeneous. Rather, it enables the researcher to examine trends in choices made by large numbers of people. Broad economic statements such as, "consumer spending will increase as a result" does not mean that all consumers will, or should, buy more. The assumption is that each individual actor will act according to their own enlightened, rational self-interest.

The purpose of this chapter is to introduce chief actors of the economy, and explain their relationship to each other and to the level of production that occurs in an economy. Special emphasis is placed on the central role financial institutions play in the economy.

Macroeconomic Actors

Consumers

Every individual in an economy is a **consumer**, and so is an actor in the economy. Everyone must consume in order to survive. People purchase goods and services in an attempt to meet their material needs and wants. Consumers are limited in their consumption by the scarcity of resources. Goods and services aren't free, so consumption has to be paid for. The sources of payment include income, gifts, transfer payments, or debt. Income comes from labor **(wages)**, capital **(interest)**, land **(rent)**, and entrepreneurship **(profit)** under the control of the individual consumer.

Not all consumers earn income. Young children, from an economic perspective, could be termed "unproductive eaters". Children, and other dependents, consume as a result of resources given to them. A **transfer payment** occurs when the government gives money or resources to a consumer without a good or service provided in return.

Should a consumer wish to purchase a good or service without first earning or receiving the needed money to do so, they often have the option of borrowing money from a financial institution. By taking on debt, the consumer is pledging a portion of their future income to the **financial institution** in exchange for current consumption.

Consumption can consist of goods or services made domestically or abroad. Consumers can do more than just consume their entire income. They could also pay taxes, save, or give their income to charity. After tax income is called **disposable** (discretionary) **income**. Savings can occur in or apart from financial institutions. Some people hold savings in a coffee can or under a mattress. Others place their savings in financial institutions that offer a positive rate of return on the savings.

Financial Institutions

Financial Institutions are firms that coordinate savers with borrowers. A saver, be it an individual, a government, or a firm, voluntarily agrees to postpone current consumption, government spending, or investment in order to gain a return on their savings that would increase their consumption, government spending, or investment ability in the future. **Banks, credit unions, credit card companies, stock markets, commodity markets, bond markets, insurance companies,** and **pension plans** are all examples of financial institutions.

Consumers can defer consumption by placing a fraction of their current income in a financial institution. If they go to their local bank or credit union, they could place their money in a **checking account**, a **money market account**, a **savings account**, or in a **certificate of deposit**. Money placed in a checking account won't typically generate interest income for the saver, but checking accounts offer easy access to the money. Access to money is called **liquidity**. Money markets are less liquid than checking accounts, but more liquid than savings accounts or certificates of deposit. A certificate of deposit specifies a period of time during which the money may not, without a fine, be withdrawn from the bank. Typically, banks entice savers to agree to less liquidity by paying higher interest rates on the savings.

Banks, credit unions, and credit card companies facilitate consumer and small business borrowing. Every time a consumer uses a credit card, they take out a loan from the credit card company. Often these loans are interest free if the entire loan is paid off by the billing due date. Otherwise the interest rate charged by credit card companies tends to be much higher than that charged by local banks, but not as high as charged by **cash advance stores**. This higher interest rate reflects the higher risk associated with making loans for nondurable consumer goods. It's virtually impossible for a credit card company to repossess the double bacon cheeseburger that was bought with a credit card.

Whether or not a bank or credit card company gives a loan to an individual or small business is dependent upon their likelihood of repayment. **Credit scores** are proxies for the credit worthiness of consumers. A low credit score means a person does not have a history of making on time payments of their debts. Low credit scores limit the availability of credit to an individual while increasing the interest rate they will have to pay to secure the loan.

There are **usury** laws in many states against charging excessive interest on loans. Some people believe that lenders who charge high interest rates to people with bad credit scores are taking advantage of these people. The truth is that if lenders can't charge enough interest to cover the likelihood of default, loans to high risk borrowers would not be made. Usury laws work to create a black market for loans where an illegally high rate of interest is charged by **loan sharks**. Loan sharks make illegal loans to people with very poor access to legal credit at illegally high interest rates. Because the loans are not enforceable by law, loan sharks often must resort to the threat or action of physical violence in order to collect on their loans.

If a small business is looking to expand, they may need to take out a small business loan from a bank. In order to determine whether or not said expansion is a profitable idea, the owner needs to compare the expected marginal benefit of the business expansion with the marginal cost. The opportunity cost of investment is the interest rate. The higher the interest rate on the small business loan, the less profitable new investment projects will be. Even if the business owner uses her own money, the interest rate is the opportunity cost of investment. If a business owner can earn a 3% rate of return by expanding their business but can save money in a certificate of deposit at 5%, then the rational business owner would choose not to expand their business even if they did not have to take out a loan to do so.

Stock Market and Commodity Markets

Rather than take a loan out from a financial institution, owners of a firm could sell a portion of their equity stake in the firm in order to raise money for a capital investment. A **share of stock** is part ownership in a firm. Stock markets are institutions where partial ownership of corporations are bought and sold. A saver may forgo current consumption in order to buy part ownership in a company they expect will make money in the future. As a part owner of the company, they are entitled to a share of the company's future profits. The **New York Stock Exchange (NYSE)** is the largest stock market in the United States and is located in New York City. The **NASDAQ** is the second largest stock market in the United States and is located in Washington DC.

The current price of a share of stock depends upon potential buyers and sellers of that share agreeing to a price for the transaction. People have varying expectations as to the future profitability of a corporation. As people's expectations begin to diverge from each other, they begin buying and selling shares based on their beliefs. All buyers and sellers of stock are speculators in that they are all acting on imperfect information regarding the future profitability of the firm.

The Dow Jones Industrial Average (DJIA or Dow) is a composite index of 30 of the country's largest corporations' stocks. It is the most often quoted index of how the stock market is doing. If the Dow goes up from one day to the next, it is often said that the stock market is up. This does not mean that the price of all stocks went higher, nor does it mean that all thirty stocks on the Dow went higher. Individual stock prices can increase or decrease independent of the Dow or **NASDAQ Composite** (an index of how companies listed on the NASDAQ perform). The **S&P 500** is a broader index of 500 companies on the NYSE, while the **Russell 2000** is an index of 2000 companies listed on the NYSE.

People who are optimistic that the stock market indices will increase in the near future are called **bulls**. People who are pessimistic that the stock market indices will increase in the near future are called **bears**. A **bull market** is a stock market whose indices are increasing while a **bear market** is a stock market whose indices are decreasing.

Bull markets occur as people begin expecting an increase in companies' future profits. As such, stock market movements attempt to predict future performance of the economy. The stock market crash of 1929 was a reflection of changes in expectations about the future profitability of US businesses. The important thing to understand is that changes in the stock market do not cause changes in economic output. Changes in economic output cause changes in the stock market. The stock market crash of 1929 was caused by the Great Depression rather than being the cause of it.

When a corporation earns profit it can **retain earnings** to be used for future investment or it can pay **dividends** to shareholders. Dividends are taxed as shareholder income. In this way income produced by corporations is taxed twice. Corporate profits are taxed at the corporate income tax rate and dividends are then taxed at the personal income tax rate.

Savers could hold their savings in assets called **commodities** with the hope that their value will increase over time. Popular commodities include precious metals such as gold and silver, industrial metals such as copper and aluminum, West Texas Intermediate (crude oil), crops such as corn and soybeans, and livestock such as lean hogs or live cattle. Not everyone who thinks that the price of lean hogs will increase will want said hogs running around their living room. Fortunately, commodity markets have evolved to allow, for periods of time, people to own commodities without actually taking delivery of them. **Futures contracts** even allow individuals to buy and sell commodities that exist only in the future.

Bond Markets, Mutual Funds, and Pensions

Alternatively, savers may wish to place their funds in to a bond market. A bond market is an institution that allows people to buy and sell the right to collect debt. A corporation or a government may wish to issue bonds in order to finance a capital improvement. A bond is an IOU that promises to pay the owner a certain amount of money over a fixed amount of time. These IOU's (bonds) are then bought and sold in bond markets. By purchasing a bond, a saver takes the risk that the debtor may default on their obligation to pay their debts. The greater the perceived likelihood of default, the greater the interest rate savers will need to be offered in order to get them to voluntarily lend their money. Bond rating agencies, such as **Moody's** or **Standard & Poor's**, make estimates about the credit worthiness of corporations and governments. In order to encourage individuals to accept a lower interest rate on government debt, the US government makes income earned from interest on government bonds tax exempt.

Rather than put all of one's life savings in a single stock, bond, or commodity, it is wiser to diversity one's **portfolio**. **Mutual funds** are collections of assets (stocks, bonds, commodities) that diversify one's assets through the purchase of a single fund. Mutual funds exist for virtually all tastes and preferences from environmentally conscious mutual funds to mutual funds that specialize in vice (gambling, tobacco, and alcohol).

Pensions are another popular way to save. They are so popular that many employers offer a pension plan for their employees as part of their compensation packages. Typically pensions are either defined benefit plans or defined contribution plans. A **defined benefit pension plan** specifies how much money a retiree will receive each year upon retirement. If a firm offers a defined benefit pension, they are legally obligated to place an actuarially determined amount of savings aside to meet all future pension promises. A **fully funded pension** system meets these actuarial requirements. Often, government pension systems are not fully funded. A **pay-as-you-go pension** system pays current retirement benefits out of current revenue.

Most private employers who offer a pension now offer a **defined contribution pension**. They contribute to an employee's **individual retirement account** a fixed amount each pay period. The amount of money an employee has upon retirement depends upon the rate of return generated by the assets in the retirement portfolio. Most retirement plans allow for the diversification of savings into stock, commodity, and bond markets.

Firms

Firms also play a key act in the economy as institutions that produce goods and services for consumers to consume. Firms include **sole proprietorships, partnerships,** and **limited liability corporations.** Firms employ resources (natural resources, labor, human capital, physical capital, technology, and entrepreneurship) in order to engage in production. They also pay taxes, donate to charity, and borrow money to invest in new capital.

The money to build a new machine, tool, or factory must come from savers. Savings predates investment. Firms use financial institutions such as banks, the stock market, and the bond market, to borrow money from savers, both foreign and domestic. Firms can also use retained earnings to finance future investment. The choice of where to place the investment, domestically or abroad is also made by firms. Their choice of where to engage in investment and production is a function of both the cost of production and the ability to get their products to their prospective consumers, both domestic and foreign.

When firms engage in production, they generate revenue which allows them to pay wages to their laborers, interest on their borrowed capital, rent on their borrowed land, and profits to their owners. This generates income for consumers. Firms also pay taxes which include capital gains taxes, corporate income taxes, license fees, and personal income taxes paid by owners of the firm. These taxes generate revenue for the government.

In a dynamic, growing economy, new firms begin production while other firms go out of business. Firms that produce goods and services and sell them at prices consumers want to pay grow, while firms that produce goods and services that people don't want or charge prices people don't want to pay shut down. When firms fail, their resources are freed up for use by more productive firms.

The Government

Federal, state, and local governments are collectively referred to as "The Government". Governments can collect taxes, engage in government spending, enact transfer payments, receive **intergovernmental transfers**, borrow, save, and regulate the economy.

Taxes can be placed on consumers or businesses. Spending can be on goods and services made domestically or abroad. Transfer payments can be made domestically or abroad to consumers, businesses, or other governments. Regulations can be placed on consumers, businesses, or lower levels of governments. While some state and local governments are required to balance their budget every year, others, including the US national government, have no such requirement. When governments spend and give away more money than they receive in taxes and intergovernmental transfers in a given year, they run a **budget deficit**. When they receive more in taxes and intergovernmental transfers than they spend and give away, they run a **budget surplus**.

In the US, the Constitution enumerates powers held by Congress and the national government. Other powers are reserved for states, as noted in the 10th Amendment. This system of divided government power is called **federalism**. By reserving some power to states, federalism allows for competition among the fifty US states in attracting firms and consumers to produce in their state. Such competition allows states to experiment with spending, taxing, borrowing, and regulatory rules to determine the mix that best meets the needs and wants of people living within each state. It also holds state and local governments accountable for poor decisions by offering US citizens a choice to live under different tax levels, spending levels, or regulatory rules. Changing political jurisdictions that better meet consumers and firms needs and wants is known as the **Tiebout effect**.

The Foreign Sector

Finally, the foreign sector is the most broadly defined economic actor. It represents consumers, financial institutions, firms, and governments that exist outside the borders of a country. Recall that exports are goods and services produced within a country and purchased by foreigners. **Imports** are goods and services produced outside of the country but purchased within the country. A **trade deficit** occurs if the dollar value of imports exceeds the dollar value of exports. A **trade surplus** occurs if the dollar value of exports exceeds the dollar value of imports.

Foreign firms can build capital in a country not their own. This is called **foreign direct investment (FDI)**. Foreigners can also borrow and save in a country's financial institutions. Japanese consumers could place money in the NYSE, and an American bank could make a loan to the Greek government. National laws and international treaties regulate domestic economic actors who engage in transactions with the foreign sector. In a globalized economy it is not uncommon for a firm in Country A to take a loan from a bank in Country B in order to invest in new capital in Country C in order to export their product to Country D. The more integrated the world economy becomes, the more important a proper understanding of the foreign sector becomes.

Chart 10.1 illustrates how the actors in the macroeconomy fit together. As production occurs, owners of resources are rewarded with income. This income in then used to purchase more output, which in turn, produces more income. The circular logic of the economy begets the name of the model, the **Circular Flow Model**. During periods of economic expansion, products are produced, people get paid, and they buy more output, causing more stuff to be made and more people to be paid. During periods of economic contraction, fewer products are made, so fewer people get paid which results in them being able to buy even less output causing output to fall more. The next chapter will analyze why the actors listed here might change their actions from one day to the next and therefore affect the growth rate in the economy.

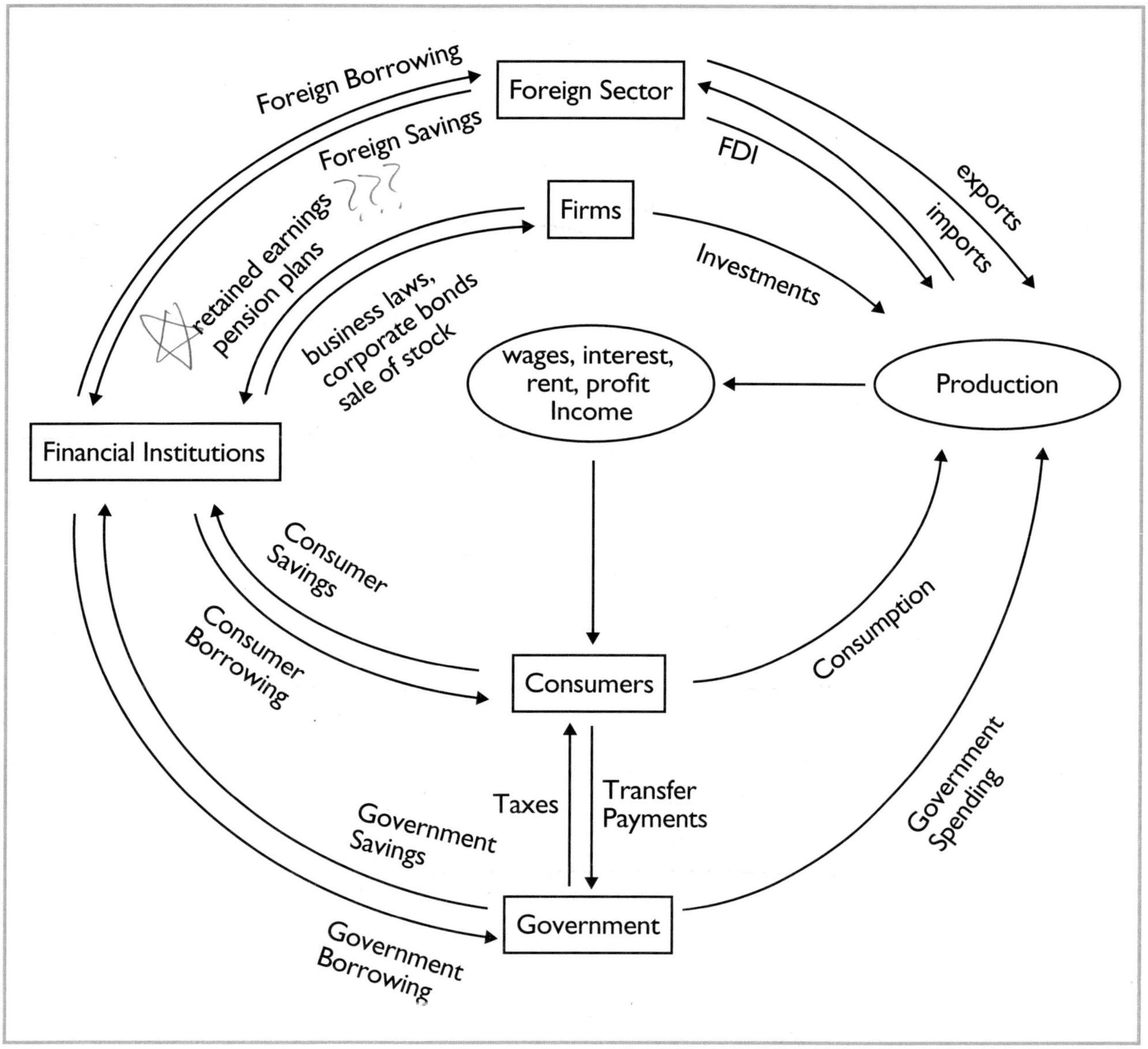

Figure 10.1 **CIRCULAR FLOW DIAGRAM**

Glossary

Bear—a stock market pessimist

Bear market—a sustained decline in stock market indices

Budget deficit—when a government spends and gives away more money than it collects in taxes and intergovernmental transfers

Budget surplus—when a government spends and gives away less money than it collects in taxes and intergovernmental transfers

Bull—a stock market optimist

Bull market—a sustained increase in stock market indices

Cash advance store—a firm that offers high interest loans to people with low credit scores

Certificate of deposit—a savings instrument that offers interest in exchange for a guarantee that the savings will not be withdrawn for a specified period of time

Checking account—a savings instrument that rarely offers interest, but provides easy access to savings

Circular Flow Model—a model that illustrates how groups of economic actors interact in the economy

Commodity—an asset which is traded in a market

Consumers—people who buy things for their personal use

Credit scores—a measure of a consumer's credit worthiness

Defined benefit pension plan—a pension plan that promises a certain payout to retirees

Defined contribution pension—a pension plan that only guarantees the amount of money an employer contributes to the plan

Disposable income—after tax income

Dividend—profit distributed to shareholders

Exports—goods and services produced domestically, but sold abroad

Federalism—a system of government that splits power between a national government and competing regional governments

Financial institutions—institutions that coordinate savings and investment, such as banks, credit unions, credit card companies, stock markets, commodity markets, bond markets, insurance companies, and pension plans

Firms—organizations created to provide goods or services for a profit

Foreign direct investment—investment made by foreign economic actors

Foreign sector—consumers, firms, and governments that exist outside the political boundaries of a country

Fully funded pension—a pension plan which sets aside an actuarially sufficient amount of money to meet future pension promises

Futures contract—a contract to exchange an asset in the future

Government—an institution which creates and enforces laws

Imports—goods and services produced abroad, but purchased domestically

Individual retirement account (IRA)—a savings instrument where initial deposits are made tax free

Interest—payment to savers in return for the use of their money

Intergovernmental transfers—grants from one government to another, typically from a higher level of government to a regional or local government

Limited liability corporations—a firm whose owners' losses are limited to the value of their stock

Liquidity—an asset's ability to be quickly used in exchange without a significant loss of value

Loan sharks—lenders who charge interest rates on loans above the legal limit set by usury laws

Money market account—a savings instrument that pays the borrower an interest rate based upon the interest rate currently offered by government and corporate securities

Moody's—a credit rating agency

Mutual funds—a collection of professionally managed stocks, bonds, and/or commodities

Pay-as-you-go pension—a pension where current retiree benefits are paid out of current revenues derived from current workers

NASDAQ—a Washington D.C. based stock exchange, the second largest stock exchange in the US which includes the stocks of many tech companies

NASDAQ Composite—a stock market composite index of over 3000 components traded on the NASDAQ stock exchange

New York Stock Exchange (NYSE)—the largest stock exchange in the United States

Partnership—a firm owned by two or more named owners

Portfolio—complete collection of assets

Profit—the portion of the sales price of a good or service that goes to the owner(s) of the firm as a reward for their entrepreneurship

Rent—the portion of the sales price of a good or service that goes to the owner(s) of land used in the production process

Retained earnings—profits earned by a firm that are held by the firm for future investment

Russell 2000—a stock index of 2000 large companies' stocks traded on the New York Stock Exchange

Savings account—a savings instrument offered by banks that pays interest; money placed in a savings account has less liquidity than in a checking account, but usually pays a higher interest rate

Share of stock—part ownership of a firm

Sole proprietorships—a firm owned by a single named individual

Standard & Poor's—a credit rating agency

S&P 500—a stock market index consisting of 500 companies' stocks listed on the New York Stock Exchange

Tiebout effect—the movement of people between political jurisdictions to better align the government policies they live under with their preferences

Trade deficit—when the dollar value of imports exceed the dollar value of exports

Trade surplus—when the dollar value of exports exceed the dollar value of imports

Transfer payment—money given to individuals by governments without an exchange of good or service

Usury—charging excessively, or illegally, high levels of interest

Wages—payment to laborers in exchange for their labor

Questions for Review

1. Who are consumers? What actions can they take? every individual.
2. What are firms? What actions can they take? investment, ~~borrowing~~ $
3. What are financial institutions? What actions can they take?
4. What is the government? What actions can they take?
5. What is the foreign sector? What actions can they take?
6. What are the four types of income? Who earns them? wage, interest, rent.
7. Which economic actors engage in production?
8. What is a stock market? What is the biggest stock market in the US?
9. What is a bond market? How do government bonds differ from corporate bonds?
10. Compare and contrast the following savings instruments: a checking account, a savings account, a money market account, and a certificate of deposit.
11. Compare and contrast defined benefit and defined contribution pensions.
12. Compare and contrast fully funded and pay-as-you go pensions. What are the advantages and disadvantages of each?

Chapter 11

Business Cycles

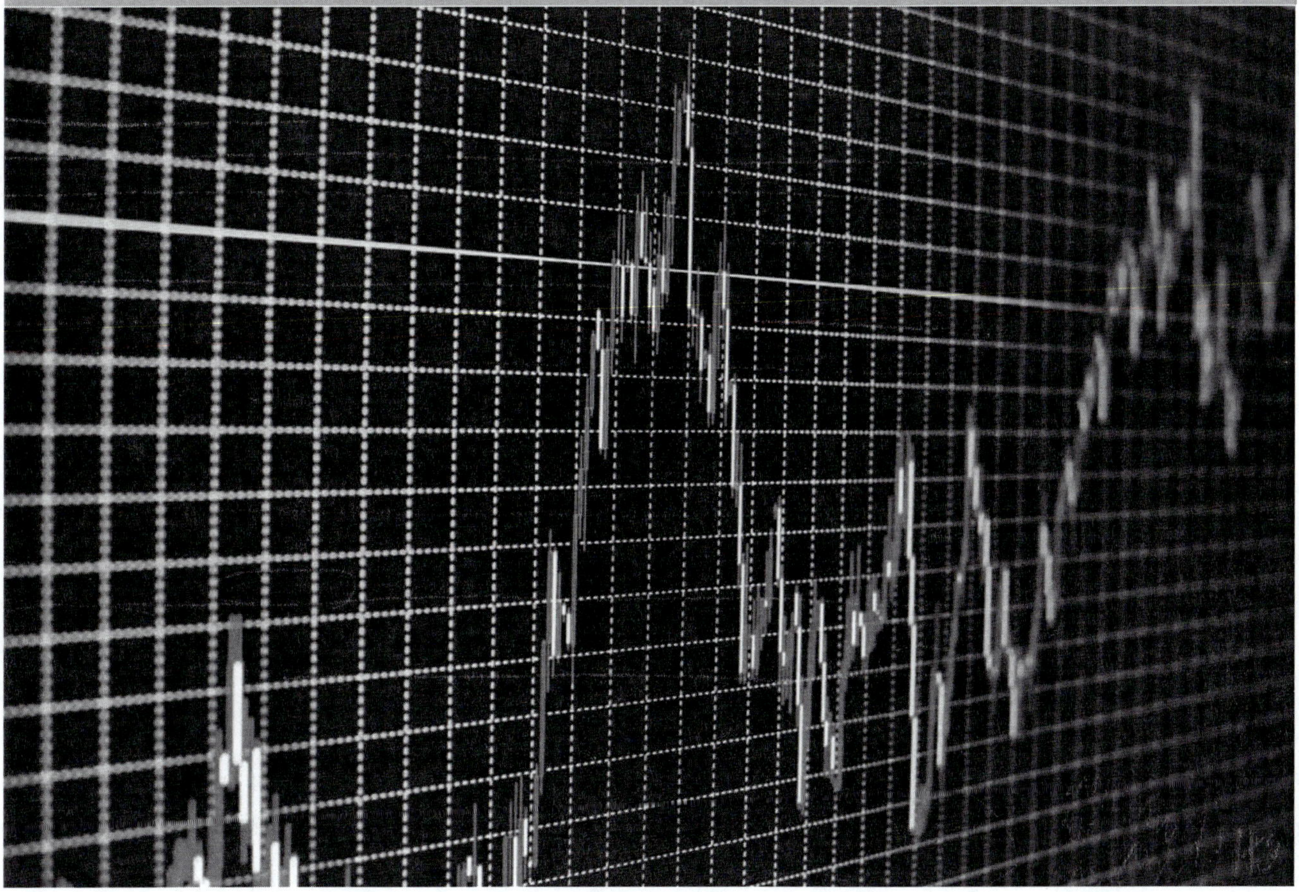

© Pincasso, 2012, under license Shutterstock, Inc.

While each economic actor can engage in multiple actions for various reasons, there are certain actions that cause firms to engage in more production. As consumers, firms, governments, and foreigners purchase more goods and services, existing inventories of unsold goods falls. This acts as a signal to producers to increase their output. Short run changes in output are the result of either changes in demand for the output of firms or a change in the firm's cost of production.

Changes in the demand for output can be broken down into four categories, changes in consumption (C), investment (I), government spending (G), and exports (X). To understand short term fluctuations in output, one must understand what causes the demand for consumption, investment, government spending, and net exports to change. Output changes as economic actors make different choices. If everyone made the same choice every day, there would not be business cycles. This chapter will explain factors that change the demand for each category of output and will outline government policies that affect demand and the cost of production.

Factors Which Shift Demand for Output

Things that Cause Consumption to Change

The level of current consumption depends upon the price of goods and services relative to consumers' income levels, the level of consumers' wealth, the amount of tax burden on consumers, the availability of credit, and consumers' expectations about the future.

All things being equal, if prices of goods and services fall, consumers can afford to buy more. This is called the **wealth effect**. Conversely, if the price levels increase, all things being equal, consumers will engage in less consumption. In the short run, if the price of gasoline increases and people find it difficult to immediately alter the amount of gasoline they consume, they will have less money left to engage in the consumption of other goods and services.

As people's incomes increase, so does their consumption of goods and services. Milton Friedman's permanent income hypothesis states that consumers will spend a relatively constant percentage of all new permanent income. They will not increase consumption based on temporary income changes. Temporary income tends to increase savings rather than consumption. If more is better, then as people's capacity to purchase goods and services increases, so too will their actual consumption.

ex. of wealth increasing not just being income

As people's wealth increases, so does their ability to engage in consumption. If Bob's income remains unchanged, but he notices that the value of the house he owns doubled in the last year, he is wealthier. Bob can now afford to consume more (assuming he wants the same amount of money available in retirement as before the increase in house prices). In this way, US consumer spending increased faster than incomes during the housing boom of the early 2000's.

Consumers can not purchase goods and services with money that is taken from them by the government. All things being equal, an increase in taxes results in a decrease in consumption. Conversely, a decrease in taxes will result in an increase in consumption, as long as people view the tax change as permanently altering their disposable income.

The purchase of higher priced consumer goods, such as automobiles, often occurs on credit. The more that credit is made available to consumers, the more access they have to shift future consumption forward. A decrease in credit availability, all things being equal, will reduce current consumption.

Consumers make consumption decisions not just based on current information, but also based upon expectations about the future. If consumers are confident that they won't get fired from their job, they are more likely to engage in consumption than if they are uncertain about the future. Expectations of higher future prices, income, wealth, availability of credit, and lower expected tax rates all will cause consumers, on average, to engage in more current consumption.

Things that Cause Investment to Change

Business investment is even more volatile than consumption. Since WWII, investment has grown less than one-third as fast as consumption but has had two and a half times the variance. During the same time period, investment levels had ten times the variance of either net exports or government spending.

Firms exist to make profit. In their pursuit of profit, they often employ new machines, tools, factories, or software. The purchase of new capital is investment. Investment decisions are based on the expected benefits over time from the fixed capital vs. the marginal costs of employing the capital.

The opportunity cost of investment is the interest rate. The higher the interest rate, the more costly it is for firms to borrow money to buy new capital. As interest rates fall, more and more capital projects become profitable to invest in. One source of variance in investment is a change in interest rates.

Similarly, changes in access to business credit can alter the pace of investment. When business credit becomes more scarce, current investment falls. As business credit standards loosen, more entrepreneurs gain access to start-up capital and investment increases. As we will examine in Chapter 22, when more loans are made by banks in a fractional reserve banking system, the money supply increases. This in turn causes a decrease in interest rates. In this way, increased business investment leads to even more business investment. On the contrary, when firms begin investing less, fewer loans are made, the money supply shrinks causing interest rates to rise, and other investment projects become more costly. As a result, the economy tends to experience booms and busts in investment, which cause and/or exacerbate business cycles.

Other factors that affect investment are the price of capital, business confidence, and business taxes/regulations. As the price of capital falls, firms are able to upgrade their capital for a lower cost. Conversely, if the price of capital increases, such as due to an increase in the price of steel raising the price of machinery, then fewer firms can afford to make new investments. The falling price of steel in the 1870's caused railroad firms to replace iron rails with steel rails. Even though steel rails for years had been more durable than iron rails, their cost had remained prohibitively high.

An increase in business taxes and regulations on capital works to decrease the amount of new investment that firms engage in. Taxes on capital, such as the capital gains tax, alter the capital to labor ratio that firms find to be profit maximizing. As taxes or regulations on capital increase, it becomes more profitable to substitute labor for capital or to build any new capital overseas. Business investment represents the true mobility of capital. While an existing factory is hard to move, when it comes to replacing the factory (i.e. new investment), capital is very mobile. New investment today translates into a larger stock of capital for tomorrow, so decisions by the government in terms of regulations or taxes on capital now not only affect today's level of investment, but tomorrow's level of potential output.

The last major source of investment variability is business confidence/uncertainty. When businesses think that their business will grow in the future, they are more likely to invest and expand their productive capacity. As firms become pessimistic about their future, new investment is curtailed. As firms face greater uncertainty due to changing regulations or taxes, this added uncertainty causes a decrease in current investment. Investment has a multi-year lifespan, so that the more uncertain business owners are about the relative profitability of capital over time, the less new investment will materialize.

John Maynard Keynes suggested that business investment is determined by "animal spirits" and is therefore unpredictable. However, because most investment in capital is expensive (relative to current cash flow) capitalists have an economic incentive to make informed investment decisions. To suggest that capitalists act irrationally based upon "animal spirits" neglects reality. Good capitalists make money and have more capital to invest later. Ill-informed capitalists lose their capital and have no further capital to invest. Time is on the side of informed investment decisions.

Things that Cause Government Spending to Change

Changes in government spending are less predictable than changes in private sector spending. People's actions concerning their own money tend to be more predictable than government officials decisions concerning other people's money. The political reward system is such that it is often in the short term benefit of politicians to increase spending and cut taxes. Because politicians face elections in the short term, they tend to emphasize these politically popular policies rather than policies that focus primarily on long run economic growth. Still, there have been periods of US history where politicians have decreased government spending, most notably at the conclusion of major military conflicts.

Historically, governments around the world have tended to spend more money in times of war than in times of peace. Constituents are usually not asked to forgo their normal government spending programs in order to finance military action.

So, rather than cut other government spending or raises taxes, most countries over time have financed wars through increased government debt. The most notable swings in government spending in the US indeed have revolved around military conflicts such as The American Revolution, The War of 1812, The Spanish American War, The US Civil War, WWI, WWII, The Cold War, and conflicts in Korea, Vietnam, Iraq, and Afghanistan. The decrease in military spending following wars is known as the **peace dividend**, because money that had been diverted to the war effort is now returned to meeting the needs and wants of consumers and businesses.

A second cause of fluctuating government spending is business cycles themselves. In response to slow economic growth or recessions since the 1930's, US politicians have often advocated the expansion of government spending in order to help stimulate the economy. President Herbert Hoover increased government spending on public works projects at the beginning of The Great Depression. President Barack Obama increased government spending for almost all government programs as a response to the 2008 recession.

Robert Higgs[1] has shown that major increases in government spending due to shocks such as wars and recessions never fully dissipate. Instead, government spending levels, though lower than their peak, rarely return to pre-crisis levels. They remain higher. For politicians, spending, and the power derived from it, can be addictive.

Things that Cause Exports to Change

People in other countries change the amount of goods and services they buy from the US for a variety of reasons. Firstly, all people in other countries are consumers. The same factors the affect US consumption affects foreign consumption. These include the prices of goods and services, foreign incomes and wealth levels, foreign tax burdens, the availability of credit, and their expectations about the future. As foreign consumers buy more generally, they also tend to buy more US exports. Therefore, increases in things like foreign income or foreign wealth increase the US's ability to sell goods abroad. In this way, one doesn't have to be altruistic to hope that other countries become wealthier over time. One can root for a growing world economy because it will benefit US exporters and therefore the US economy.

[1] Robert Higgs. "Crisis, Bigger Government and Ideological Change: Two-Hypotheses on the Ratchet Phenomenon." *Explorations in Economic History* 22 (1985): 4.

Of particular note to foreign consumers or businesses is the relative price difference of products between countries. When one country's prices increase relative to those of another, fewer consumers, both domestic and abroad, will want to buy that country's goods and services. Conversely, when the relative prices of a country's goods fall, more people around the world will want to buy them.

These spending categories (consumption, investment, government spending, and exports) are known as **injections**. To sum up demand side explanations for business cycles, when consumption, investment, government spending, or exports increase, GDP increases. When they fall, GDP falls. After all, GDP calculations are made by summing up consumption, investment, government spending, and net exports.

In the short run, consumers could choose to save more and consume less. Because an increase in saving causes a decrease in consumption, savings are known as a **leakage** in the short term. Leakages are items that if increased, tend to slow down GDP in the short run. Savings can make their way back into the economy through investment, but it may take time to do so. Likewise, taxes and imports are two other common leakages. When taxes increase on consumers, they can afford to engage in less consumption. When taxes are increased on businesses, they can afford to engage in less investment. While these taxes may find their way back into the economy via higher government spending, there is no requirement that they do so.

When consumers choose to buy foreign made products, they replace domestic consumption (and therefore production) with products that increase foreign production. While the purchase of foreign goods increases foreign incomes and could therefore cause future exports to increase, there is no guarantee that people in other countries, once wealthier, will want to buy more American made products. Yet, free trade overall increases wealth.

Government Polices to Boost Demand

There are numerous policies that a government can enact to change demand for output. These policies can have short run benefits or long run benefits, but typically benefits today come at the cost of benefits in the future and vice versa.

Policies that Target Consumption

Current consumption generally increases when taxes are lowered and when consumers are confident that future government policies will lead to lower taxes and more economic growth. Governments have often attempted to increase consumption by redistributing money from high income individuals to low income individuals on the belief that lower income individuals will spend a larger percentage of their income than did the people who once held the money. While this policy attempts to increase consumption, it also works to decrease investment, because the expectation of future income transfers decreases the future profitability of current investment. Policies designed to boost short run consumption typically come at the cost of future consumption due to slower economic growth.

Policies that Target Investment

Government policies to increase investment come in two varieties: increasing investment over time (including now), and increasing investment in the short run (at the expense of future investment). In order to increase investment over time, governments can create a tax and regulatory environment that is conducive to investment (see Chapter 5). Legal changes that make taxes and regulations more capital friendly will boost investment levels both now and later.

The second strategy does not increase capital accumulation over time, but merely alters when in time investment occurs. For instance, if the Federal Reserve increases the money supply to lower interest rates, they lower the cost of borrowing with the intent of spurring current investment. Inflation neutral monetary policy dictates that today's loosening of monetary policy necessitates a future tightening. In this way, the Federal Reserve signals that today's investment will cost less, and tomorrow's investment will cost more. Therefore, tomorrow's investment should be moved forward to today. Likewise, investment tax credits which apply to now, but not later, provide an incentive to move investment forward.

To the extent that this strategy is effective, an economy gets more investment today accompanied by less investment tomorrow. The 2009 "Cash for Clunkers" program saw a temporary increase in car sales followed by a large reduction in car sales as consumers planning to buy cars in the near future just moved up their consumption by a couple of months. Excessive use of monetary easing or investment tax credits causes artificial investment bubbles that can, and do, burst.

In order to bring the US out of the 2001 recession, the Federal Reserve eased monetary policy, which caused businesses to bring investment forward. Because monetary policy was so loose for so long, a large amount of investment was brought forward. In fact, so much was brought forward that excess capacity was created in everything from industrial plants, to condos, to office space. This excess capacity caused investment to come to a virtual halt in the US, helping to trigger the 2008–2009 economic recession.

Policies that Change Government Spending

Government policies that cause government spending to change over time include balanced budget rules, pay as you go rules, or binding spending constraints. Governments with binding spending constraints, either in terms of dollars, a percentage of output, or as a function of tax receipts, have less discretion over changing government spending than do governments with no such rules.

As governments become more in debt, future government spending becomes imperiled. Therefore, a strategy of government borrowing to increase current government spending can lead to less government spending over time. Historically, government's decisions to go to war also have had profound impacts on current spending levels for domestic causes.

Policies that Target Net Exports

Government policies that cause net exports to increase in the short term include increased trade barriers, export subsidies and depreciation of their currency's value. However, in the long run other countries retaliate by putting trade barriers on US exports, devalue their currency, and subsidize their country's exports. Over time, these actions serve to lower exports and slow down economic growth.

Over time a country can increase its net exports by lowering its national debt and taxing consumption rather than production. By lowering its national debt, governments take away the option of foreigners storing domestic currency in government bonds. Instead, they would be forced to buy goods, services, or assets in the domestic economy, thereby spurring exports. Tax codes that tax production handicap producers selling to the international market. Tax codes that tax consumption export some of the domestic tax burden to international producers.

Things that Cause the Cost of Production to Change

Business cycles can be also be caused by quick and unexpected changes in the cost of production faced by a majority of firms in a country. These include changes in cost of inputs, productivity, technology, the quantity of inputs (immigration, disasters, or war), government regulations, and business taxes.

When OPEC increased the price of oil in the 1970's the US economy suffered. Energy is a major input into the production process and the increase in the price of energy increased both production and distribution cost of goods throughout the US economy. This worked to slow the economy down.

In the 1990's, the internet revolution dramatically lowered information and communication costs. This increased worker productivity and lowered the cost of production for many goods and services throughout the economy. As a result, the economy grew quickly.

Wars and natural disasters decrease the productive capacity of an economy by destroying existing capital. This destruction lowers current output while creating the need to rebuild capital can increase the pace of economic growth following the end of military hostilities. Germany and Japan's economies were devastated by the Allied troops' bombings. However following WWII, both economies grew quickly, as they worked to replace destroyed capital.

Once again, government policies can affect the cost of production. In particular, increases in government regulations and business taxes increase the cost of production which in turn, slows down production and therefore economic growth.

Conclusion

Government policies often have multiple and conflicting motives. Policies such as increasing the minimum wage, forced usage of union labor, and environmental protections are imposed to protect workers and the environment. The tradeoff is that these regulations increase the cost of production and therefore slow down economic growth. Each government regulation would need to be examined on a case by case basis to determine if the marginal benefit to workers or the environment exceeded the marginal cost imposed upon society through slower growth.

Government policies on war and immigration can affect the productive capacity of an economy at any given time. More resources lead to more output. Changes in business taxes along with changes in education policy can also affect the cost of production.

The economy is ever changing. Changes made by any number of actors have the potential to cause business cycles in the US economy. Consumers, firms, governments, and foreign economic actors all play a part in a growing economy. While the economy grows, it does not always do so at an even rate. The following chapters will examine how John Maynard Keynes modeled short run business cycles in the economy along with his policy prescriptions for governments and central banks. This analysis will also include critiques of his prescriptions.

Glossary

Injections—things that if increased, increase the current demand for domestic production

Leakages—things that if increased, decrease the current demand for domestic production

Peace dividend—a decrease in military spending that frees up resources to be used for the benefit of consumers

Wealth effect—a fall in prices increases the purchasing power of consumers

Questions for Review

1. What causes consumption levels to change?
2. What causes investment levels to change?
3. What causes government spending levels to change?
4. What causes exports to change?
5. What government policies can spur current consumption?
6. What government policies can spur current investment?
7. What government policies can spur current government spending?
8. What government policies can spur current exports?
9. What causes the cost of production to change?
10. What government policies can cause the cost of production to change?
11. Identify which component(s) of GDP change(s) as a result of each of these scenarios:
    a. capital gains taxes are increased
    b. the DOW rises
    c. mortgage rates fall
    d. new tariffs are implemented

Chapter 12

Aggregate Demand and Aggregate Supply

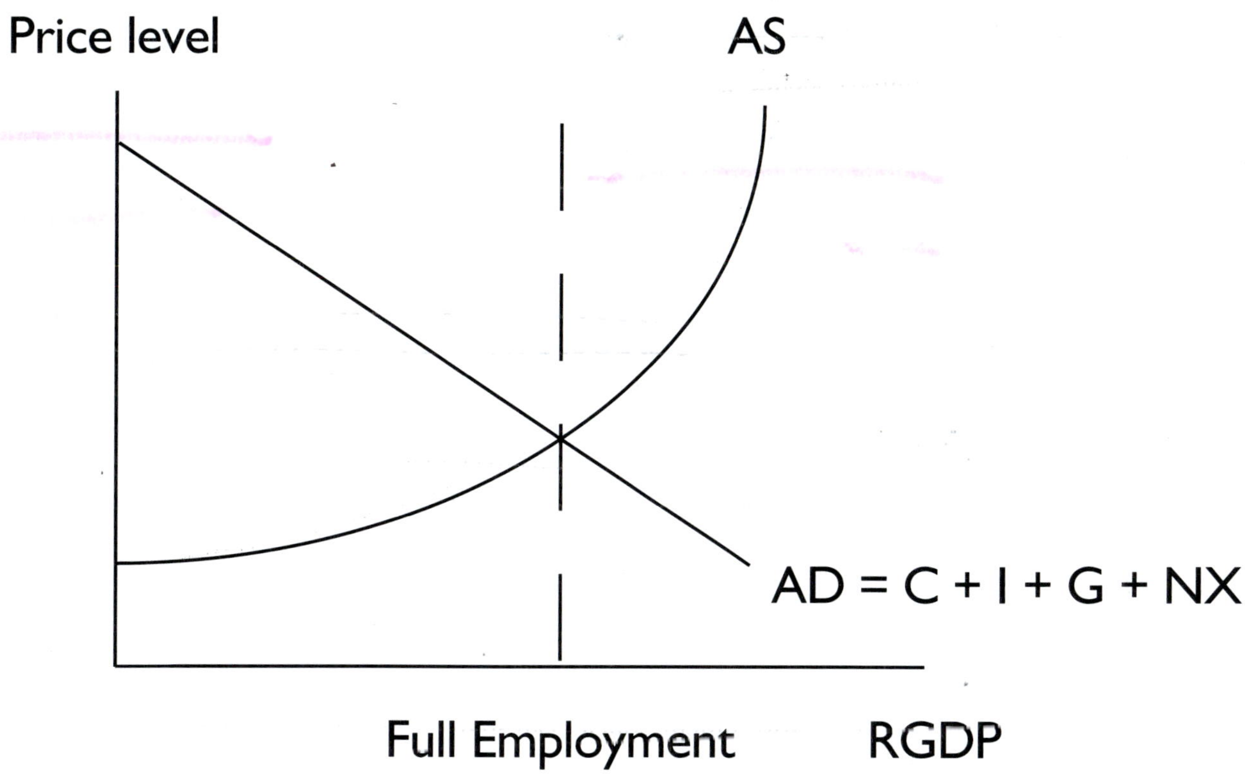

Models, but for the ones on runways, are theoretical abstractions. Economic models are no different. Macroeconomic models make simplifying assumptions about actors in the economy in order to understand and predict levels of unemployment, inflation, and economic output. As noted in the previous two chapters, a myriad of economic actors make decisions relative to making their lives better, their company's profits higher, or their re-election more likely. John Maynard Keynes created the aggregate demand and aggregate supply model to attempt to explain unemployment, inflation, and output by examining the demand for domestically made goods and services relative to their supply. This chapter outlines the aggregate demand and supply model and discusses how shifts in aggregate demand or supply affect the macroeconomic equilibrium.

Aggregate Demand

Aggregate demand (AD) is the sum total of all domestic goods and services that consumers, businesses, the government, and foreign actors want to buy at any given price level. It is theoretically derived by adding the demand for apples to the demand for cars to the demand for bread to the demand for every other good or service. Mathematically, aggregate demand equals the demand for consumption plus investment plus government spending plus net exports at every price level. Recall that these are the same variables used to calculate GDP via the expenditure approach.

$$AD = C + I + G + NX$$

For individual goods and services, the **law of demand** states that as prices fall, the quantity demanded of a good or service increases. The aggregate demand curve is downward sloping because consumers, businesses, governments, and foreigners can all afford to buy more goods and services as prices fall. This is due to three factors: the wealth effect, interest rate effect, and foreign trade effect.

The **wealth effect** occurs as lower prices enable economic actors to engage in larger purchases of goods and services with the same amount of income. In this way, consumers feel wealthier as their money goes further due to the lower prices. At the same time, lower price levels typically lower the cost of borrowing money. The **interest rate effect** states that as the cost of borrowing money falls, firms will be better able to afford investment in new capital, consumers will be more able to purchase homes and durable consumer goods, and governments will find it cheaper to borrow, enabling them to run larger budget deficits. Even if firms, consumers, or governments are using their own funds for these purchases, the opportunity cost of doing so decreases as prices fall. Finally, lower domestic prices will encourage residents and foreigners to purchase more domestically produced goods and services, thereby lower imports and increasing exports. This is known as the **foreign trade effect**. All three of these effects then cause the aggregate demand curve to slope downward.

Note that when the prices of individual goods are aggregated, they yield the **average price level**. In reality, the average price level is measured and reported by examining a market basket of goods defined by the Bureau of Labor Statistics (Chapter 9). As such, prices of individual products can change at different rates or even in different directions from the government reported average price level. Rather than stand for an actual price, the price on the y-axis is meant to measure changes in the average price level (i.e. inflation or deflation). Recall that an increase in the average price level is inflation, while a decrease is deflation.

The x-axis of the aggregate demand curve represents the sum total of all goods and services produced in the economy, or RGDP. As discussed earlier, RGDP sums all domestic production (just as GDP does) while also controlling for inflation. In this way the x-axis is a measure of actual economic output. An increase in RGDP reflects economic growth, while a decrease in RGDP is an economic

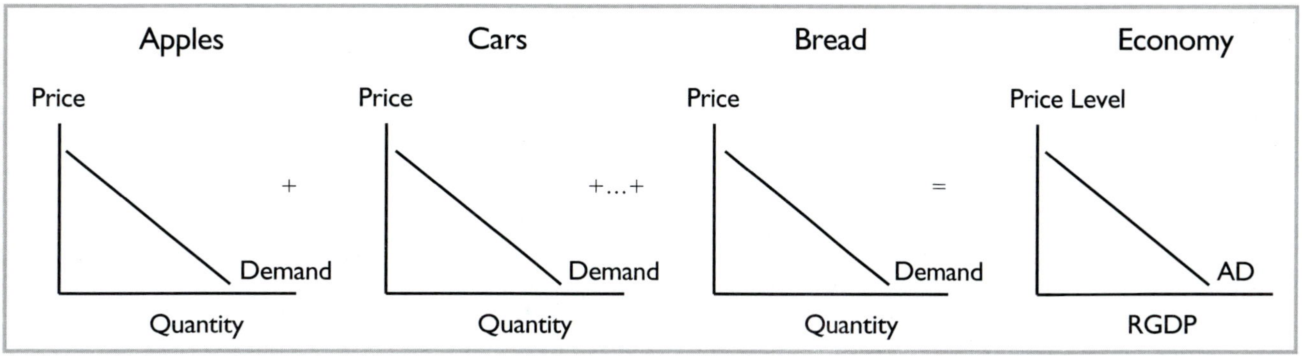

Figure 12.1
CREATION OF AGGREGATE DEMAND VIA THE SUMMING OF INDIVIDUAL DEMAND CURVES

contraction, or recession. Figure 12.1 illustrates how aggregate demand then is the sum of each individual demand curve in an economy.

Aggregate demand constantly shifts as actors in the economy act and react to each other. Aggregate demand shifts to the right (increases) when consumption, investment, government spending, or net exports increase. Aggregate demand shifts to the left (decreases) when consumption, investment, government spending, or net exports decrease. The previous chapter describes the many factors which can cause consumption, investment, government spending, investment, and net exports to change. In Figure 12.2, AD represents the initial level of aggregate demand while AD' represents the new level of aggregate demand following a change in consumption, investment, government spending, or net exports.

Aggregate Supply

Aggregate supply is the sum total of all goods and services firms and governments are willing and able to produce at any given price level. It is theoretically derived by adding the supply of apples to the supply of cars to the supply of bread to the supply of every other good or service. Figure 12.3 illustrates this relationship.

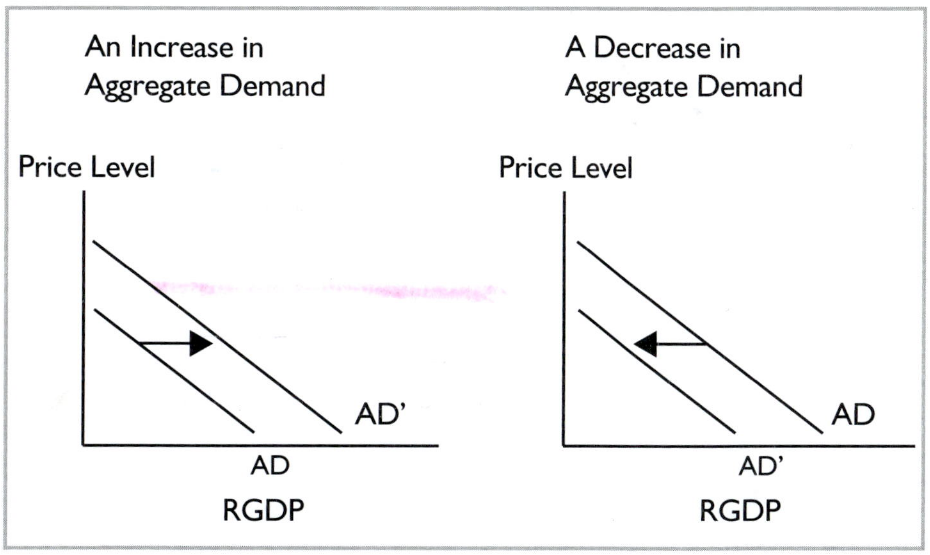

Figure 12.2
SHIFTS IN AD

The aggregate supply curve's shape varies from flat to upward sloping and then to vertical. At any given point in time, an economy can only produce on or within its production possibilities frontier. When output in the economy is extremely low as is the case in a severe recession, a large number of productive resources are unused. Multiple existing factories are idle, skilled workers are laid

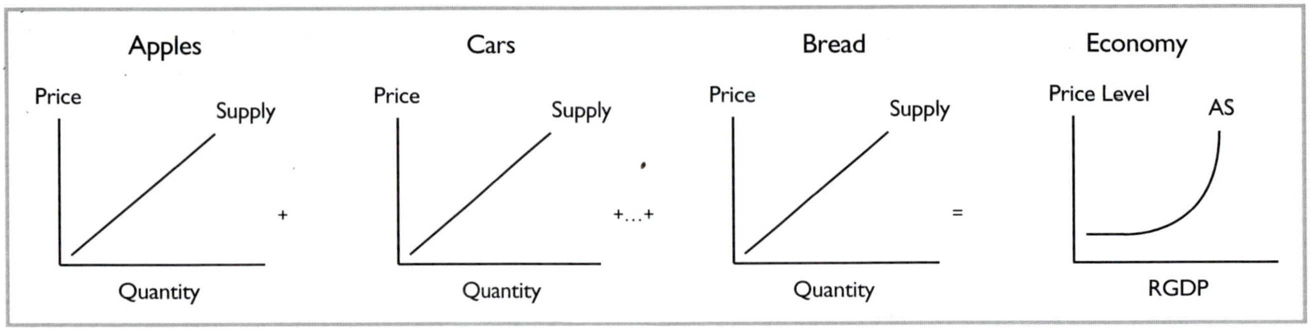

Figure 12.3
CREATION OF AGGREGATE SUPPLY FROM INDIVIDUAL SUPPLY CURVES IN THE ECONOMY

off, and land is left fallow. In this state of affairs, producers are said to have **excess capacity**. Firms can increase production without substantial increases in cost by employing workers that are already trained and utilizing capital that was sitting unused. In this way, aggregate supply is relatively flat at low levels of economic output because production can increase without increases in the price level.

At the other extreme, when production is near full capacity the aggregate supply curve is vertical. The vertical portion of aggregate supply represents the constraint resulting from the production possibilities frontier. Even if consumers want to buy more products, producers cannot operate above full capacity. So despite higher price levels, production cannot increase beyond this point without economic growth, and so aggregate supply is vertical here.

For most levels of production, aggregate supply is upward sloping. As production increases toward full capacity, more and more resources are employed in the production process. The most fertile land is plowed first. The most productive capital and workers are also employed first. As production increases, producers needing more resources are then forced to employ less productive resources in the production process. This increases the cost of production and yields higher prices for output. As a result, in this range of aggregate supply increased output corresponds to a higher price level.

Just as aggregate demand shifts from changes in a variety of factors affecting GDP, aggregate supply shifts when anything changes the cost of producing. As the cost of production increases, aggregate supply shifts to the left (decreases); at any given price level, producers will now be able to bring fewer products to market. As the cost of production decreases, aggregate supply shifts to the right (increases); at any given price level, producers will now be able to bring more products to market. As noted in the previous chapter, the cost of production can be affected by changes in government regulations, business taxation, the quantity of resources available for production, resource productivity, wars, and natural disasters.

While different industries will face different changes in their cost structure, aggregate supply is meant to measure overall changes in the cost of production. Changing energy and labor costs, for instance, tend to have widespread impact on numerous firms. In Figure 12.4, AS represents the initial level of aggregate supply while AS' represents the new level of aggregate supply following a change in the cost of production.

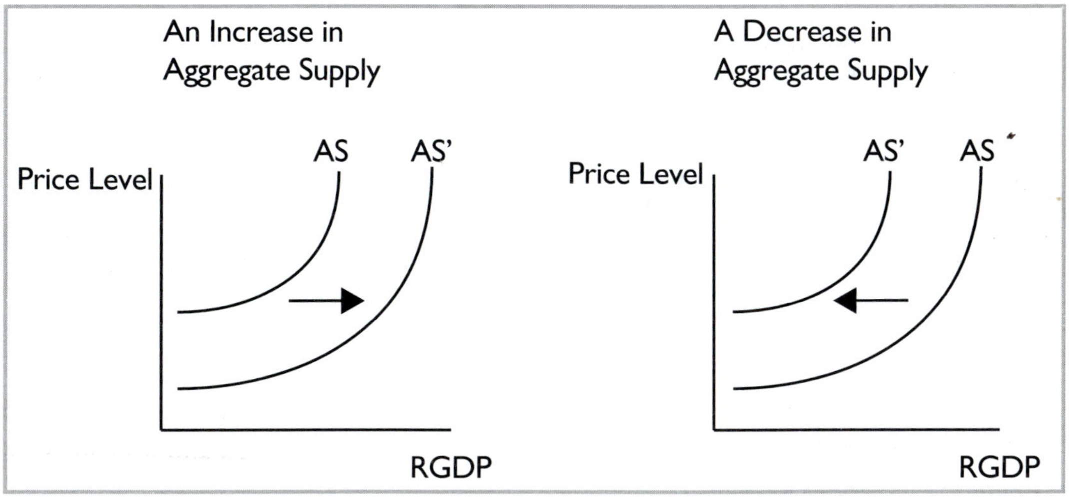

Figure 12.4
SHIFTS IN AS

Macroeconomic Equilibrium

Theoretically, the intersection of the aggregate demand and aggregate supply curves represents the **macroeconomic equilibrium**. This is where the quantity of domestic goods and services demanded in the economy equals the quantity of domestic goods and services supplied. This equilibrium dictates the current price level, the current level of real GDP, and the current unemployment rate. An increase in aggregate demand or a decrease in aggregate supply causes inflation (the equilibrium average price level increases). A decrease in the aggregate demand or an increase in aggregate supply causes deflation (the equilibrium average price level decreases).

Likewise, RGDP changes as a result of a change in aggregate demand or aggregate supply. An increase in RGDP, occurs when aggregate demand or aggregate supply increase. Real GDP decreases, as aggregate demand or aggregate supply decrease. While the x-axis explicitly represents output or RGDP, it implicitly represents unemployment. Reductions in output are typically accompanied by a reduction in the workforce, as fewer workers are needed to produce fewer goods and services. Economic growth is usually accompanied by an increase in the workforce, as more workers are needed to produce a larger number of goods and services. As such, a decrease aggregate demand or aggregate supply causes an increase in unemployment while an increase in aggregate demand or aggregate supply causes a decrease in unemployment. The one caveat to note is that changes to aggregate supply caused by changes in worker productivity can cause output to change without changing levels of unemployment.

Recall that full employment is where cyclical unemployment equals zero, but the overall unemployment rate is between 5 and 5.5%. When aggregate demand and aggregate supply intersect at the full employment level of output (FE), the economy is said to be at equilibrium at its "happy place." This is illustrated in Figure 12.7. The next chapter discusses what happens when the economy moves away from this "happy place" due to shifts in aggregate demand or aggregate supply.

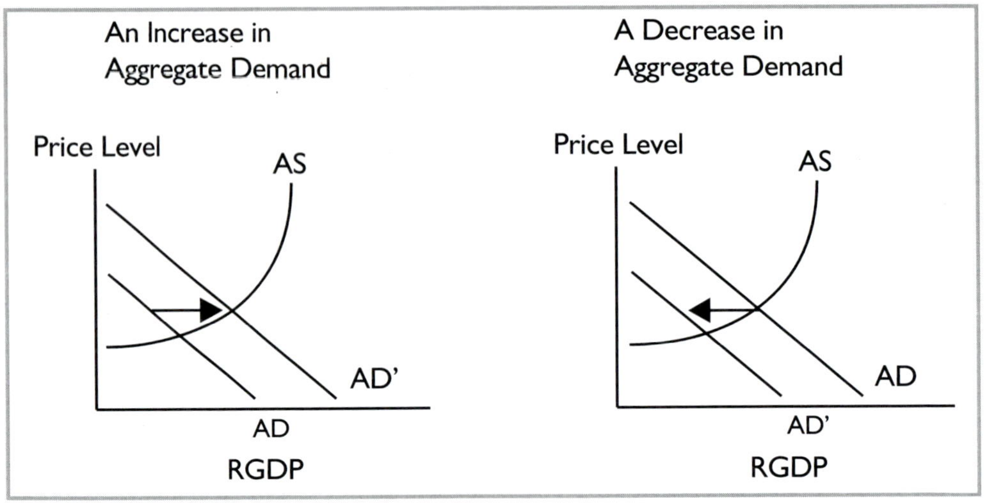

Figure 12.5

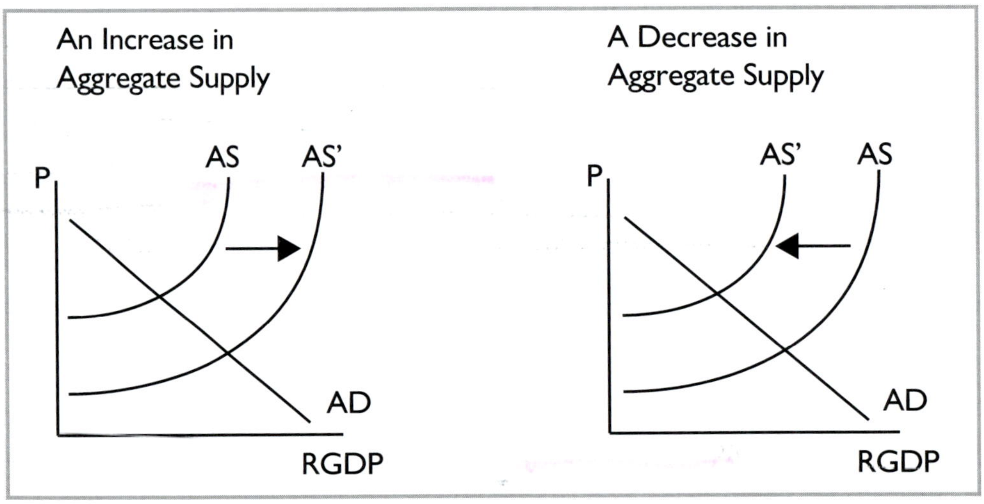

Figure 12.6

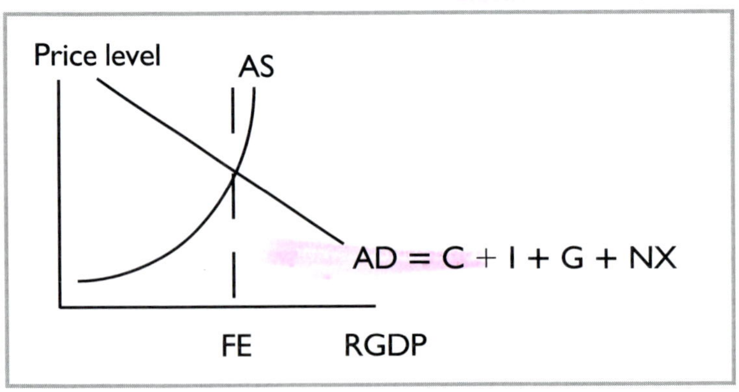

Figure 12.7
THE ECONOMY AT ITS HAPPY PLACE

Glossary

Aggregate demand—the sum total of all domestic goods and services that consumers, businesses, the government, and foreign actors want to buy at any given price level

Aggregate supply—the sum total of all goods and services firms and governments are willing and able to produce at any given price level

Average price level—the cost of purchasing the market basket of goods and services as constructed by the Bureau of Labor Statistics

Excess capacity—high levels of unused resource; this occurs when production is inside the production possibilities frontier

Foreign trade effect—the effect caused by lower domestic prices encouraging residents and foreigners to purchase more domestically produced goods and services, thereby lower imports and increasing exports

Interest rate effect—the effect that occurs as prices and interest rates lower, causing a reduced opportunity cost of investment and a greater incentive to invest

Law of demand—as prices fall, the quantity demand of a good increases

Macroeconomic equilibrium—where the quantity of domestic goods and services demanded in the economy equals the quantity of domestic goods and services supplied

Wealth effect—the effect caused by lower prices enabling economic actors to engage in greater purchases of goods and services with the same amount of income

Questions for Review

1. What does the aggregate demand curve look like? How do the three different factors each work to give it that slope?
2. What causes aggregate demand to increase? Decrease?
3. What does the aggregate supply curve look like? What determines its different possible slopes? What types of economic situations are common for each of the three possible slopes?
4. What causes aggregate supply to increase? Decrease?
5. How are equilibrium levels of prices, output, and employment determined in the economy?
6. What happens to the average price level, RGDP and unemployment when aggregate demand increases? When aggregate demand decreases?
7. What happens to the average price level, RGDP and unemployment when aggregate supply increases? When aggregate supply decreases?
8. Does the presence of a macroeconomic equilibrium mean that the quantity demand of all individual goods and services in an economy equals their quantity supplied? Why or why not?
9. Examine each of the following events. What impact will they have on aggregate demand, aggregate supply, the average price level, RGDP, and unemployment? Graph the shift in AD or AS and label the changes that occur as a result.
   a. the US experiences an increase in worker productivity
   b. interest rates increase making it more expensive to borrow money
   c. the European Union bans the importation of US made products
   d. the federal government raises the minimum wage to $100 an hour
   e. the federal government lowers the corporate income tax rate
   f. the federal government spends $100 billion on building new bridges in the US
   g. the federal government imposes a carbon tax on all carbon emissions from US plants
   h. consumers become optimistic that the economy will begin to grow quickly in the near future

Chapter 13

Recessionary Gaps, Inflationary Gaps, and Stagflation

Once upon a time (the 1930's), in a land far, far, away (the United Kingdom), John Maynard Keynes proposed the aggregate demand and aggregate supply model to explain current levels of unemployment and inflation and to provide theoretical analysis with policy alternatives to reach full employment. Full employment (the economy's happy place where no cyclical unemployment occurred) was seen as the ideal place to which the economy should be directed.

Unfortunately, the economy routinely suffered "shocks" that knocked it out of the full employment equilibrium. These shocks were modeled as being exogenous to the economy. That is, they came out of nowhere, and were not expected events. In reality, no one knows the future, so every day contains shocks to someone. Furthermore, these shocks are not exogenous to the economy but rather they are endogenous, as they result from actions made by actual economic actors that take part in the economy. Nevertheless, the analysis of the Keynesian model will treat "shocks" as being exogenous. This chapter examines the scenarios created when such shocks occur.

The Recessionary Gap

Assume the economy is operating at full employment. Next, assume that businesses become pessimistic about their future profitability and this pessimism leads to a decrease in new investment. This unexpected decrease in business investment is considered to be an exogenous shock to the economy. Recall that aggregate demand is composed of consumption, investment, government spending, and net exports. As investment falls, aggregate demand falls as well. Consequently, aggregate demand will intersect aggregate supply to the left of full employment, and the economy is said to be experiencing a **recessionary gap**.

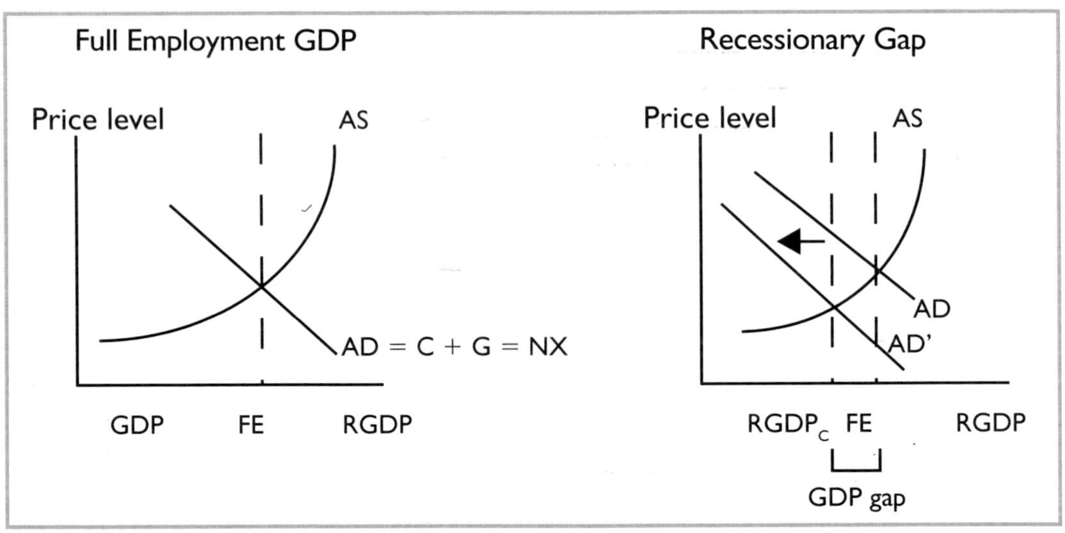

Figure 13.1 **A RECESSIONARY GAP RESULTS FROM A DECREASE IN AD BELOW FULL EMPLOYMENT**

As aggregate demand falls, real GDP decreases (to RGDPc in Figure 13.1). Since fewer businesses want to buy new capital, workers are laid off, and less capital is produced. As a result unemployment increases. All things being equal, there will also be downward pressure on prices. While lower output and higher unemployment are generally viewed as negative economic phenomena, deflation (as noted in Chapter 9) helps creditors and consumers buy more with their income, but could hurt producers or debtors.

The recessionary gap is so named because a prolonged decrease in output is referred to as a recession. The GDP gap refers to the gap between current real GDP and full employment GDP. In other words, it is the amount of production the economy is forgoing due to cyclical unemployment. Note that no one actually knows the size of a recessionary gap while it is occurring. It is anyone's guess as to what level of GDP corresponds to full employment. Economic data regarding the present output levels of the economy are neither immediate nor wholly accurate. Recall from Chapter 3, GDP data are calculated for each quarter of the year. The government's final estimate of a quarter's production only comes three months after the completion of the quarter. This estimate still is not perfect for reasons also cited in Chapter 3.

A recessionary gap is caused by aggregate demand being "too low." It intersects aggregate supply to the left of full employment. Anything that would cause a reduction in consumption, investment, government spending, or net exports, then would lead to a recessionary gap. The result is high unemployment, a decrease in output, and deflation.

The Great Depression in the US is said, according to this model, to have been a really large recessionary gap. Consumption[1] and investment[2] dramatically slowed down in the US economy. The Smoot-Hawley Tariff also caused US exports to decline. This fall in consumption, investment, and exports caused a large downward shift in US aggregate demand. As a result, the unemployment rate reached 25%, real GDP fell by 33% between 1929 and 1932, and deflation led to a 33% fall in prices.

The Inflationary Gap

What happens when aggregate demand shifts in the opposite direction? First assume once again that the

[1] Peter Temin argued that an unexplained fall in consumption led to the Great Depression.

[2] John Maynard Keynes argued that an unexplained fall in investment led to the Great Depression.

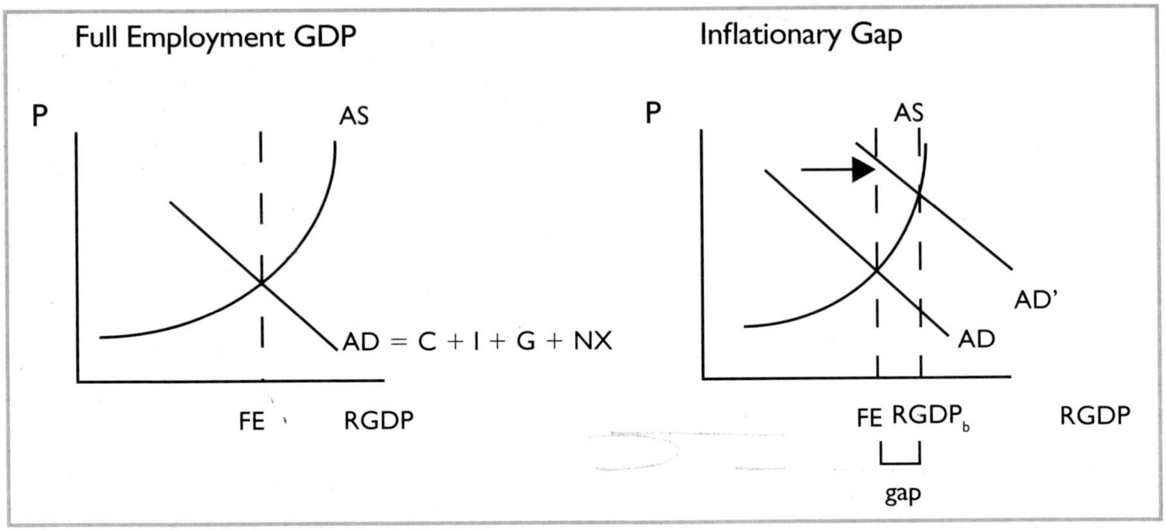

Figure 13.2
AN INFLATIONARY GAP IS CAUSED BY AN INCREASE IN AD BEYOND FULL EMPLOYMENT

economy starts out operating at full employment. Now suppose the government declares war on another country and dramatically ratchets up military spending. This increase in government spending will cause a shift rightward in the aggregate demand curve. When the aggregate demand curve intersects the aggregate supply curve to the right of full employment, the economy is said to be experiencing an **inflationary gap**.

As the government demands to buy more tanks, more workers are hired to produce them. Unemployment falls, while real GDP increases. These two economic phenomena are usually considered to be good things. More people have jobs and more output is being made. Still, output that is available to consumers typically falls in times of war. The production of tanks, fighter jets, and ammunition requires the use of scarce resources. As the production of military equipment increases, the production of consumer and investment goods decreases. In WWI, the US converted Ford automobile plants into tank factories. More tanks led to fewer autos.

The inflationary gap derives its name from the fact that this increase in aggregate demand has resulted in an increase in the average price level, i.e. inflation. There is also now a gap between full employment GDP and current real GDP, as is illustrated in figure 13.2 as RGDP shifts to $RGDP_b$. As more products than normal are demanded, buyers bid against each other for access to scarce output. As output increases, it does so by utilizing less productive inputs (less fertile land, lower skilled labor, etc.). The use of less productive inputs drives up the production costs to firms who in turn pass these cost increases, in part, onto buyers. Those groups (see Chapter 9) that are most hurt by inflation, such as creditors, small businesses, and people on fixed incomes, will not see the inflationary gap as a good thing.

Thus, an inflationary gap is caused by aggregate demand being "too high." It intersects aggregate supply to the right of full employment. Anything that would cause an increase in consumption, investment, government spending, or net exports past full employment would lead to an inflationary gap. The result is low unemployment, an increase in output, and inflation.

In the 1960's, military spending increased due to the Vietnam conflict. At the same time, the government began implementing President Lyndon Johnson's Great Society programs. This increase in government spending pushed the US economy into an inflationary gap. While unemployment rates fell, inflation rates soared.

Like the three bears' bowls of porridge, aggregate demand can be too low (a recessionary gap), too high (an inflationary gap), or just right (full employment). As the aggregate demand curve shifts, there is a tradeoff between unemployment and inflation. As aggregate demand increases, unemployment falls, but inflation increases. As aggregate demand decreases, unemployment increases but inflation decreases. Because unemployment and inflation are often observed moving in opposite directions, some people began to believe that they must always do so.[3] The **Phillips Curve** was introduced to economics by William Phillips and it represented an inverse relationship between unemployment and inflation. However, the Phillips Curve proved to be incorrect once the economy was observed suffering from stagflation, or a decrease in aggregate supply.

Stagflation

What happens when aggregate supply decreases? Again assume that the economy is operating at full employment. Suppose that the government declares industry carbon emissions bad for the environment and introduces a tax on all carbon emitted in the production process. This increase in government regulation and taxation will cause a decrease in the aggregate supply curve. When the aggregate supply curve decreases (so that now it intersects the aggregate demand curve to the left of full employment), the economy is said to be experiencing **stagflation**.

As the cost of production increases, firms are willing to sell less output at every price. This reduction in output puts the economy in a contraction and causes workers to be laid off, thereby creating higher unemployment. The increased cost of production gets passed on to consumers via higher prices (inflation).

Stagflation derives its name from the fact that output is stagnant (not growing) while the economy is experiencing inflation. The presence of stagflation

[3] Phillips, A.W. (1958). "The Relationship between Unemployment and the Rate of Change of Money wages in the United Kingdom 186 to 1957". *Economica* 25 (100): 283-299.

Stagflation

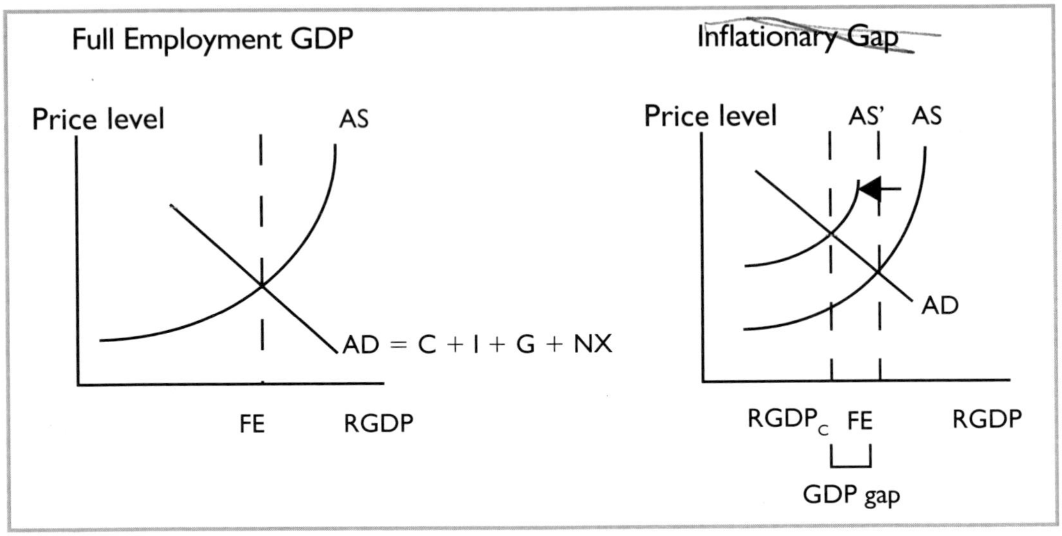

Figure 13.3
STAGFLATION RESULTS FROM A DECREASE IN AS BELOW FULL EMPLOYMENT

during the late 1970's served to disprove the Phillips curve. Unemployment and inflation can indeed rise at the same time if production costs in the economy are increased.

One historical example of stagflation occurred in the 1970's as **OPEC** dramatically increased the price of oil. Oil is (and was even more so then) an important energy source for the production and transportation of goods in the economy. As the price of oil increased, the US economy experienced a simultaneous increase in unemployment and inflation. As a presidential candidate, Jimmy Carter's campaign coined a new economic term called the misery index. The misery index is the unemployment rate plus the inflation rate. Carter used **the misery index** to point out how the economy had gotten worse under President Ford. Unfortunately for President Carter, rising oil prices continued during his term to increase the misery index from 12.72 to 19.72. This contributed to his loss to Ronald Reagan in the 1980 presidential election.

Thus, stagflation is caused by aggregate supply shifting to the left such that it intersects aggregate demand to the left of full employment. Anything that would cause an increase in the cost of production (see earlier chapters for examples) would result in stagflation. The result is high unemployment, a decrease in output, and inflation. Rising prices accompanied by higher unemployment and lower output is the worst possible economic problem for an economy to face.

Long Run Economic Growth

So far, the problems caused by aggregate demand shifting away from full employment or aggregate supply shifting leftward have been discussed. What happens when aggregate supply shifts rightward? Actually, increases in aggregate supply are good for the economy. This scenario is illustrated in Figure 13.4.

When the cost of production falls, aggregate supply shifts to the right. Firms are able to produce more output at every possible price level. This increase in

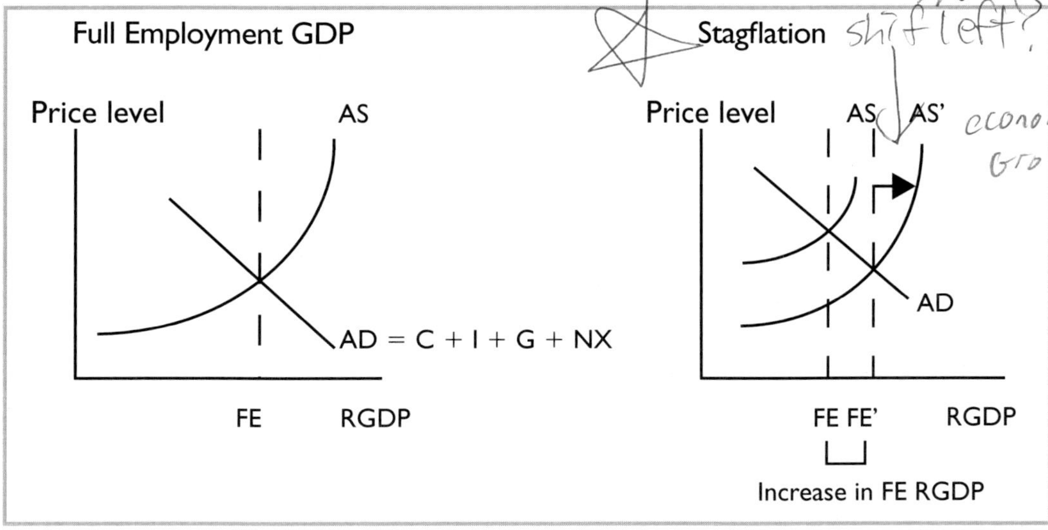

Figure 13.4
ECONOMIC GROWTH IS CAUSED BY AN INCREASE IN AS BEYOND FE.

output is called long run economic growth, and as such, the production possibilities frontier for the economy shifts outward. More production options become available for the economy, corresponding to a higher average standard of living.

If the decrease in the cost of production arises from increased worker productivity, then as the aggregate supply curve shifts rightward, so too does the full employment level of output. Each worker, if more productive, can make more output per unit of input; therefore, the full employment level of output will be greater and a new "happy place" for the economy will be created. If the increase in the aggregate supply curve is due to an increased number of resources, then the full employment output will again be increased. In this way, the full employment level of output for today's economy is larger than where it was fifty years ago.

The internet revolution of the 1990's dramatically lowered information costs for producers and consumers in the economy. This caused a reduction in the cost of production for many firms. As a result, the US economy experienced a period of low unemployment accompanied by low inflation and fast economic growth. (In absence of Federal Reserve policy, there would have been deflation).

Indeed, few people complain about the absence of inflation, fast economic growth, and low unemployment. This is why the "Holy Grail" of economics revolves around shifting the aggregate supply curve to the right and why the authors of this text devote so many chapters to analyzing how that can happen. The next chapter examines how the economy can self-correct when such shocks occur and explores the concepts behind supply side economics.

Glossary

Inflationary gap—an increase in output and prices accompanied by a decrease in unemployment due to decreased demand for domestic goods and services

Misery index—the unemployment rate plus the inflation rate

OPEC—a cartel of oil exporting countries

Phillips Curve—a curve that states an inverse relationship between unemployment and inflation which was disproven with the rise of stagflation in the late 1970's

Recessionary gap—a decrease in output and prices accompanied by an increase in unemployment due to decreased demand for domestic goods and services

Stagflation—a simultaneous increase in unemployment and inflation caused by increased cost of production

Questions for Review

1. When is inflation and unemployment inversely related? When are they directly related?
2. What causes a recessionary gap?
3. What causes an inflationary gap?
4. What causes stagflation?
5. What causes long run economic growth?
6. What problems arise from a recessionary gap? Inflationary gap? Stagflation?
7. Why isn't the rightward shift of the aggregate supply curve generally not frowned upon?
8. Below is a list of economic shocks. List whether they cause a recessionary gap, an inflationary gap, stagflation, or long run economic growth. Also graph the impact of these shocks on aggregate demand or supply and note what happens to prices, unemployment, and real GDP as a result of each shock:
   a. consumers decide to go a spending binge because they want to live for today
   b. foreigners decide to boycott US made goods due to America's invasion of foreign countries
   c. a drought decimates US agricultural output for the year
   d. new solar power technology dramatically lowers energy costs

Chapter 14

Say's Law, the Self-Correcting Economy, and Supply Side Economics

John Maynard Keynes is considered by many to be the father of modern macroeconomics. His analysis of short term fluctuations in the economy (as discussed in the previous chapter) served as the discipline's standard for half of a century. It is important, however, to note that his analysis was entirely limited to the short run economy. The **short run economy** is considered to be an economy during a single business cycle.

Prior to the 1930's, the study of **political economy** was primarily interested in analyzing the **long run economy**. The long run economy is considered to be an economy over multiple business cycles. Adam Smith's *Wealth of Nations* was an analysis of the long run economy. He examined why some countries were wealthier than others over time. This chapter highlights how the economy work to self-correct from shocks and explores the idea behind supply side economics, while providing examples of both from US economic history.

Say's Law

The predominant strain of economic thought in the eighteenth and nineteenth centuries was known as the **Classical School**. Adam Smith, David Ricardo, Jean-Baptiste Say, Thomas Malthus, and James Mill were some of the major economists associated with this school of thought. Their view of the short and long run economies are best summed up by **Say's Law**. Say's Law states that "products are paid for with products."[1] A restatement of this principle is that production creates the wealth needed for consumption, or supply creates its own demand.

According to Say's Law, there could be some firms whose products are unwanted by consumers therefore causing a glut of those specific products. This glut, however, was balanced by a shortage of goods that consumers actually desired. No general glut of all goods and services could exist in the economy. As producers whose products are unwanted go out of business, resources are freed up to be used by firms whose products consumers demand.

In this way, swings in unemployment rates are primarily due to increases in structural unemployment as workers are forced to leave industries whose products are not in demand. It takes time for them to be retrained and gain employment in industries whose products are in demand. The classical school believed that this change in production and employment would happen naturally as individuals responded to incentives that they faced. Short term fluctuations in unemployment were temporary, and in the long run, the economy would always return to full employment on its own. In the long run, then, the economy faces a vertical aggregate supply curve at full employment.

Says law contradicts **under-consumption theory**, popularized by Keynes. Under-consumption theory states that the economy, if left alone, will experience general gluts of output where consumers are unable or unwilling to consume that which has been produced. Cyclical unemployment, he surmised, then became the chief cause of fluctuations in the unemployment rate. People were unemployed because of a lack of aggregate demand. Under-consumption theory is a rejection of Say's Law. It assumes that consumption drives production rather than production being the catalyst of consumption.

[1] Treatise and Coordination of Economic Activity. 1803. 153

When it comes to advocating policies to intervene in the short run economy, economists who adhere to under-consumption theory focus on changing aggregate demand (see Chapter 15). Those who believe in Say's Law focus either on letting the economy self-correct, or on policies designed to increase aggregate supply. Adherents to Say's Law tend to focus on the long run health of an economy. On the other hand, those who advocate Keynesian views of intervention in the economy tend to hold Keynes' view that "In the long run we are all dead."[2] Put another way, long term ramifications of market intervention are not important to **neo-Keynesians**. Their focus is on solving today's problems today regardless of future implications.

The Self-Correcting Economy

Self-correction in a Recessionary Gap

As previously noted, adherents to Say's Law believe that specific gluts in specific industries will work themselves out over time. As consumers do not buy a firm's output, that output piles up. Firms cannot indefinitely afford to pay their workers or pay for the use of other resources without generating revenue from the sale of their products. As firms go bankrupt, the resources they were using are freed up to be used by firms who are producing products that people want to buy at prices they want to pay.

Market self-correction consists of a different dynamic under Keynesian analysis. Since general gluts or general shortages exist in the Keynesian view, markets cannot self-correct simply by moving resources from one industry to the next. From this perspective, a solution must require a change in all industries. How, then, will an economy self-correct from a recessionary gap, an inflationary gap, and stagflation under the Keynesian framework?

Recall that a recessionary gap is caused by aggregate demand being too low. Unemployment is higher than normal; prices and output are lower than they were at full employment. Unemployment can be viewed as a surplus of workers. More people want a job than are currently being hired in the market. Markets clear surpluses by placing products on sale. Any clothing store that has a surplus of jackets will have to put the jackets on sale in order to move their inventory.

The economy works the same way with a surplus of workers; it figuratively places them "on sale." Because there are a number of people unemployed during a recessionary gap, there is greater competition among workers for any given job opening. This competition for jobs by workers enables producers to offer lower wages than normal and still hire skilled workers. In the recessionary gap, **real wages** (which represent the purchasing power of workers' hourly labor) are bid down.

---

[2] *A Tract on Monetary Reform* (1923).

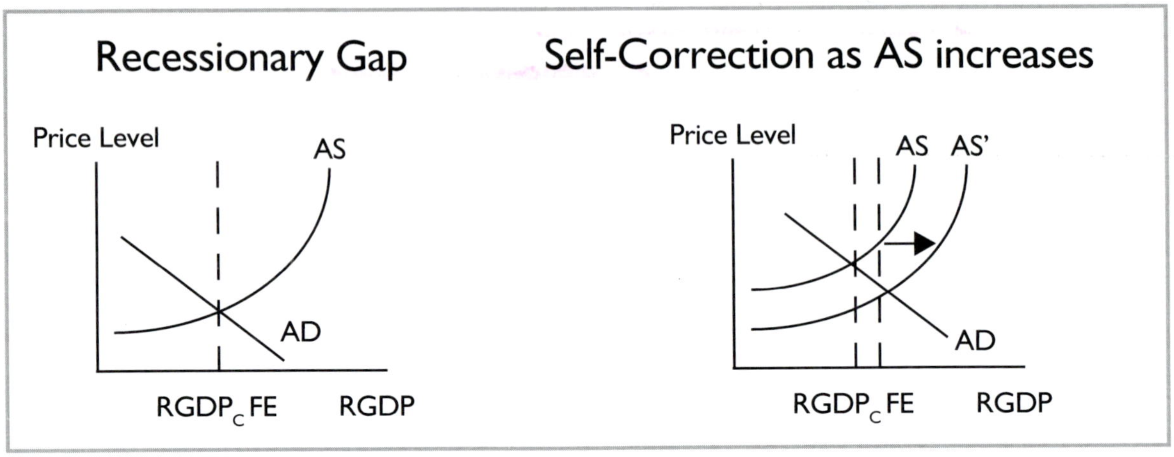

Figure 14.1
THE SELF-CORRECTION PROCESS IN A RECESSIONARY GAP.

A change in the real wage is the self-correcting mechanism of the economy. As producers are able to pay less for labor, the cost of production falls. This decrease in the cost of production causes aggregate supply to increase. As long as cyclical unemployment exists, there will be downward pressure on real wages, shifting aggregate supply rightward until it again intersects aggregate demand back at full employment.

Keynes acknowledged that a decrease in real wages would indeed bring the economy back to full employment. However, he stated that wages are "sticky downwards." People don't like taking pay cuts, and unions which represent workers will fight wage decreases. Therefore, Keynes chief critique of the self-correcting economy during the recessionary gap is that it took too long to work.

Note that for the self-correcting economy to work, people don't necessarily have to take nominal pay cuts, though that does sometimes happen. People just have to have a reduction in their real wages. If an inflation rate of 3% exists, while workers receive a nominal wage increase of 1%, then real wages fall by 2%. A change in nominal wages minus the inflation rate equals the change in real wages. Typically during a recession, people's wages don't tend to keep up with inflation, and they take real wage cuts. Another way to take a real wage cut is to require more worker output for the same salary. This too would lower the cost of production to firms allowing room for aggregate supply to increase and for the economy to self-correct.

Self-correction in an Inflationary Gap

The inflationary gap is exactly the opposite of the recessionary gap. Output and prices are higher than normal, but unemployment is lower than normal. In fact, the economy, by cutting into frictional and structural unemployment, is facing a shortage of workers. As an economy approaches its production possibilities frontier, producers can only produce more of their output if other producers produce less. The scarcity of qualified workers becomes more acute than normal.

As producers compete with each other to hire or retain qualified employees, real wages are bid up. As it becomes more expensive to compensate workers, aggregate supply decreases. The upward pressure on real wages will continue shifting the aggregate supply curve leftward until it intersects the aggregate demand curve back at full employment.

Workers don't tend to protest wage increases. Producers cannot profit if they lack the needed workers to produce more output. As a result, unlike the recessionary gap, the economy can self-correct quickly out of the inflationary gap. On the downside, inflation, which is already a problem, gets worse as the economy returns to full employment. Figure 14.2 illustrates the resulting increase in inflation.

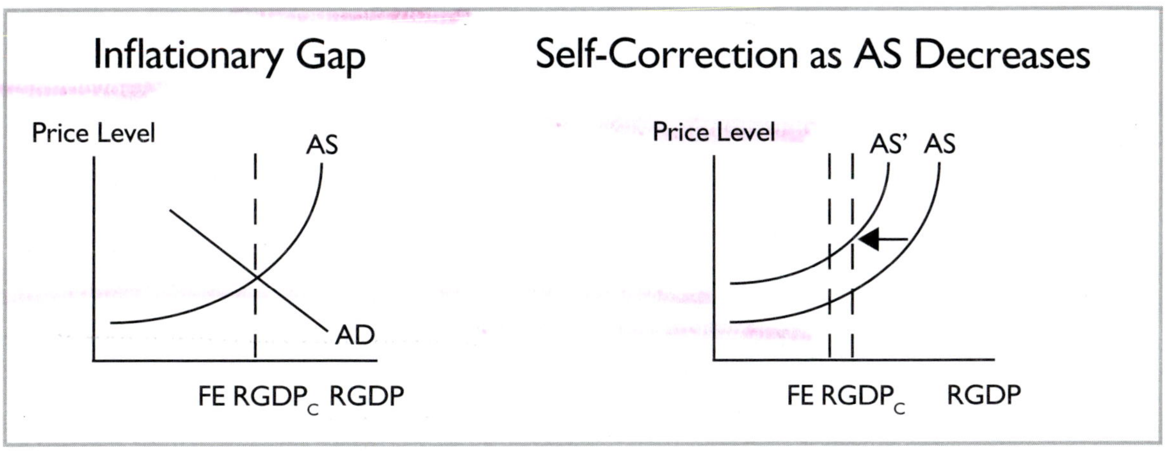

Figure 14.2
THE SELF-CORRECTION PROCESS IN AN INFLATIONARY GAP.

Self-correction in Stagflation

The market self-corrects from stagflation in the same way as it does from a recessionary gap. High levels of unemployment continue to put downward pressure on real wages, shifting the aggregate supply curve rightward until it again intersects the aggregate demand curve back at full employment. The problem, just as in the recessionary gap, is that wages may be sticky downwards.

The Self-Correcting Economy in American History

Throughout the eighteenth, nineteenth, and early twentieth centuries, the American economy self-corrected with relative ease. Large increases in unemployment were accompanied by large reductions in real wages. Unregulated labor markets adjusted quickly to changing market conditions. This occurred even as large numbers of Americans moved from the agricultural industry to the manufacturing and service industries.

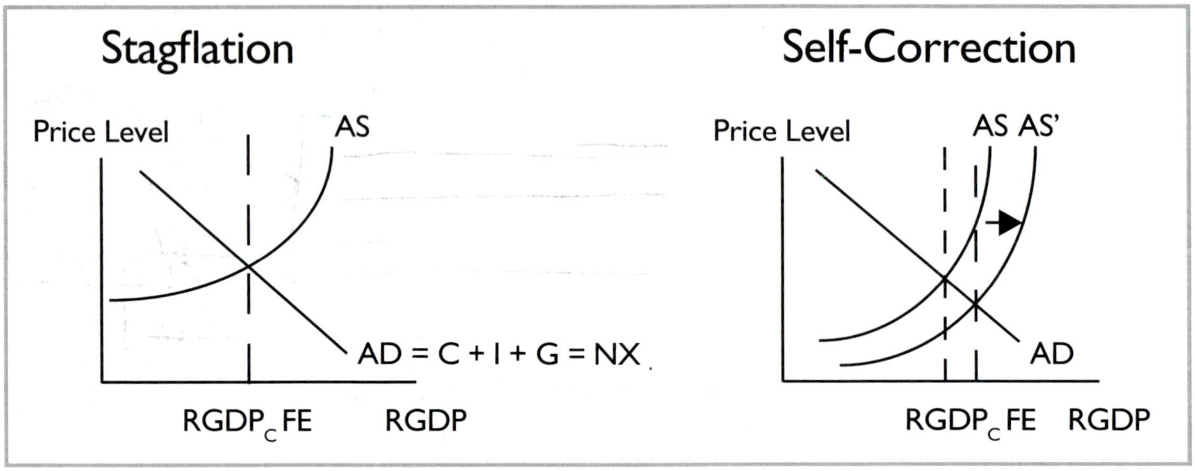

Figure 14.3
THE SELF-CORRECTION PROCESS IN STAGFLATION.

Throughout the twentieth century, the labor market took longer to adjust to market conditions. Increased union membership in the first half of the twentieth century created a climate where existing workers obtained more leverage over their wages at the expense of the currently unemployed. Government mandating of minimum wages also prevented market correction in wages for low skilled jobs. If the labor market for unskilled labor will only clear at a wage below the legally allowed minimum, then mandated minimum wages prevent this adjustment and result in higher unemployment levels.

The development of unemployment insurance benefits and government make work programs also reduced the pace of labor force adjustment. In the past, the loss of a job necessitated a quick search for a new job, lest a worker be unable to meet the needs of themselves or their dependents. Unemployment benefits or a government make work job reduce the immediate urgency of finding a new job and therefore reduce the downward pressure placed on real wages, slowing their decline and prolonging the return to full employment.

As the percentage of laborers employed by governments has increased, so too has the percentage of employees who have been awarded tenure. University professors, school teachers, and many government workers have labor contracts that don't permit their loss of a job without explicit employee malfeasance. While the real wages of tenured employees can, and do, fall during recessions, the market is prevented from reallocating labor between industries.

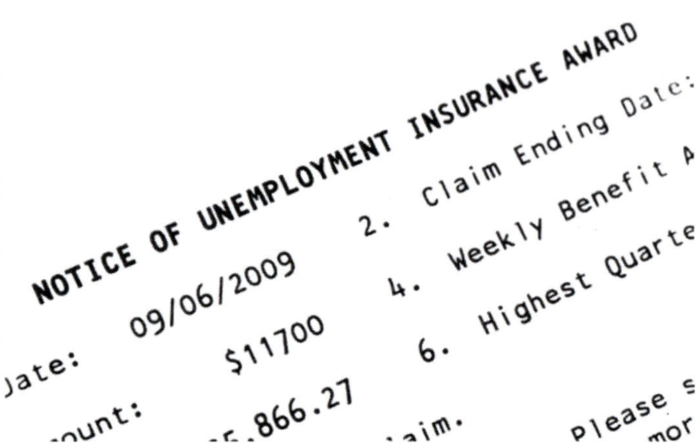

Homeownership can also impede self-correction in labor markets. A laborer who loses his job may only be able to find a new job in a different city or state than where he currently lives. When few people had a high percentage of their wealth stored in the value of their homes, labor was more mobile. One reason that unemployment stayed so high for so long after the 2007–2008 recession is that homeowners had a difficult time selling their homes and relocating due to the large number of unsold homes on the market.

Supply Side Economics

The US economy experienced severe stagflation in the late 1970's and early 1980's. This decrease in aggregate supply was caused by a dramatic increase in the price of oil. President Reagan's economic team led by Arthur Laffer attempted to develop a set of economic policies to shift the aggregate supply curve rightward. While the economy's self-correcting mechanism would eventually shift aggregate supply rightward, these policies attempted to not only bring the economy back to full employment, but also increase long term economic growth. This set of policies became known as **supply side economics** for its attempt to increase aggregate supply.

Supply side economics refers to any attempt by policy makers to increase the productive capacity of the economy. The supply side economic policies implemented by the Reagan administration have been coined **Reaganomics**. The main features of Reaganomics included deregulation and reductions in marginal income tax rates, savings tax rates, corporate income tax rates, and capital gains tax rates.

A reduction in government regulations reduces the cost of production, as firms face fewer restrictions on using the resources at their disposal as they see fit in order to profit. Fewer government regulations free up firms' resources to be used for production rather than to ensure compliance with government regulations. As the cost of burdensome government regulations falls, aggregate supply increases.

Lower tax rates should also work to increase aggregate supply. When Reagan took office, the top marginal federal income tax bracket in the US was 70%. The top rate had actually been even higher under Presidents Roosevelt, Truman, and Eisenhower. President Kennedy proposed cutting the top income tax bracket from 91% to 70%. His famous justification for doing so was that "a rising tide lifts all boats." This meant that if entrepreneurs were discouraged from working when nearly all of their income was confiscated, perhaps letting them keep more of their income would incentivize them to work harder, producing wealth that is enjoyed by everyone. By increasing labor supply, lower marginal tax rates should work to shift the aggregate supply curve rightward.

Art Laffer supposed that even 70% marginal tax rates worked as a disincentive for people to work. He created the **Laffer Curve** to illustrate the relationship between marginal tax rates and tax revenue. At a 0% tax rate, the government would not generate any tax revenue. As tax rates increase, so, too, does tax revenue—to a point. While the higher tax rates mean a larger percentage of earned income becomes revenue for the federal government, it also means a larger disincentive for work. So, at low tax rates, tax revenues increase with the rate. After that, increases in marginal tax rates actually resulted in lower tax revenue as the reduced incentive to work overtakes the higher revenue stream. At a 100% tax rate people would not voluntarily work and report their income because it would be confiscated in its entirety. Figure 14.4 illustrates the Laffer Curve.

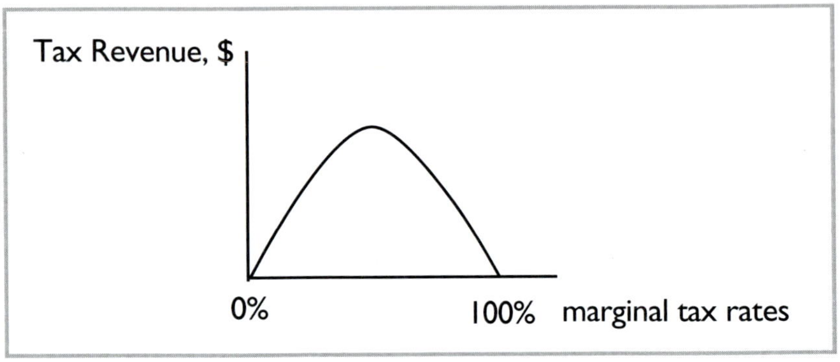

Figure 14.4 **THE LAFFER CURVE**

High marginal tax rates encourage people to hide income from the government or not earn income in the first place. While the shape of the Laffer Curve is not controversial amongst economists, there is much disagreement about where the revenue maximizing tax rate is. People who describe themselves as supply side economists typically assign a lower estimate of the revenue maximizing tax rate than do economists who do not consider themselves to be supply side economists. A survey of economists by the *Washington Post* places the range between 20% and 70%.[3] Under President Reagan, the top rate was reduced from 70%to 28%. In reality, the short term revenue maximizing tax rate is higher than the long term revenue maximizing tax rate, as it take time for people to respond to economic incentives.

If tax rates are reduced and the marginal tax rate is above the revenue maximizing point, then a reduction in tax rates will generate increased tax revenue. This idea was lampooned by candidate George H.W. Bush during the 1980 Republican primary as "voodoo economics." Later, he served as President Reagan's vice president. Still, when he became president, George H.W. Bush increased many of the same tax rates that President Reagan had lowered.

Nobel Prize winning economist Edward Prescott has shown that changes in marginal tax rates have indeed led to a divergence in the number of hours worked by the average American relative to the average European in the last half of a century.[4] He finds that in the early 1970's, the average German and Frenchman worked five percent more hours per year than the average American. At the same time, the average British worker worked ten percent more hours and the average Japanese worker worked twenty-seven percent more than the average American worker. Then, marginal tax rates fell in the US as they rose in Europe. By the mid

---

[3] "Where does the Laffer curve bend?"Dylan Matthews August 9, 2010. http://voices.washingtonpost.com/ezra-klein/2010/08/where_does_the_laffer_curve_be.html

[4] "Why Do Americans Work So Much More Than Europeans?" *Federal Reserve Bank of Minneapolis Quarterly Review Vol. 28, No. 1. July 2004, 2-13.* http://www.minneapolisfed.org/research/QR/QR2811.pdf

1990's the average American worked 26% more hours than the average German or Frenchman. They worked 23% more hours than the average Japanese worker and 33% more than the average Britain.

Lowering taxes on savings also works to increase aggregate supply. A reduction in taxes on savings increases the rate of return on savings. In theory, this makes savings more lucrative and should cause consumers to spend less and save more. This increase in savings makes it easier for firms to invest in new capital. By increasing the amount of capital in the economy, aggregate supply increases.

Likewise, a reduction in the capital gains tax increases the profitability of individuals saving money by placing it in appreciating assets, like shares of stock. Since saving money in government bonds generates tax free income, any reduction in the capital gains tax increases the relative profitability of providing capital to private sector production over government debt. Lowering the capital gains tax also frees up investment funds for firms owning appreciating capital. The long run capital gains tax rate fell from 39.875% in the mid 1970's to 20% in the early 1980's.

When President Reagan took office the top corporate income tax rate in the economy was 46%. When he left office it was 34%. As corporation's tax rates were lowered, the rate of return on corporations' capital and labor increased. Firms were able to hold onto more of their own profit which they could reinvest in new capital or use to hire new workers. An increase in capital and labor increases the productive capacity of the economy.

While Reaganomics had been billed as a set of policies to solve stagflation, its immediate effect on the economy did not bring the economy instantly back to full employment. To the extent that reductions in the capital gains and corporate income taxes increased investment in the economy, investment immediately increased aggregate demand more than aggregate supply. Capital, only once it has been built, increases the productive capacity of the economy. Therefore the principle benefits of Reaganomics helped the economy experience faster growth in the decade following their implementation rather than in the months immediately thereafter.

Likewise, a reduction in the marginal income tax rate took time to be felt in the economy. Workers do not shift occupations or career fields instantaneously in response to new tax incentives. Worker training and education take time. Even deregulation takes time for firms to adjust to before they are able to change their business practices.

Reductions in taxes on savings did not yield the desired increase in the US savings rate. In fact, the US savings rate fell. As Americans saw their existing retirement savings grow more quickly, they started placing less money in their retirement plans. One often placed criticism against Reaganomics is the fact that the national debt tripled during President Reagan's term. Some mistakenly suggest that so many tax reductions left government coffers empty. In reality, tax revenues increased from $517 billion in 1980 to $909.3 billion in 1988 even with large reductions in multiple tax rates. The increase in the national debt in the 1980's can largely be attributed to the massive increase in government spending during the decade. While tax revenues grew, government spending grew much faster. Government spending rose from $591 billion in 1980 to $1,065 billion in 1988.

Another criticism of Reaganomics is that it increased income inequality. The term "trickle- down economics" is a pejorative term that implies that Reaganomics was designed to reward the wealthy with the hope that an increase in their wellbeing would trickle down to other members of the economy. The idea that the purchase of a yacht by a wealthy businessman would generate jobs for middle class yacht builders is no different than that of the Keynesian spending multiplier. Economic activity is generated beyond those specifically targeted by changes in taxes or government spending.

If the tax code is designed to allow productive people to keep more of the wealth that they create, then more wealth does get created, but income inequality also increases. Assume that there are two workers in an economy. Jack makes $10,000 a year while Jill makes $100,000. There is $90,000 worth of income inequality. Now suppose that a growing economy increases each of their incomes by 10%. Jack now makes $11,000 to Jill's $110,000. There is now $99,000 worth of income inequality. Jack and Jill are both wealthier, but income inequality has increased.

During the 1980's the rich got richer faster than the poor, so income inequality increased, but the poor did get richer. Absolute poverty exists if people are unable to pay for the necessities of life. Absolute poverty fell in the 1980's. Relative poverty exists if some people make more money than others. The phrase "the rich got richer while the poor got poorer" is only true in the 1980's if relative, rather than absolute, poverty serves as the method of comparison.

President Bill Clinton was one of many politicians who campaigned against "trickle-down" economics. The irony is that his administration effectively implemented some supply side polices of its own without using the term. President Clinton's supply side policies included creating and expanding an investment tax credit and a research and development tax credit for firms along with deficit reduction that enabled more savings to flow to private investment. The chapter that follows examines the use of fiscal policy to manipulate economic outcomes.

Glossary

Classical School of Economic Thought—a body of Eighteenth and Nineteenth Century economic thought that emphasized natural economic order

Laffer Curve—a graph that shows the relationship between marginal tax rates and tax revenue that states that the revenue maximizing marginal tax rate is below 100%

Long run economy—an economy over multiple business cycles

Neo-classicalists—economists who see prices, output, and consumption as functions of supply and demand in the free market

Neo-Keynesians—economists who have attempted to synthesize the macroeconomic theories of John Maynard Keynes with neo-classical economics

Political economy—the study of how laws, customs, and government regulations influence production and consumption

Reaganomics—a set of economic policies passed during President Reagan's tenure which include a reduction in personal and corporate income tax rates, a reduction in tax rates on savings and the capital gains tax rate, and deregulation

Real wages—hourly payment for labor, controlling for changes in the average price level

Say's Law—Products are paid for with products, that is, consumption follows production

Short run economy—an economy over one business cycle

Supply side economics—the study of how to increase the productive capacity of an economy to boost long term consumption and the standard of living

Under-consumption Theory—a theory which states that the economy, if left to itself, will experience general gluts of output where consumers are unable or unwilling to consume that which has been produced

Questions for Review

1. What is Say's Law? What does it imply?
2. Why is the rejection of Say's Law the starting point for Keynes' advocacy of fiscal policy?
3. What is the self-correcting mechanism in the Keynesian aggregate demand and aggregate supply model?
4. How does the economy self-correct out of the recessionary gap?
5. How does the economy self-correct out of the inflationary gap?
6. How does the economy self-correct out of stagflation?
7. What was Keynes' chief gripe with the self-correcting mechanism coming out of the Great Depression?
8. Which economist is most known for promoting supply-side economics?
9. What does supply-side economics attempt to do?
10. Name and describe five supply-side policies implemented under President Reagan.
11. In what ways were Reagan's supply-side policies successful? Unsuccessful?
12. Draw the Laffer Curve. What does the Laffer Curve imply?

Chapter 15 Keynesian Fiscal Policy

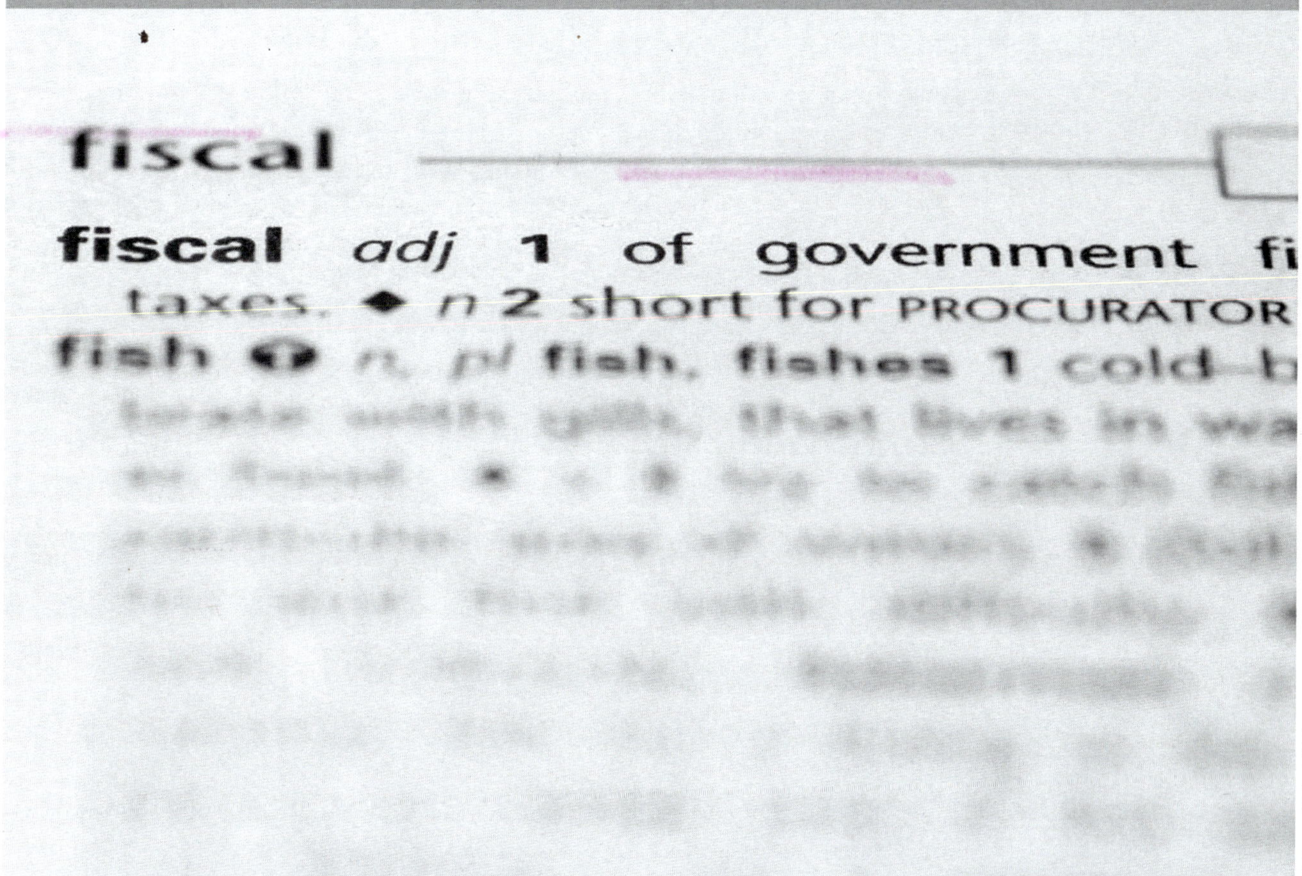

Some believe that the economy is unable to self-correct or else should not be given the time to self-correct. This type of Keynesian fiscal policy was born out of the Great Depression. Keynes theorized that government intervention in the economy could bring the economy back to full employment faster than the economy could self-correct. By changing levels of taxes and government spending, the government could manipulate aggregate demand until it intersected aggregate supply back at full employment.

The practice of Keynesian fiscal policy is meant to smooth business cycles. When the economy needs a boost, such as in a recessionary gap or stagflation, the federal government can either increase government spending or reduce taxes. **Expansionary fiscal policy (fiscal stimulus)** is an increase in government spending or a reduction in taxes that is meant to increase aggregate demand. When the economy overheats, as it does in an inflationary gap, the federal government can either increase taxes or reduce government spending. **Contractionary fiscal policy** is an increase in taxes or a reduction in government spending that is meant to lower aggregate demand. This chapter examines the ways in which expansionary or contractionary fiscal policy work to return the economy back to full employment.

Time Lags

Fiscal policy is not instantaneous. There is no easy button to push to dispense the appropriate amount and makeup of fiscal policy. There are three specific time lags associated with fiscal policy. The **recognition lag** is the time it takes to realize that a problem exists in the economy. Since macroeconomic data takes weeks or months to accrue, the economy may be experiencing a recessionary gap, inflationary gap, or stagflation before policy makers are aware that a problem exists.

While Bill Clinton campaigned for president in 1992 by advocating a fiscal stimulus package, by the time he took office in January 1993, the economy had already self-corrected. Real GDP increased by 4.3% in the fourth quarter of 1992. Because it was no longer needed, Congress, though controlled by members of the president's own party, voted against a fiscal stimulus package.

Once a problem is recognized, there exists a **policy lag**, which is the time it takes to enact a policy designed to fix the problem. When both houses of Congress are controlled by members of the same party as the president, the policy lag may be short. Politicians whose ideologies and constituents are similar are more likely to come to agreement on fiscal policy than politicians of differing ideologies or differing political parties When differing parties control differing houses, then policy lags can be quite long.

Once a change in taxes or spending makes it out of committee in the House of Representatives, it has to be passed by the House, taken up by a committee in the Senate, and passed verbatim by the Senate. If the Senate bill differs from the House bill, the bill must go to a conference committee made up of selected House and Senate members, returned to both the House and Senate for an up or down on the same language, and sent to the President's desk to be signed into law. At that point, the President could veto the legislation, which would require a two-thirds majority in the House and Senate to override.

Once a policy is enacted, it will then face an **implementation lag**, which is the time it takes for a policy to have an impact on the economy. If an increase in government spending involves the building of a new highway, for instance, once the government decides to build the road, it must acquire right of way for the road, have firms bid on the design and construction of the road and award the bids. Then the building of the road is not instantaneous. Payments to construction workers happen over time as they provide their labor to the construction project. Each successive round of spending, as hypothesized by the spending multiplier, takes even more time to materialize. The call for "shovel ready" projects in the 2009 stimulus bill was a recognition of the fiscal challenges faced by the implementation lag. Even then, only one-third of the $787 fiscal stimulus had been spent in the year following its passage.[1]

Together the recognition, policy, and implementation lags make it even harder to fine tune fiscal policy to bring the economy back to full employment. The economy doesn't stand still while it waits for policy makers. It is constantly changing. Conducting fiscal policy is like trying to hit a moving target through one's rear view mirror with the knowledge that pulling the trigger will release a bullet sometime tomorrow.

Expansionary Fiscal Policy

Recall that in Keynes' model, a recessionary gap is caused by aggregate demand being too low. High levels of unemployment and low levels of output are the result of inadequate demand for goods and services in the economy. The Keynesian policy prescription to a recessionary gap is to engage in fiscal stimulus in the form of increased government spending and/or a reduction in taxation.

If the government increases spending by building roads or bridges, then construction workers would gain jobs and output would be increased. This increase in government directed economic activity translates into higher levels of real GDP. Keynes' belief in fiscal stimulus spending was so great that he stated that the object of the increase in government spending was irrelevant. He noted that if the government hired ditch diggers to dig a ditch and then hired more workers to fill in the ditches, the economy would still be stimulated.

Bridge to nowhere

On paper, real GDP would be increased by the amount of money the government spent on ditch diggers and ditch fillers. According to the expenditure approach, GDP is a function of consumption, investment, government spending, and net exports. Any increase in government spending, regardless of where it was spent, would therefore increase real GDP. Of course, a ditch dug and then refilled leaves the world with no actual new wealth. How, then, is the economy made better off from stimulus spending?

Assume that the ditch digger earns $100 in income in return for his labor. The initial increase in government spending is that $100. The ditch digger now has an extra $100 of income in his pocket.

[1] "Bulk of Stimulus Spending Yet to Come" *Wall Street Journal* February 17, 2010. http://online.wsj.com/article/SB10001424052748704804204575069772167897834.html

An increase in income to a consumer could go one of three places: to pay taxes, to increase savings, or to increase consumption. If the ditch digger faces income tax liability as a result of his new income, he won't be able to spend all of his new income.

The **marginal propensity to consume (MPC)** is the change in consumption the average consumer engages in divided by the change in income they receive. If the average American consumer spends 80% of all new income they receive, then the MPC for the US economy is said to be .8. If the ditch digger is representative of the average American, then an extra $100 of income will translate into an additional $80 worth of consumption. This increase in consumption also serves to increase aggregate demand. If the ditch digger spends his $80 at the bakery, then the baker now has an extra $80 of income. If the baker then spends 80% of his new income at the butcher shop, then his $64 of new consumption will also cause aggregate demand to increase.

Table 15.1 THE RESULT TO THE ECONOMY OF AN INITIAL INCREASE OF $100 IN GOVERNMENT SPENDING

New spending	Total change in spending
100	100
80	180
64	244
.	.
.	.
.	.
0	500

The amount that real GDP is expected to increase as a result of increased government spending in the Keynesian model is determined by taking the initial increase in government spending and multiplying it by the **spending multiplier**.

$$\text{THE SPENDING MULTIPLIER} = \frac{1}{(1\text{-MPC})}$$

If the MPC in the economy is .8 then the spending multiplier is 5. The spending multiplier is created by an infinite series. As each consumer increases spending by a percentage of a positive number, spending keeps increasing at smaller and smaller amounts for infinity.

In order to determine the appropriate amount of government stimulus needed to solve a recessionary gap, an economic advisor would need the following information: the full employment level of real GDP, the current level of real GDP, and the marginal propensity to consume for an economy. The full employment level of real GDP requires a theoretical guess. The second piece of information, the current level of real GDP, is impossible to know given the lag in collecting economic data, but it can be approximated by looking at the most recent GDP data. The final piece of information, the marginal propensity to consume, is also impossible to know. By collecting historical spending data, economists can create an estimate of past MPC levels in the US economy. However, because consumers make choices for themselves, there is no way to know what their MPC will be at a future in time until they have already spent their money. Consumer confidence and consumer uncertainty can play key roles in changing people's MPC over time. The MPC may also depend upon whose income is increased. Some economists theorize that poor people's MPC is higher than wealthier people's MPC and therefore an increase in the income of poorer people will create a larger spending multiplier than would be created by the same increase in the income of wealthier people.

In the US, Congress and the President control fiscal policy. If one believes as Keynes did that said politicians or the bureaucrats that work for them are smart enough to know where the economy is, where it should be, and what the spending multiplier is, then the appropriate size of fiscal stimulus spending is relatively easy to determine.

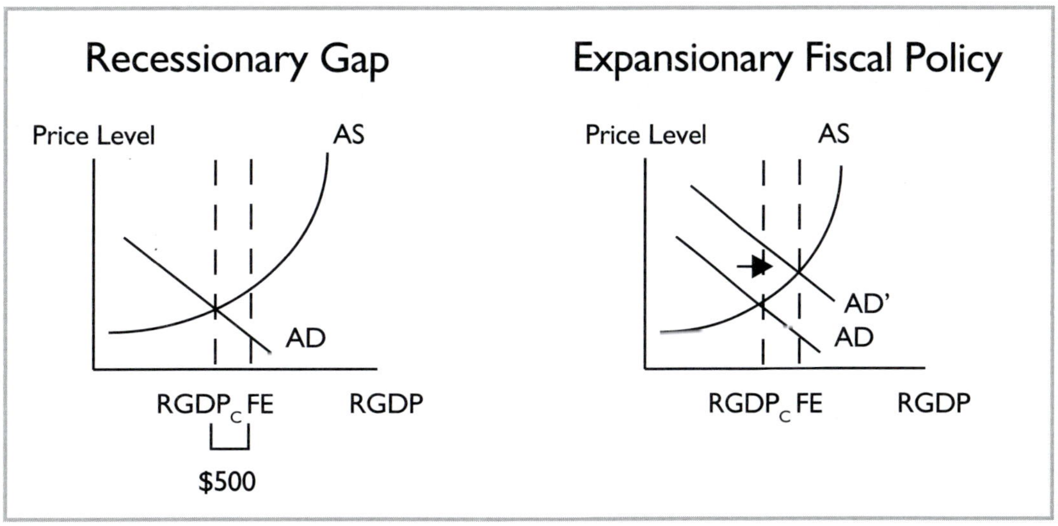

Figure 15.1
EXPANSIONARY FISCAL POLICY USED IN A RECESSIONARY GAP.

In Figure 15.1 case, the economy is facing a $500 GDP gap. This is the distance between the current level of real GDP and full employment GDP. If the MPC in the economy is .8, then the appropriate amount of stimulus spending to bring the economy back to full employment is $100.

CHANGE IN REAL GDP = INITIAL CHANGE IN GOVERNMENT SPENDING X SPENDING MULTIPLIER

$500 = $100 X 5

So, government spending would need to change by $100 to increase real GDP by $500, given a spending multiplier of 5. This formula only holds if the aggregate supply curve is horizontal (as Keynes saw it during recessionary gaps). If an increase in aggregate demand occurs on the flat portion of the aggregate supply curve, then the increase in aggregate demand equals the increase in real GDP. If, however, the increase in aggregate demand occurs on the upward sloping portion of the aggregate supply curve, then the resulting higher prices faced by consumers will offset some of the potential gains in real GDP. Consumers will spend more money, but some of their increased spending will be to accommodate higher prices of existing products. When the aggregate supply curve is vertical, any increase in aggregate demand results only in higher prices with no change occurring to real GDP.

In 2009, Congress and President Obama passed a $787 billion stimulus bill. That's a very specific number. Why not $750 or $800 billion? To be sure, some economists argued for less stimulus spending while others argued for more. The reason for the public disagreement between economists is that each economist was forced to make their own assumptions about where the economy was, where it was supposed to be, and how large the spending multiplier would be. Furthermore, some economists disagreed with the entire Keynesian approach and preferred to let the economy self-correct.

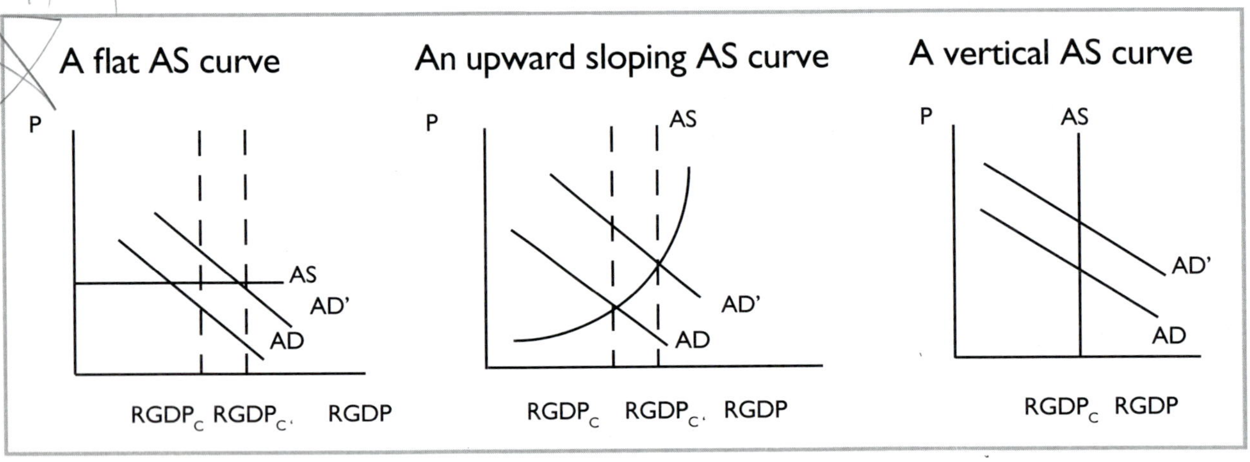

Figure 15.2 THE SAME SIZED INCREASE IN AGGREGATE DEMAND UNDER THREE SCENARIOS

Work by Robert Barro found that the spending multiplier for this stimulus program was .8. For every dollar that was spent by the government, GDP only increased by eighty cents.[2] Because fiscal policy deals with so many unknowns, users of fiscal policy run the risks of not doing enough or doing too much fiscal policy and as a result either not solving the existing problem or creating new ones.

There are other problems with the Keynesian approach to fiscal stimulus spending. The problem of deciding which projects are chosen to receive government support can affect both the short term and long term growth pattern of the economy. This problem is explained in more depth in Chapter 19. Stimulus money must come from somewhere. If the federal government was previously

[2] "Stimulus Spending Doesn't Work" *The Wall Street Journal* September 30, 2009.

running a balanced budget, or a budget deficit, an increase in government spending or a reduction in taxes means the government will be forced to borrow money to finance these policies. Today's stimulus creates an economic hangover for tomorrow. The short and long term consequences of government debt are examined more thoroughly in Chapter 18.

Instead of increasing government spending to stimulate an economy, the government could reduce the tax burden or increase transfer payments. As consumers are allowed to keep a larger percentage of their income, or are given more income, they have more money with which to consume and save. According to Keynes, however, a dollar reduction in taxes or increase in transfer payments does less than a dollar increase in government spending to increase GDP.

Assume that a baker receives a $100 tax cut or transfer payment. If his MPC is .8, he will consume $80 worth of new goods and services so GDP will increase by $80. Much like the spending multiplier, a change in taxation is magnified by the **tax multiplier**.

$$\text{THE TAX MULTIPLIER} = -\left(\left(\frac{1}{(1-MPC)}\right) - 1\right)$$

$$\text{THE TRANSFER MULTIPLIER} = \left(\frac{1}{(1-MPC)}\right) - 1$$

If the spending multiplier is 5, then the tax multiplier is one less and negative, or -4. The tax multiplier is negative because an increase in taxes slows down the economy while a reduction in taxes speeds it up. A decrease in taxes increases spending, and vice versa. The difference in magnitude is due to the absence of the first round of government spending. If the government buys $100 worth of cakes, then cakes have been produced. If the government merely gives the baker $100 in tax cuts, no extra cake in made. The rounds of spending for a $100 tax cut with an MPC of .8 are given below.

Table 15.2 THE EFFECT OF A $100 TAX CUT OR TRANSFER PAYMENT ON THE ECONOMY

New spending	Total change in spending
80	80
64	144
.	.
.	.
0	400

Because Keynes felt that dollar per dollar changes in government spending were more powerful than changes in taxes, most Keynesians prefer to increase government spending rather than cut taxes. According to empirical work done by many prominent economists, however, the opposite appears to be true.[3] The tax multiplier has been empirically found to be larger than the spending multiplier. This means that economists who are concerned with the size of the national debt should prefer tax cuts to increases in government spending during recessionary gaps in order to speed up the economy the most for the least future cost.

In addition to the empirical questions of whether tax cuts or increases in government spending stimulate the economy more are the political and ethical considerations revolving around changes in taxation and government spending. Politicians who represent constituents with little or no tax burden but who receive government support payments may be more in favor of higher levels of government spending or transfer payments than they are lowering their non-constituent's taxes. Politicians who represent constituents with high tax burdens but who receive few government support payments may be more inclined to support tax breaks. Further discussion of these spending (Chapter 16) and taxing (Chapter 19) issues appear later in this text.

Contractionary Fiscal Policy

When an economy is overheating and inflation is on the rise, contractionary fiscal policy serves as the Keynesian approach. A decrease in government spending would cause aggregate demand to fall, as would an increase in taxes that leave consumers with less money to spend. The idea, as illustrated in figure 15.3, is to actively slow down the economy by reducing aggregate demand until it intersects aggregate supply back at full employment.

Contractionary fiscal policy faces many of the same hurdles as expansionary fiscal policy. In order for its use to be successful, policy makers must know what the current level of real GDP is, what the desired level of real GDP is, and the marginal propensity to consume will be. Assuming that these are all known, then determining the amount of needed fiscal policy is similar to how it is determined in the recessionary gap. Once the size of the inflationary gap is determined, the spending, transfer payment, or tax multiplier can be applied to determine the optimal amount of fiscal contraction.

[3] Greg Mankiw."Spending and Tax Multipliers" Greg Mankiw's Blog. December 11, 2008. http://gregmankiw.blogspot.com/2008/12/spending-and-tax-multipliers.html

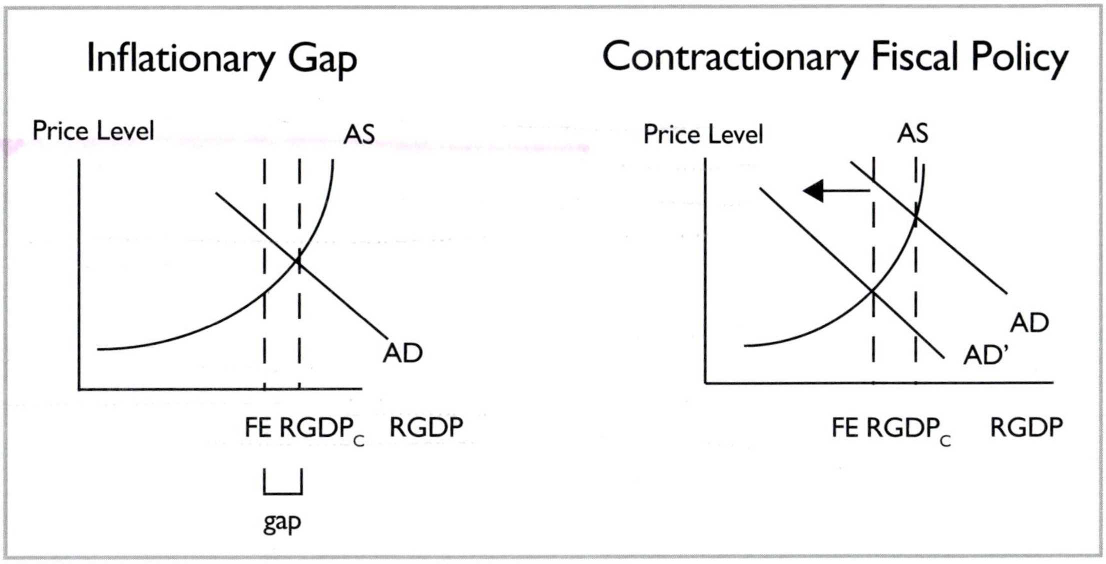

Figure 15.3 CONTRACTIONARY FISCAL POLICY

There is, however, an additional hurdle faced by the use of contractionary fiscal policy. Its use is usually politically unpopular. Most voters do not appreciate having their taxes increased. Nor do they like it when government programs or transfer payments that they themselves benefit from are reduced. As a result, the policy lag for contractionary fiscal policy tends to be longer than it is for expansionary fiscal policy.

Just as empirical research has been done on fiscal stimulus packages, work has also been done analyzing **austerity** (contractionary) **packages**.[4] Research indicates that the most economically successful packages are the ones where the reduction in government spending is roughly three times the size of the tax increases. Research indicates that cutting taxes is more efficient than increasing government spending at stimulating an economy and cutting government spending rather than raising taxes is better for long run job creation. The theme from the research is that the private sector does a better job than the public sector at using resources to create wealth over time. Taxes that distort economic incentives away from private sector wealth creation slow down the long run economic growth of an economy.

Fiscal Policy During Stagflation

While the economy is operating below full employment during stagflation, it is not a given that politicians following the Keynesian approach would necessarily advocate an increase in government spending or a reduction in taxes. Doing so, like in the recessionary gap, would work to increase aggregate demand until it intersected aggregate supply back at full employment. This would increase RGDP,

[4] "Canada's Budget Triumph" David R. Henderson. Working Paper No 10-53, August 2010. Mercatus Center. http://mercatus.org/sites/default/files/publication/Canada%27s%20Budget%20Triumph.WP_.pdf

but would also lead to much higher inflation since it would occur on the steeper portion of the aggregate supply curve.

If politicians were more concerned with fighting inflation than fighting unemployment, then the correct Keynesian response to stagflation would be higher taxes or lower government spending. This would cause the aggregate demand curve to shift leftward. The result would be lower inflation but at the cost of significantly higher levels of unemployment.

The use of Keynesian fiscal policy during periods of stagflation places policy makers between a rock and a hard place. Since a shift in aggregate demand creates a tradeoff between unemployment and inflation, they can only solve one problem by making the other problem much worse.

Ideology and Automatic Stabilizers

Given that politicians, rather than economists, are in charge of fiscal policy, politicians' ideologies play a role in the selection of the approved policy. Ideology is a doctrine or belief that guides an individual, an institution, or a social movement. Stereotypically, conservative politicians in America tend to favor tax cuts during recessionary gaps and reductions in government spending during inflationary gaps. Conversely, liberal politicians in America tend to favor government spending increases during recessionary gaps and tax increases during inflationary gaps. Since the 1930's, most politicians of both above ideologies have favored the use of Keynesian fiscal policy. President Nixon famously announced that "we are all Keynesians now".[5] Libertarian politicians in the US prefer to let the economy self-correct. Their focus on taxing and spending policies tend to be focused on making long run structural reforms to lower the amount of government influence and interference in the economy.

Some taxing and spending policies put in place in the past act as automatic stabilizers for the economy. An automatic stabilizer is something that helps the economy return to full employment without explicit government action. Examples include unemployment insurance, welfare, and the personal income tax.

During a recession, unemployment is higher than normal. Without changing government policies, more people qualify for unemployment insurance and welfare, while income tax collections fall due to lower income levels. This automatic increase in transfer payments and decrease in taxes works to help keep aggregate demand from falling further. During an inflationary gap, fewer people collect unemployment insurance and welfare due to the fact that more people have jobs. They also pay more in income taxes. These actions work to keep aggregate demand from increasing further.

[5] Hanke, Seve H. "We wer all Keynesians – then" *Forbes Magazine* February 22nd, 1999.

Typically the unemployed in the US can qualify for up to six months of unemployment insurance benefits. During recessions, however, there is increased political pressure to extend those transfer payments. President George H.W. Bush refused to extend unemployment benefits during the 1991 recession and failed to get re-elected. President George W. Bush extended unemployment benefits to a year during the 2001 recession. President Barack Obama increased unemployment insurance to almost two years during the 2009 recession. While increasing unemployment insurance is meant to stimulate aggregate demand, it also reduces aggregate supply as workers take longer to re-enter the workforce. Thus, like everything else, the benefits must be weighed against the costs when determining whether or not to extend unemployment benefits.

The next chapter will examine different types of government spending in more detail.

Glossary

Austerity package—a law that increases taxes or lowers government spending or transfer payments

Automatic stabilizers—things that help the economy get back to full employment without explicit use of fiscal or monetary policy

Contractionary fiscal policy—an increase in taxes or a decrease in government spending designed to reduce aggregate demand

Expansionary fiscal policy—an increase in government spending or a decrease in taxes designed to increase aggregate demand

Fiscal stimulus—a synonym for expansionary fiscal policy

Implementation lag—the time it takes for a policy, once enacted, to be felt by the economy

Marginal propensity to consume (MPC)—the percentage of each new dollar of income that the average consumer spends

Policy lag—the time it takes policy makers to develop a set of policies to address an economic problem

Recognition lag—the time it takes policy makers to realize a problem exists in the economy

Spending multiplier—a tool to understand the total impact on real GDP resulting from an original change in spending, $\frac{1}{1\text{-MPC}}$

Tax multiplier—a tool used to understand the total impact on real GDP resulting from an original change in taxes, $-((\frac{1}{1\text{-MPC}})-1)$

Questions for Review

1. According to Keynes, what is the appropriate fiscal policy to employ during a recessionary gap? Why? Expansionary fiscal policy.
2. According to Keynes, what is the appropriate fiscal policy to employ during an inflationary gap? Why? Contractionary fiscal policy.
3. Why is the use of fiscal policy complicated if the economy is experiencing stagflation? b/c supply curve is steeper. b/c unemp and inflation happens at the same time.
4. List and describe three time lags as they impact fiscal policy. ① Policy lag. ② Recognition lag. ③ Implementation lag.
5. How does ideology impact the use of fiscal policy? Ideology affects politicians when making a new policy.
6. What information do policy makers need in order to correctly engage in fiscal policy? Full employment level of real GDP, current level of real GDP, marginal propensity.
7. How does the shape of the aggregate supply curve impact the effectiveness of fiscal policy.
8. List two examples of automatic stabilizers and how they help keep aggregate near full employment. unemployment insurance, welfare.
9. Why might empirical evidence of spending and tax multiplier differ from Keynesian theory?
10. If the federal government hires ten thousand workers to count blades of grass on Capitol Hill, would wealth be created? Why or why not?

~~No. Keb.~~

Chapter 16
Government Spending

© Antonio Abrignani, 2012, under license Shutterstock, Inc.

In order to understand how the government might increase or decrease spending over time, it is important to learn the process determining how the government spends money. The US government's budget year goes from October 1st until September 30th. The 2010 budget year, then, started on October 1, 2009. In 2010, the federal government spent roughly $3.456 trillion. This spending can be divided into two main categories: discretionary and mandatory spending. This chapter examines the differences between discretionary and mandatory spending, trends in each, and the intricacies of the Social Security and Medicare budgetary shortfalls facing the United States.

Discretionary spending is money that is authorized to be spent by Congress with the passage of an appropriations act. Fiscal policy utilizes discretionary spending changes to influence the economy. Congress is required to pass appropriations bills each year to fund discretionary spending. When they fail to do so, they must either pass continuing resolutions to temporarily fund government operations or engage in a **government shutdown**. A government shutdown is where the government ceases to spend money due to a lack of legal authority to do so. The 2011 federal budget was actually passed on April 15, 2011, seven months into that fiscal year.

Mandatory spending is money that is required to be spent according to current law. When Congress and the President create **entitlements**, they set up rules regarding who qualifies for federal money rather than stating how much money those programs will have. An entitlement is a legal guarantee to benefits. Rather than vote each year on how much money to spend on Social Security, Congress and the President created a formula to determine Social Security spending. In this way, mandatory spending is often referred to as being programmatic or automatic spending. Congress and the President can at any point pass new laws to change how the entitlement spending is handed out, but are under no legal obligation to do so.

Table 16.1 lists government spending as a percentage of GDP during selected years. In the last forty years, there have only been two presidents who have overseen a decrease in the size of the federal government as a percentage of the economy: President Reagan and President Clinton.[1] President Clinton famously remarked in his 1996 State of the Union Address, "The era of big government is over." However, by 2009 the relative size of government spending was at its largest post WWII amount at 25% of GDP. Even as the government spent a smaller percentage of US GDP in 2010, the level was still higher than at any year since 1983. These federal outlays include government spending and transfer payments.

Table 16.1 FEDERAL OUTLAYS AS A % OF GDP[2]

1972	19.6	1992	22.1
1976	21.4	2000	18.4
1980	21.7	2008	20.9
1988	21.3	2010	23.8

Mandatory Spending

In 2010, mandatory spending made up 60.5% of federal government outlays. The five largest programs that fall under mandatory spending include Social Security,

[1] Richard Nixon began his second term in 1972. Jimmy Carter began his term in 1976. Ronald Reagan began his two terms in 1980. George H.W. Bush began his term in 1988. Bill Clinton began his two terms in 1992. George W. Bush began his two terms in 2000. Barack Obama began his first term in 2008.

[2] Source: Congressional Budget Office.

Medicare, Welfare, Medicaid, and pensions. **Social Security** is a federally managed retirement system for US workers. **Medicare** covers health care expenditures for the elderly. **Welfare** (including Temporary Aid to Needy Families and food stamps, among other programs) provides assistance to those in poverty. **Medicaid** covers health care expenditures for low income people. The pension's portion of entitlement spending refers to pension payments made to former federal government employees.

The elderly receives a larger portion of entitlement spending than the poor. Even wealthy retirees can collect Social Security and Medicare benefits. In this way, entitlement spending is more a reflection of organized political lobbying than of physical need. The elderly also receive much more entitlement spending than do young people, perhaps because the elderly can vote while those under age 18 are not allowed to do so. Table 16.2 illustrates the distribution of entitlement spending.

Table 16.2 2010 UNITED STATES ENTITLEMENT SPENDING IN BILLIONS OF DOLLARS[3]

Social Security	$701
Medicare	$520
Welfare	$437
Medicaid	$272
Pensions	$139

The nature of the federal government has changed greatly over the last half century. Entitlement spending has grown from being 28% of federal outlays in 1965 to accounting for 60.5% of federal outlays in 2010. The primary function of the federal government has become income redistribution to the elderly and the poor. In 2010, the federal government spent more on Social Security than on national defense, even with troops in Iraq and Afghanistan. As life expectancy in the US has increased, entitlement programs meant to help people at the very end of their lives are now being used by the average elderly person for over a decade.

The 2003 extension of Medicare to cover prescription drugs is an example of entitlement reform that has resulted in more spending. As entitlement spending increases to a larger percentage of the economy, this leads to more government control of the economy unless there is a comparable sized decease in discretionary spending. The Welfare Reform Act of 1996 dramatically reduced welfare entitlement eligibility. This helped to account for the large decrease in mandatory spending as a percentage of GDP under President Clinton. Table 16.3 illustrates the historical trend in mandatory spending.

entitlement spending ↑'s more gov. control over economy...

[3] Ibid.

Table 16.3 US MANDATORY SPENDING AS A PERCENTAGE OF GDP[4]

1972	8.6%	1992	11.5%
1976	10.9%	2000	10.5%
1980	10.7%	2008	12.4%
1988	10.1%	2010	14.4%

In 2010, mandatory spending almost equaled tax revenues. That is, even if discretionary spending were reduced to zero, the federal government would almost run a budget deficit based on mandatory spending alone. As the percentage of its spending devoted to entitlements increases, the federal government reduces its ability to engage in Keynesian fiscal policy.

Social Security and Medicare

What makes entitlement spending so large? Social Security and Medicare are the two largest entitlement programs in the US. Both of these programs are aimed at helping the elderly. The Social Security Act that created the program was signed into law by President Franklin Delano Roosevelt in 1935. Social security taxes were collected for the first time in 1937 with benefits starting in 1940. Since its inception as a worker retirement system, Social Security benefits have been expanded to include survivors' benefits to a deceased worker's spouse and children (1939), disability benefits (1956), and an automatic cost of living increase (1972). President Lyndon B. Johnson signed Medicare into law in 1965.

At its beginning, the Social Security retirement age was set at age 65, which also happened to be the average life expectancy in the US at the time. In this way, Social Security was originally designed to help those who "unexpectedly" lived longer than average and therefore hadn't saved enough to fund their own consumption. The retirement age is now 67 years, but life expectancy is over 78 years in the US. This means that the average American can expect to receive over a decade of Social Security payments and Medicare benefits.

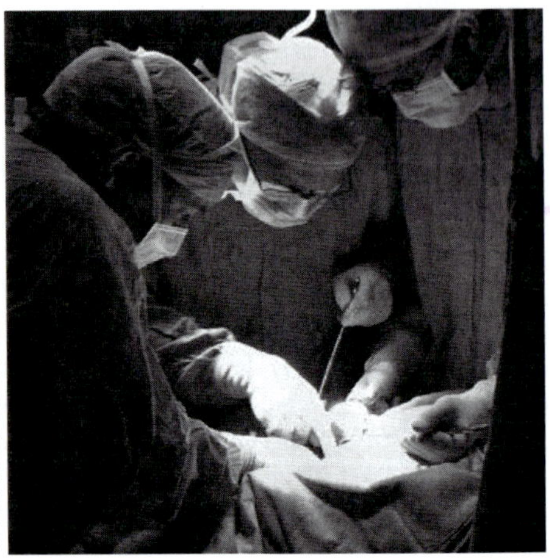

An increase in life expectancy is generally viewed as a good thing. However, the increased number of entitlement beneficiaries has placed a strain on the fiscal sustainability of both Social Security and Medicare. In 1945, there were 42 workers per retiree. Today there are only three workers per retiree. What accounts for this shift? As young people have stayed in school longer to achieve higher levels of education, they have delayed their entrance to the labor force. As educated workers have been able to quickly earn wealth, they have also been able to retire at younger ages. Finally, the increase in life

[4] Ibid.

expectancy, combined with the demographic bubble known as the baby boom, has contributed to a change in the ratio. A large number of boomers went from being workers to retirees.

When the federal government created Social Security in the 1930's, they had the choice of how to design the retirement system. Their choices included a fully funded pension plan, a partially funded pension plan, or a pay as you go pension plan. A fully funded pension plan would have entailed workers funding their own retirement. In a fully funded pension, enough money is put away during workers earning years to actuarially cover their promised benefits. Private employers who offer defined benefit pensions are legally required to fully fund their plan. Social Security, though a defined benefit pension, is not fully funded.

A pay as you go pension plan (pyramid scheme) has current workers pay retirement benefits to current retirees. Such a plan works well if each generation is substantially larger than the previous one so that the number of workers per retiree doesn't decrease rapidly. Social Security began as a pay as you go pension, but policy makers realized that the baby boom generation would place undue strain on the system if, as workers, they were only required to fund current retiree's benefits. As a result, by 2010, the **Social Security Trust Fund** contained $2.6 trillion in assets. These assets reflect that baby boomers partially funded their own retirement.

The assets in the Social Security Trust Fund are US government bonds. That is, as the Social Security system ran budget surpluses, the federal government took all of that money and replaced it with IOU's. Therefore the trust fund merely contains a promise that the government will pay future benefits out of future tax revenues. In this way, Social Security once again became a pay as you go pension plan. Even so, the Social Security 2011 Trustee Report indicates that the disability trust fund will begin running a deficit in 2013 and completely exhaust the fund by 2018. The old age retirement trust fund will begin running a budget deficit in 2023, and will be completely exhausted by 2035. The 2011 Medicare Trustee's Report indicates that the Medicare Trust Fund will be completely exhausted by 2024.

Exhaustion of trust funds means that both Social Security and Medicare are on paths to become completely pay as you go plans. The problem is that, as entitlements, benefits for these programs are fixed at rates that cannot be supported by the current payroll tax rates. Table 16.4 illustrates changes to the payroll tax that have been made to extend the life of the programs. At first, new revenues came from higher tax rates. Then higher tax rates were accompanied by higher earnings limits. An earnings limit is the amount of money a person can make beyond which they pay no Social Security Tax. Since 1990 the payroll tax rate has remained constant while the maximum taxable earnings have increased.

Table 16.4 **HISTORICAL SOCIAL SECURITY AND MEDICARE TAX RATES**

Year	Combined Employer-Employee Tax Rate	Maximum Taxable Earnings	Year	Combined Employer-Employee Tax Rate	Maximum Taxable Earnings
1937	2%	$3,000	1973	11.7%	$10,800
1950	3%	$3,000	1978	12.1%	$17,700
1954	4%	$3,600	1979	12.26%	$22,900
1957	4.5%	$4,200	1981	13.3%	$29,700
1959	5%	$4,800	1982	13.4%	$32,400
1960	6%	$4,800	1984	14.0%	$37,800
1962	6.25%	$4,800	1985	14.1%	$39,600
1963	7.25%	$4,800	1986	14.3%	$42,000
1966	8.4%	$6,600	1988	15.02%	$45,000
1967	8.8%	$6,600	1990	15.3%	$51,300
1969	9.6%	$7,800	2010	15.3%	$106,800[5]
1971	10.4%	$7,800			

Social Security and Medicare have uncertain futures. One of three (or a combination thereof) scenarios will come to pass. First, if there is no reform to either benefits or payroll taxes, then benefits that exceed the amount collected by the payroll tax will have to come from other federal tax revenues such as the income tax. This would require a corresponding decrease in other entitlement or discretionary spending.

Secondly, Congress and the President could raise payroll tax revenues by either increasing payroll tax rates or increasing the maximum earnings limit for Social Security. Medicare already faces no such limit on earnings. As noted in the Table 16.4, increased taxes have been the primary mode of entitlement adjustment in the past. A removal of the cap on Social Security earnings would immediately increase the marginal tax rate of wealthy self-employed income earners by 15.3 percentage points. On top of the 35% personal income tax they already pay, the payroll tax would place their marginal tax burden over 50%, even before they pay state and local taxes.

Thirdly, Congress and the President could reduce benefits. They could raise the retirement age to reduce the number of retirees. They could change the Social Security payment formula to reduce benefits to each retiree or change the way the

[5] Since 1994 there has been no top limit on taxable earnings for Medicare.

cost of living increase is calculated for benefits. Another option is to means test benefits. In this way only poorer old people would get Social Security checks or receive health care assistance. As the current benefit schedule already redistributes income from wealthier to poorer retirees, this would increase the progressivity of the program.

A reduction in Medicare benefits could entail a lowering of reimbursement costs to health care providers. Significant decreases may result in less access to health care, particularly by the elderly in rural areas. Increases in patient copayments or out of pocket maximums could also save Medicare money. Bureaucrats could end up determining which medical procedures are approved and their corresponding waiting times.

To fix the future social security shortfall, President George W. Bush advocated letting people place a portion of their payroll tax into a private account that they could invest in the stock market to earn a potentially higher rate of return. Any such movement to go from a pay as you go system to one that becomes partially or fully funded would require major benefit or tax changes. As current workers' money is diverted to their own retirement accounts, money no longer exists to pay benefits to current retirees.

Turning Social Security into a fully funded pension plan could require that a generation of taxpayers would be willing to fund the retirements of their parents plus their own. It isn't likely that any generation will voluntarily do that. Instead, a conversion to a fully funded pension plan could require that the government borrow enough money to cover current pension payments. The burden of the higher national debt could then be shared by generations to come. However, there are certainly obstacles to taking on more debt as is discussed in later chapters. Policymakers not only have to figure out how to fix this shortfall caused by mandatory spending, they have to decide which future projects to fund via discretionary spending.

Discretionary Spending

Only under Presidents Reagan and Clinton did nondefense domestic discretionary spending fall as a percentage of GDP. This spending includes items such as the court system, domestic law enforcement, infrastructure, education, agriculture, energy, and national parks. In 2009 and 2010, the stimulus package spending led nondefense domestic discretionary spending to levels not seen since the early 1980's. Table 16.5 illustrates this in its historical context.

One example of discretionary spending is spending on farm subsidies. Table 16.5 notes that corn farmers receive more support from taxpayers than any other agricultural commodity. Seventy-four percent of farm subsidies go to the richest 10% of farmers. Agricultural subsidies enrich corporate farmers who have been able to

Table 16.5 US NONDEFENSE DOMESTIC DISCRETIONARY SPENDING AS A PERCENTAGE OF GDP[6]

1972	3.8%	1992	3.4%
1976	4.5%	2000	3.0%
1980	4.7%	2008	3.4%
1988	3.1%	2010	4.2%

Table 16.6 FARM SUBSIDIES 1995-2010 IN BILLIONS OF DOLLARS[7]

Corn	$77	Rice	$13
Wheat	$32	Sorghum	$6.1
Cotton	$31	Dairy	$4.9
Soybeans	$24	Livestock	$3.7

effectively lobby their Congressional representatives for money. The Federal Agriculture Improvement and Reform Act of 1996 phased out agricultural subsidies by 2000, only to have Congress and President Bush bring them back with the Farm Security and Rural Investment Act of 2002.

Defense spending, as a percentage of GDP, trended downward from the early 1970s until 1980, as the US ended its intervention in Vietnam. Under President Reagan, defense spending rose in an effort to bring the Cold War to an end. The **Cold War** was an unofficial war between the US and the Soviet Union which began in 1946 and came to an end with the fall of the Soviet Union in 1991.

Following the end of the Cold War, the US was able to benefit from the **peace dividend**; as resources were freed up due to the absence of a military conflict, they were diverted to meet other needs and wants for society. The US response to the September 11th attacks in 2001 brought with it an increase in military spending as the US invaded Afghanistan and Iraq. These trends are reflected in Table 16.7.

Relative to other advanced industrialized economies, the US spends a much larger percentage of its economy on national defense. Canada, for instance, spends less than one third as much as the US on national defense as a percentage of GDP. Germany

[6] Ibid.

[7] Environmental Working Groups's 2011 Farm Subsidy Database, http://farm.ewg.org/.

Table 16.7 US DEFENSE SPENDING AS A PERCENTAGE OF GDP[8]

1972	6.7%	1992	4.8%
1976	5.2%	2000	3.0%
1980	4.9%	2008	4.3%
1988	5.8%	2010	4.7%

Table 16.8 INTERNATIONAL DEFENSE SPENDING AS A PERCENTAGE OF GDP[9]

US	4.7%	Canada	1.5%
UK	2.7%	Germany	1.4%
China	2.2%	Japan	1.0%

and Japan, who are in part protected by US military bases located in their countries, are able to free up resources to be used satisfying nonmilitary needs and desires.

Discretionary spending undertaken by the federal government does not have to reflect national priorities. An **earmark** is spending that directs approved funds to be spent on specific projects. A Congresswoman may want a bridge to be built in her district. If she is able to sit on the committee that originates the spending bill, she may be able to add her earmark to the bill. She could also add her earmark by engaging in **logrolling**. Logrolling is vote trading. She may agree to vote for spending that one of her colleagues likes but she doesn't care for, in exchange for a vote for her earmark. In this way, many urban congresspersons over the years have voted for farm subsidies in exchange for more urban spending.

When Congress wishes to engage in fiscal policy the 'devil is in the details' as to where and on what the spending is spent. Government roads and bridges are named after powerful congresspersons for a reason. They have been able to use their seniority on committees to direct spending to their district or state. While spending has been discussed in this chapter, spending is largely dependent upon revenue. The next chapter examines the sources of tax revenue for the US federal government and compares its tax rates with those of other nations.

[8] Source: Congressional Budget Office.

[9] Source: Stockholm International Peace Research Institute's Military Expenditure Database.

Glossary

Cold War—an unofficial war between the US and the Soviet Union which began in 1946 and came to an end with the fall of the Soviet Union in 1991

Discretionary spending—money that is authorized to be spent by Congress by the passage of an appropriations act

Earmark—spending that directs approved funds to be spent on specific projects

Entitlement—a legal guarantee to benefits

Government shutdown—when the government ceases to spend money due to a lack of legal authority to do so

Logrolling—the trading of votes used to generate sufficient support for legislation that would not pass on its own

Mandatory spending—money that is required to be spent according to current law

Medicaid—a federal program that covers health care expenditures for low income people

Medicare—a federal program that covers health care expenditures for the elderly

Peace dividend—resources that are freed up due to the absence of a military conflict

Social Security—a federally managed retirement system for US workers

Social Security Trust Fund—government bonds purchased with surplus revenues from the Social Security tax

Welfare—a set of government programs that provide assistance to those in poverty

Questions for Review

- Mandatory: required to be spent according to current law.
- Discretionary: money that is authorized to be spent by congress with the passage of an appropriations act.

1. How does mandatory spending differ from discretionary spending?
2. Why have government outlays been increasing as a percentage of GDP over time?
3. Under which Presidents since 1970, if any, has discretionary spending as a percentage of GDP fallen? Reagan.
4. Under which Presidents since 1970, if any, has mandatory spending as a percentage of GDP fallen? Clinton.
5. How does US defense spending compare to other industrialized countries? #1.
6. What type of pension system is Social Security? pay as you go.
7. Under current law, when will Social Security exhaust its trust fund? ~~2018~~ 2035
8. Under current law, when will Medicare exhaust its trust fund? 2024.
9. Does Social Security need to be reformed? Why or why not?
10. What are the possible Social Security reforms? Which do you prefer? Why?
11. Does Medicare need to be reformed? Why or why not?
12. What are the possible Medicare reforms? Which do you prefer? Why?

Chapter 17 Taxes

"No taxation without representation" was a popular phrase used by American revolutionaries to generate anti-British sentiment in support of the American Revolution. The revolutionaries believed that British Parliament should not have the power to directly tax American colonists since colonists lacked representation in Parliament. However, American colonists only paid a fraction of the taxes that other British subjects paid.

Table 17.1 INDEX OF PER CAPITA TAX BURDENS IN 1765 (GREAT BRITAIN = 100)[1]

Great Britain	100
Ireland	26
Pennsylvania	4
Maryland	4
Massachusetts	4
New York	3
Connecticut	2
Virginia	2

In 1932, US federal tax revenues as a percentage of GDP were 2.8%. By 1944, they had risen to 20.9%. President Franklin Delano Roosevelt oversaw a dramatic shift in the size and scope of the US government, as New Deal spending was accompanied by New Deal tax increases. This chapter lays out the current US tax code, compares state tax rates, places the US tax code in an international comparison, and examines the code's efficiency and fairness.

The Current Federal Tax Structure

The amount of revenue generated by the federal government is dependent upon both the tax code and the health of the US economy. As the economy grows, so too does the number of taxable economic transactions. Tax revenues, then, are variable over the course of the business cycle.

Examining tax revenues as a percentage of GDP over the last forty years reveals that the presidents who oversaw an increase in tax revenues as a percentage of GDP were all Democrats. However not all democratic presidents have had tax revenues rise. Presidents Carter and Clinton saw tax revenues as a percentage of GDP increase, while Presidents Ford, Reagan, and both Presidents Bush (all Republicans) saw tax revenue as a percentage of GDP fall during their tenure. In spite of this trend, the biggest decrease in tax revenue, has occurred during

[1] Source: Gerald A. Gunderson, *A New Economic History of America* (New York: McGraw-Hill, 1976): 98.

President Obama's presidency. President Obama extended the Bush tax cuts while also cutting the payroll tax for 2011. Combined with a slowing economy, US government revenues as a percentage of GDP were lower in 2011 than any year since 1943. This is illustrated in Table 17.2.

Table 17.2 FEDERAL TAX REVENUES AS A PERCENTAGE OF GDP[2]

1972	17.6%	1992	17.5%
1976	17.1%	2000	20.9%
1980	19.0%	2008	17.7%
1988	18.2%	2010	14.9%

The modern income tax came into being with the passage of the 16th Amendment to the US Constitution in 1913. Before then, it was unconstitutional for the federal government to tax income. Today, the two largest sources of tax revenue for the US government are the personal income tax and the payroll tax. The first applies to all forms of income, while the latter applies only to wage labor. Corporate taxes and other excise taxes, such as the national gas tax, account for only small portion of federal tax revenues. Table 17.3 highlights the sources of the federal tax revenue of 2010.

Table 17.3 2010 FEDERAL REVENUES BY SOURCE (IN BILLIONS)[3]

Personal Income Tax	$899
Payroll Tax	$865
Corporate Income Tax	$191
Other	$171

The payroll tax (FICA) is a tax paid by employers and employees based on their wages. An employer must pay 7.65% of their worker's income to the federal government. Each employee must also pay 7.65% of their income, for a total of 15.3%. The payroll tax applies to all wage income earned up to $106,800 in 2010.

---

[2] Source: Congressional Budget Office.

[3] Ibid.

Wage income earned above that level is subject only to the Medicare portion of the payroll tax (2.9% split between the employer and employee).

Table 17.4 lays out the federal income tax brackets for 2010. A **marginal tax rate** is the percentage of a new dollar in economic activity that must be paid to the government. Tax brackets represent marginal tax rates. Married households pay a tax rate of 10% on their first $16,750 of annual taxable income, whether they earn $20,000 or $2 billion a year. Married couples earning more than $16,750 pay 15% on all income past $16,750 and up to $68,000 earned. For those with taxable income greater than $68,000, 25% of this added income up to the next cutoff of $137,300 is paid to the federal government, and so forth. In this way, taxpayers in the top tax bracket do not pay 35% of their entire income in federal income taxes, but instead pay according to each tax bracket up until they exceed $373,650 cutoff. Then they pay 35% of all additional dollars earned past the cutoff.

Table 17.4 **2010 FEDERAL INCOME TAX BRACKETS**[4]

Marginal Tax Rate	Married Couples Filing Jointly Adjusted Gross Income	Single Filers Adjusted Gross Income
10%	Not over $16,750	Not over $8,375
15%	$16,750-$68,000	$8,375-$34,000
25%	$68,000-$137,300	$34,000-$82,400
28%	$137,300-$209,250	$82,400-$171,850
33%	$209,250-$373,650	$171,850-$373,650
35%	Over $373,650	Over $373,650

The **average tax rate** is the total taxes paid divided by the income. The average income tax rate is lower than the marginal income tax rate for two reasons. First, most people's first dollar of income is taxed at a lower marginal rate than their last dollar of income. Second, not all income is taxable. This is due to **deductions** and **exemptions** that serve to complicate the tax code. A deduction is an amount that can be deducted from taxable income. Money given to charities, interest paid on a home loan, or state and local property tax payments are just a few examples of deductions that exist in the tax code. A person who gives half of their income away to charity has their taxable income fall by 50%, and so only pays taxes on the remaining half. The 10% tax bracket then kicks in on the first taxable dollars of income. Since the average tax rate is determined by actual income, the average tax rate in this case will be much lower than the marginal tax rate. Those who don't choose to itemize their deductions could have opted for a $5,700 standard

[4] Source: Internal Revenue Service.

deduction in 2010 if they were single or an $11,400 deduction if they were married filing jointly.

An exemption is a portion of one's income that is not subject to taxation. For instance, interest earned on US government bonds is not considered to be taxable income. That income is tax exempt. The US personal income tax code also has a personal exemption. A taxpayer does not have to pay any taxes on their first $3,650 of income. They get an additional $3,650 exemption for each dependent in their household. A family of four in 2010 could have earned $26,000 ($14,600 in exemptions plus the standard deduction) before it was subject to the income tax. In addition to no federal tax burden for an above mentioned family of four who makes $20,000 a year, they also qualify for the **earned income tax credit**. The earned income tax credit pays low income earners based on their income and family size. The **child tax** credit pays people based on the number of children they have. In this way, many Americans face no federal income liability and instead get checks from the government. The bottom 50% of income tax earners in 2008 only paid 2.7% of the nation's income taxes. Table 17.5 illustrates the share of income taxes paid by various percentages of the population. It also demonstrates the progressive nature of the US federal income tax.

Table 17.5 **INCOME TAXES PAID BY VARIOUS GROUPS, 2008**[5]

All Taxpayers	Group's Share of Adjusted Gross Income	Group's Share of Income Taxes
100%	100.00%	100.00%
Top 1%	20.00%	38.02%
Top 10%	45.77%	69.94%
Top 25%	67.38%	86.34%
Top 50%	87.25%	97.30%
Bottom 50%	12.75%	2.70%

Cross Country Comparison of Tax Rates

With regard to income taxes, the United States is neither at the top, nor at the bottom when their top federal and local income tax rates are compared to other countries. Table 17.6 notes that Sweden, Belgium, the Netherlands, Denmark, and Japan all impose 50% plus marginal tax rates on income earners. Conversely, the Czech Republic and the Slovak Republic cap their marginal income tax burden at 15%. In North America, Canada's top marginal income tax rate at 46.4% is

[5] Ibid.

higher than that in the US. However, Mexico's 28% rate gives them a much lower rate that the US's combined federal and local rate of 41.9%.

The United States has the highest marginal corporate income tax rate in the industrialized world at 35%. Switzerland, Ireland, Germany and Canada have all been able to attract corporations and their production in exchange for low tax rates. The result is that their corporate tax revenues may even exceed those of the US. Low rates applied to more firms can yield higher tax revenues. In this way, the US has placed itself at a comparative disadvantage for attracting corporate job growth. In fact, the current corporate tax code encourages US corporations to move their operations (and accompanying jobs) overseas to lower their tax bills.

The single largest difference between the US tax code and most of the industrialized world is the absence in the US of a broad based national sales tax or **value added tax (VAT)**. A value added tax is a sales tax applied to every transfer of a good based on the increased worth of that good since it was last exchanged. Many European countries have double digit VAT's. A sales tax, or VAT, can apply to all income earners. Therefore, the **tax base** for a VAT is larger than for an income tax. A tax base is the number of people who pay the tax.

b/c EVERYONE buys not EVERYONE WORKS.

Table 17.6 TOP MARGINAL PERSONAL INCOME TAX RATES FOR EMPLOYEES[6]

Czech Republic	15%	United States	41.9%	Denmark	51.6%
Slovak Republic	19%	Canada	46.4%	Netherlands	52.0%
Mexico	28%	Germany	47.5%	Belgium	53.7%
UK	40%	Japan	50.0%	Sweden	56.5%

Table 17.7 CENTRAL GOVERNMENT CORPORATE TAX RATES[7]

Country	Tax Rate	Country	Tax Rate
Switzerland	8.50%	Japan	30.00%
Ireland	12.50%	Belgium	33.99%
Germany	15.825%	France	34.40%
Canada	16.50 %	United States	35.00%

[6] Source OECD Taxation of Wage Income (2010).

[7] Source: OECD Taxation of Corporate and Capital Income (2011).

The larger the tax base, the lower the marginal rates must be to achieve the same level of revenue. The almost total reliance on income taxes by the US government leaves them subject to downturns in tax revenues during recessions and periods of high unemployment.

A Comparison of US State Taxes

State governments primarily rely on tax revenue from income and sales taxes. While some states also impose property taxes, local governments collect the majority of all property taxes paid. Eight US states have no state income tax, while three: California, Hawaii, and Oregon, all have double digit income tax rates. High income earners, because they often have a choice of where to live in the US, can move to reduce or eliminate their state income tax burden. States compete for taxpayers by offering bundles of government spending and taxation that appeal to citizens. People can choose to sort themselves among political jurisdictions in order to find their preferred taxing and spending levels. This process of voting with one's feet is called the **Tiebout Effect**. Table 17.8 lays out the eight lowest and highest state income tax rates.

Table 17.8 TOP AND BOTTOM 2011 INCOME TAX RATES FOR US STATES[8]

Alaska	0%	Maine	8.50%
Florida	0%	Vermont	8.95%
Nevada	0%	New Jersey	8.97%
South Dakota	0%	New York	8.97%
Tennessee	0% (6% on interest and dividend income)	Iowa	8.98%
Texas	0%	California	10.30%
Washington	0%	Hawaii	11.00%
Wyoming	0%	Oregon	11.00%

Six US states don't have statewide sales taxes, while the top sales tax rate belongs to California at 8.25%. Oregon, though it has the nation's highest income tax, has no sales tax. Their neighboring state, Washington, has no income tax. People who work in Washington but purchase goods in Oregon can avoid both income and sales taxes. Table 17.9 illustrates the highest and lowest state sales tax rates.

[8] Source: State Individual Income Tax Rates, 2000-2011, Tax Foundation.

Table 17.9 TOP AND BOTTOM 2011 STATE SALES TAX RATES FOR US STATES[9]

Alaska	0%	Indiana	7.00%
Delaware	0%	New Jersey	7.00%
Montana	0%	Rhode Island	7.00%
New Hampshire	0%	Tennessee	7.00%
Oregon	0%	California	8.25%

Tax Efficiency and Fairness

An efficient tax system raises revenue without causing a significant disruption in economic activity. A perfectly efficient tax would be one that costlessly collects tax revenue while not causing any economic actor to change their behavior. Because the amount of land on earth (or in a country) is constant, a land tax would be able to generate tax revenue without the destruction of land. However, costs of collection would still exist. Property taxes generally tax both land and the improvements to the land. By taxing improvements, property taxes can dissuade people from making improvements to land.

As the US Supreme Court once held, "The power to tax is the power to destroy".[10] A high sales tax rate can cause people to engage in less consumption, both because consumers then have less money to spend and because the relative return to savings increases. Consumers can also choose to buy goods and services where they face a lower sales tax, or in the black market where no taxes are collected. Many states have tried to tax internet sales in an attempt to keep their citizens from avoiding state sales taxes. Because sales taxes are already collected by most states, there would be little administrative burden in collecting a national sales tax.

When it comes to personal and corporate income taxes, the marginal tax rate serves as a disincentive to increase earnings. As marginal tax rates increase, the opportunity cost of leisure increases and people may choose to substitute leisure for work, on the margin. An efficient income tax code would have low marginal tax rates and few, if any, deductions or exemptions. As it currently stands, the numerous personal and corporate tax loopholes work to push marginal tax rates higher and discourage economic activity. A simplified tax code would also serve to lower the compliance costs associated with filing income taxes. The current complexity of the tax code causes millions of Americans to pay professional tax preparers to help them file their tax forms. This added cost of compliance means that people pay compliance costs that the government cannot recoup. People could keep more

[9] Source: Combined State & Local Sales Tax Rates (as of January 1, 2011) Tax Foundation.

[10] McCulloch v. Maryland (1819).

of their money and the government could generate more revenue by reducing the complexity of the tax code.

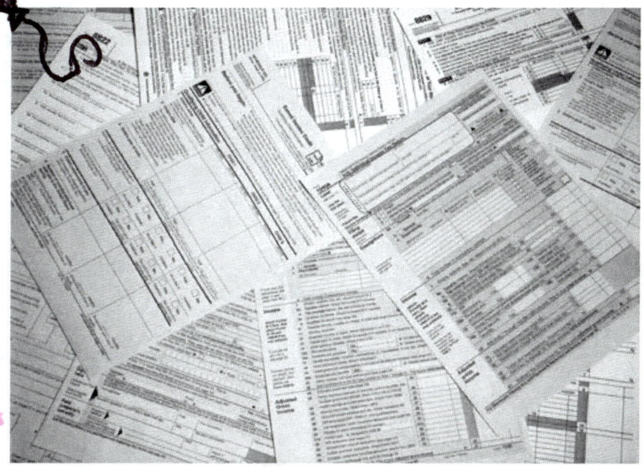

A tax can either be progressive, proportional, or regressive. A **progressive tax** is one where the average tax rate paid increases with income earned. A **proportional tax** is one where the average tax rate paid stays the same as income increases. A **regressive tax** is one where the average tax rate paid decreases as income increases. With its multiple tax brackets and many deductions and exemptions, the US income tax is highly progressive. The payroll tax is proportional up to the earnings limit on Social Security taxes. Sales taxes, if they are applied to all goods and services, tend to be regressive. Lower income individuals tend to spend a larger percentage of their income on goods and services than do higher income individuals. As a result, lower income individuals tend to pay a larger percentage of their income in sales taxes.

The question of which type of tax system is most *fair* depends on one's own ethical considerations and is often disputed between the two major political parties in the United States. Overall, the US tax system is progressive, but the debate over how progressive it should be has no foreseeable end in sight. Often the choice of tax code involves tradeoffs. A broad based sales tax is the most efficient revenue raiser but is also regressive. A steeply progressive personal or corporate income tax rate is very inefficient because it lowers economic activity and is costly to collect, but is seen by some as being fairer.

The answer to the efficiency vs. fairness tax debate comes down to whether people are more concerned about absolute or relative poverty. **Absolute poverty** means that people are unable to afford the basic necessities of life. **Relative poverty** is a measure of income inequality reflecting that some people can afford to buy less than others. An efficient tax code allows the economy to grow faster than it would under an inefficient tax code. This economic growth creates benefits for people of all incomes. There is less absolute poverty in the US than in Honduras because of faster economic growth over time. Still, this reduction in absolute poverty could cause an increase in relative poverty which some people find undesirable.

Glossary

Absolute poverty—people are unable to afford the basic necessities of life

Average tax rate—the total taxes paid divided by income

Child tax credit—a payment to people based on the number of children they have

Deduction—something to be deducted from taxable income

Earned income tax credit (EITC)—a payment to low income earners based on their income and family size

Exemption—a portion of one's income that is not subject to taxation

Marginal tax rate—the percentage of a new dollar in economic activity that must be paid to the government

Progressive tax—a tax where the average tax rate paid increases with income earned

Proportional tax—a tax where the average tax rate paid stays the same as income increases

Regressive tax—a tax where the average tax rate paid decreases as income increases

Relative poverty—a measure of income inequality where some people can afford to buy less than others

Tax base—the number of people or transactions that apply to a specific tax

Tiebout Effect—the sorting of individuals among political jurisdictions in order to find their preferred taxing and spending levels

Value added tax (VAT)—a sales tax applied to every transfer of a good based on the increased worth of that good since it was last exchanged

payroll tax - taxes employers pay

Ford, Reagan, 2 Bush ↓ Clinton ↑, Carter ↑,

Questions for Review

1. How does the US government generate most of its revenue?
2. How have federal tax revenues changed over time? All democrat presidents ↓ tax R% GDP
3. What is a progressive tax? A proportional tax? A regressive tax? Give examples of taxes in each category. Which is most efficient? The most fair? Why?
4. How do US personal and corporate income tax rates compare to those of other industrialized countries? very high. Personal : 41.9% (8th) Corporate : 35% (top)
5. What are the pros and cons of the US not having a national sales tax or VAT? Con: Cors move to overseas. pro:
6. Which political party tends to favor lower levels of federal taxation? Why do you think that is the case? Democrat
7. What percentage of personal income taxes does the top 25% of income earners pay? 86.34%
8. Which US states have no income tax? No sales tax? Alaska.
9. When did the US income tax become legal?
10. How would you reform the current tax code? Why would you advocate those changes?

Chapter 18
The National Debt

"I'll gladly pay you Tuesday for a hamburger today."

— *J. Wellington Wimpy*

"Neither a borrower nor a lender be,
For loan oft loses both itself and friend,
And borrowing dulls the edge of husbandry."

— *William Shakespeare*[1]

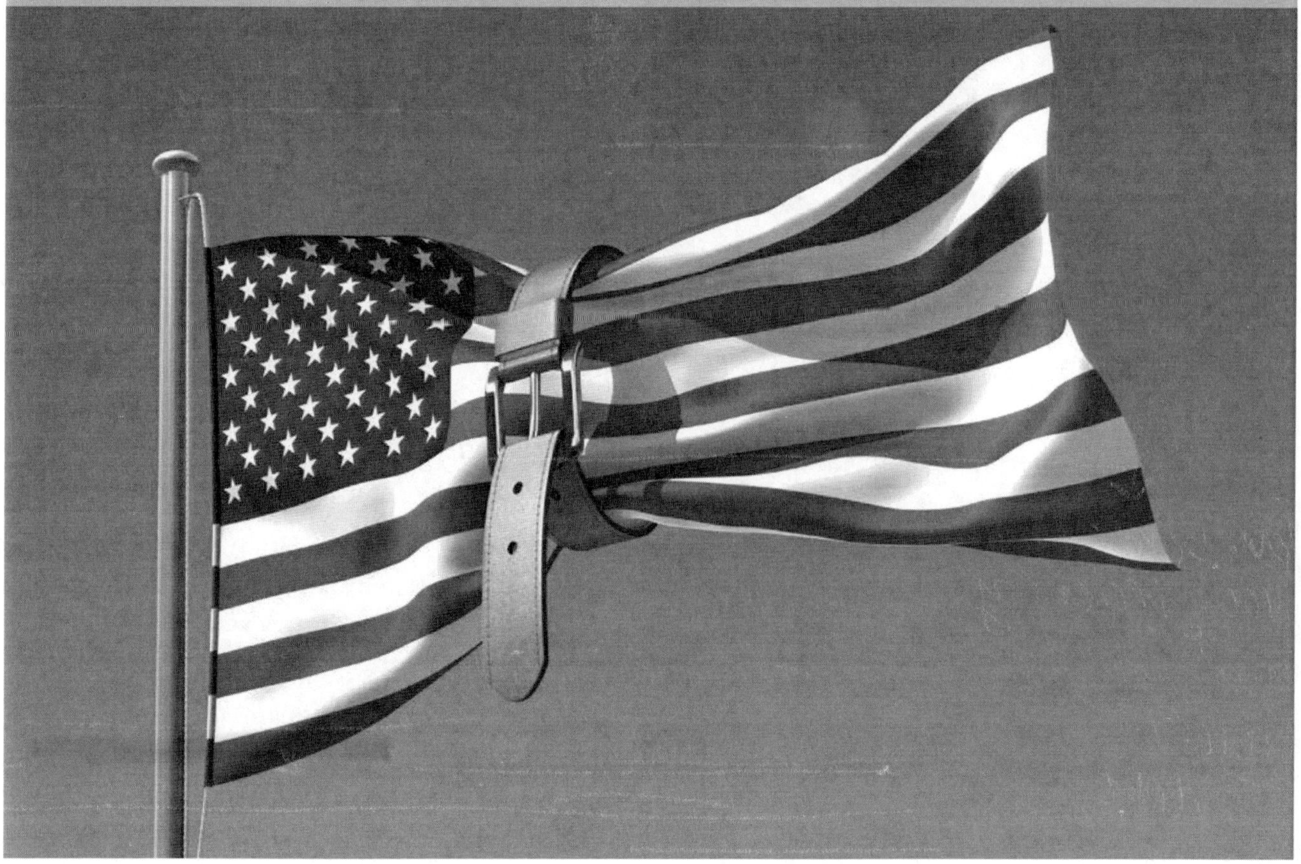

[1] Hamlet Act 1, scene 3, 45-77.

The prior two chapters discuss spending and revenue collection for the US federal government. But what happens when current revenues are insufficient to cover desired expenditures? Debt can be used as tool to finance long term investment. Businesses take on debt to finance new factories or equipment. Consumers take on debt to finance the purchase of new homes or a college education. In these cases, the benefits from the accumulated capital accrue over many years. These multiyear benefits may not be possible if businesses or consumers had to pay for large capital purchases up front.

Debt can also serve as a weight around borrowers' necks. If a business borrows money to finance capital for which there is little demand or use, then the service of that debt will take away scarce resources. If a consumer uses their credit card to finance current consumption, such as eating at expensive restaurants, they will be forced to service very high interest payments while forgoing future consumption.

Debt is growth enabling if the proceeds from the debt are used to increase future earnings enough to exceed interest payments on the debt. Another use for debt is consumption smoothing. If people know they will be wealthier in the future and want to spread their consumption more evenly over time, they can use debt to consume more today at the cost of consuming less tomorrow. When it comes to government debt, it is important to understand why a government takes on debt in order to determine the optimal level of public debt. This chapter examines government debt, where it came from, whether it is growth enhancing or detracting, and the path of future government debt.

US National Debt

The United States government is the largest debtor in the world. As of August 1, 2011, the US national debt stood at $14.3 trillion, roughly $46,000 for each American. The next day Congress and the President authorized a change in the **debt ceiling** to increase the amount of money the federal government could borrow by as much as $2.4 trillion more. Of the $14.3 trillion, $9.8 was owed to the public while $4.5 trillion were **intergovernmental holdings**. As noted in Chapter 16, the Social Security Trust Fund consists of government bonds. It, and other federal agencies, own government bonds and collectively this debt held by government agencies is known as intergovernmental debt. As government agencies cash in their bonds to meet spending commitments, the government will either have to generate more tax revenues, cut discretionary government spending, or borrow the money from the public to meet these government commitments.

Pension funds, mutual funds, banks, insurance companies, local governments, and individuals can all own government bonds. They own these bonds because the federal government pays interest on the bonds and that interest is tax free income to the owners of the bonds. To the extent that the US debt is owed to US citizens, repayment of the debt merely involves the transfer of income from US taxpayers to US bondholders, with the money staying in the US economy. Debt owed to foreign interests, however, means that money will be transferred from future US taxpayers to foreign interests, which represents a loss of money for the US economy.

Of the $9.8 trillion in debt owned by the public, roughly $4.6 trillion is owed to foreign entities. The government of China has loaned the US more than $1 trillion. Being a trillion dollars in debt to another world power has foreign policy implications. Secretary of State Hillary Clinton noted in 2010 that "We cannot sustain this level of deficit financing and debt without losing our influence, without being constrained in the tough decisions we have to make".[2]

The United States was an indebted country at its birth. Fighting the American Revolution required the Continental Congress to borrow money, principally from the French, to fund the war effort. When the US Constitution became ratified, $75 million in war debt became the property of the new federal government. In order to pay down this debt, the federal government ran budget surpluses and had paid off $30 million worth of the debt by 1812, when the US returned to war with Great Britain. Between 1816 and 1835 the federal government paid off its entire debt. President Andrew Jackson started rebating taxes to states and left a nominal national debt balance of $34,000 in 1835.

War is expensive. Throughout its history (until the 1950's) the US government has borrowed money to engage in war and then has run budget surpluses to pay down on that debt. This was true for the American Revolution, The War of 1812, The Mexican-American War, The US Civil War, and WWI. Because the benefits of peace presumably accrue to future generations, future generations are asked to help pay for current wars. Still, the American ethos was one that disliked government debt, so repayment of the national debt typically followed the end of wars. That has changed since the late 1950's.

Table 18.1 HISTORICAL US NATIONAL DEBT

Year	Debt	Year	Debt	Year	Debt
1791	$75 million	1849	$63 million	1919	$27.9 billion
1812	$45 million	1857	$29 million	1930	$16.2 billion
1816	$127 million	1866	$2.8 billion	1946	$269 billion
1835	$34 thousand	1893	$1.5 billion	1951	$255 billion

[2] Adrew Quinn, Reuters May 27, 2010.
http://www.reuters.com/article/2010/05/27/security-obama-clinton-idUSN2714967820100527?type=marketsNews

The national debt has grown every year since 1958. The US has engaged in military conflicts since then including, but not limited to, the Vietnam War, the Cold War, and the War on Terror. The principle of borrowing to finance wars with repayment to follow the war's conclusion is only fiscally sustainable if the economy experiences long stretches of peace. With the war on terror reaching no obvious conclusion, borrowing to finance the war is akin to borrowing for consumption rather than for investment. Indeed, Adam Smith argued that if countries were prohibited from running budget deficits in times of war, there would be fewer wars.[3]

Table 18.2 **RECENT DEBT HISTORY**

Year	Debt	Year	Debt
1972	$427 billion	1992	$4.1 trillion
1976	$620 billion	2000	$5.7 trillion
1980	$908 billion	2008	$10.2 trillion
1988	$2.6 trillion	2010	$13.5 trillion

As Table 18.2 demonstrates, more than sixty percent of the US's national debt has accrued since 2000. The national debt rose at its slowest pace in the last forty years during the Clinton Administration in the 1990's. Strong economic growth coupled with tax and welfare reform reduced the rate at which the federal government was borrowing. The national debt almost tripled in size during the Reagan Administration in the 1980's.

The Burden of Government Debt

If an individual borrows $500,000 to purchase a house, is paying off this type of debt reasonable? To a large extent, the answer to this question depends on the individual's income. For someone earning a six figure income, a $500,000 debt should not be terribly difficult to pay off. For someone working for minimum wage, it is unlikely they would be able to pay off such a large debt.

Similarly, the best measure to determine the burden of government debt on an economy is the debt/GDP ratio. It looks at an economy's debt with respect to its ability to pay it back. If debt is funding growth enhancing projects, the added government debt will lower the debt/GDP ratio over time. If the debt is growth inhibiting, the added debt increases the debt/GDP ratio over time and is a sign that government borrowing is being used to finance current consumption.

[3] An Inquiry into the Nature and Causes of the Wealth of Nations. Adam Smith, 1776.

Seventy-five million dollars was a lot of debt for the revolutionaries in the 1700's, but would not be terribly burdensome for a $15 trillion economy. By 1945 the debt to GDP ratio had risen to 121.2% of GDP. Even without paying down on the debt after 1958, economic growth exceeded deficit spending, so the debt/GDP ratio fell to 62.5% in 1981. By 2011, the US debt to GDP ratio had increased to 99.5% as Table 18.3 demonstrates.

Research by Reinhart and Rogoff[4] (studying debt and economic growth data from 44 countries over 200 years) indicates that countries with a debt/GDP ratio under 30% historically have had the highest average rate of economic growth. These countries have averaged growth at a 4.1% annual rate. In comparison, countries with a higher than 90% debt/GDP ratio have had an average -.1% economic growth rate. In other words, by running up debt, these economies actually grew poorer in the future. Not only does the fiscal imbalance entail an intergenerational transfer of wealth, it also impoverishes future generations by slowing down their trajectory of economic growth. Put another way, countries with debt/GDP ratios over 90% end up taking money from future generations to give it to the current relatively wealthier generation.

Large amounts of public debt can be harmful for multiple reasons. The higher the debt, the greater the annual interest payments are on the debt. These payments take government revenues that would otherwise have been used to fund other current government initiatives. Discretionary spending and entitlements have to fight over ever smaller government revenues in a world of rising debt.

The more the government borrows, the less savings are available to private firms who would have been interested in investment. As the government borrows increasingly larger amounts of money, the price of borrowed money, the interest rate, increases and firms and individuals who want loans are forced to compete for a smaller pool of savings. Government borrowing decreases private investment, as it drives up interest rates and decreases funds available for private companies. Larger debts also increase the likelihood of default, causing savers to demand a higher rate of return on their loans. These higher interest rates discourage private investment and therefore slow down long term economic growth. This process is referred to as **crowding out**.

As long as savers can get a positive return on low risk government bonds, they may choose to keep their savings out of the private sector. In the absence of government bonds, savers looking for a return to their savings must embrace the private sector. When the federal government ran budget surpluses following the US Civil War, the government used these surpluses to pay down debt. This allowed money to be made available for private investment, and private investment soared. This process is referred to as **crowding in**.

Government debt is inherently redistributive in nature. The government chooses to allocate resources based on its preferences rather than the preferences

[4] Reinhart, C. M., and K. S. Rogoff (2010), "Growth in a Time of Debt", draft December 31, 2009, presented American Economics Association, January 2010.

of individual decision makers. Debt also redistributes wealth from future generations unless citizens privately save more to compensate for increased public debt. Japan's large public debt is less burdensome on their economy because most of their debt is held by Japanese citizens. Repayment of debt is also redistributive. It redistributes income from future workers to bondholders. By raising marginal tax rates on future workers, said workers will likely adjust to these higher marginal rates by providing less work to the economy, thereby causing slower growth rates.

Table 18.3 **2011 DEBT AND DEFICITS**

Country	Debt/GDP[5]	Deficit/GDP[6]	Country	Debt/GDP	Deficit/GDP
Japan	229.1%	7.9%	Hong Kong	4.5%	2.7% (surplus)
Greece	152.3%	8.4%	Estonia	6.3%	1.3%
Italy	120.3%	4.0%	Luxembourg	17.9%	1.1%
Ireland	114.4%	11.4%	Australia	24.1%	2.3%
Iceland	103.2%	5.4%	South Korea	28.8%	1.5% (surplus)
US	99.5%	9.1%	New Zealand	35.8%	7.5%
Belgium	97.3%	3.8%	Sweden	37.3%	.1% (surplus)
Singapore	93.7%	0.3% (surplus)	Czech Republic	41.7%	4.5%
Portugal	90.6%	6.5%	Slovenia	42.3%	4.7%
France	87.6%	5.9%	Slovakia	45.1%	5.1%

Table 18.3 lists the top ten advanced countries with the lowest debt/GDP ratios and the bottom ten advanced countries with the highest debt/GDP ratio. These are the countries that are doing the best and worst jobs of paying for current consumption with their current revenues. Although there is great variation in the amount of public sector involvement in the countries listed, countries in the first column have all kept their spending in line with the revenues they collect. Five countries have a debt/GDP ratio under 30%: Hong Kong, Estonia, Luxemburg, Australia, and South Korea. Conversely, there are currently seven advanced (many more in the developing world) economies that fall over the 90% threshold: Japan, Iceland, Greece, Italy, Belgium, US, and Singapore. These countries are in a serious need of budget reform to lower their debt/GDP ratio. The three countries that stand out are Iceland, Greece, and the US, as they continue to borrow money at a record pace. It is this path of continued borrowing that led S&P to

[5] Source: IMF April 2011 Economic Outlook.

[6] *The Economist Magazine*. June, 2011.

Table 18.4 **TOP TEN GOVERNMENTS MOST LIKELY TO DEFAULT ON THEIR DEBT (2ND QUARTER 2011)**[7]

Rank	Country	Risk of Default (5 year CPD%*)	Rank	Country	Risk of Default (5 year CPD%*)
1.	Greece	80.6	6.	Argentina	34.9
2.	Venezuela	51.4	7.	Ukraine	28.6
3.	Portugal	47.6	8.	Lebanon	22.2
4.	Ireland	47.2	9.	Vietnam	21.8
5.	Pakistan	44.9	10.	Dubai	21.7

*CPD is the cumulative probability of default

downgrade the US bond rating in August, 2011. Table 18.4 lists the 10 countries with the highest risk of default for early 2011.

Debt and Unfunded Liabilities for US States

Government debt in the US is not confined to the federal government. Table 18.5 illustrates the states with the largest and smallest debt/GSP (**gross state product**) ratios. It reveals that seven US states have a debt/GSP (gross state product) ratio under 1%. They are Nebraska, Iowa, Wyoming, Tennessee, South Dakota, Colorado, and North Dakota. But for Tennessee, this group is largely concentrated in the Great Plains. What they have in common are constitutional rules that dictate balanced budgets.

The states with the highest debt/GSP ratios are Hawaii, Massachusetts, Connecticut, and New Jersey. They all have debt/ GSP ratios over 8%, so they possess more than eight times as much debt as the most prudent US states. While California has a high public debt, it also is the most populous state in the country. As a percentage of gross state product, California's debt does not place them in the bottom ten states in terms of debt/ GSP. However, the raw size of the amount of money California needs to borrow combined with its inability to make spending cuts/raise taxes has left California with the worst bond ratings of any US state.[8]

In addition to their existing debt, all US states have some unfunded pension liability they are responsible for. The Pew Center for the States estimated that

---

[7] Source: CMA Sovereign Risk Monitor Global Sovereign Debt Credit Risk Report, 2nd Quarter 2011.

[8] "California's credit rating cut to lowest of all 50 states" LA Times January 3, 2009. http://latimesblogs.latimes.com/money_co/2009/02/california-cred.html

Table 18.5 **2010 TOP TEN MOST AND LEAST INDEBTED STATES AS A PERCENTAGE OF GROSS STATE PRODUCT**[9]

Rank	State	Debt/GSP	Rank	State	Debt/GSP
1.	Nebraska	.0%	50.	Hawaii	9.5%
2.	Iowa	.2%	49.	Massachusetts	9.0%
3.	Wyoming	.2%	48.	Connecticut	8.8%
4.	Tennessee	.7%	47.	New Jersey	8.1%
5.	South Dakota	.7%	46.	Mississippi	6.1%
6.	Colorado	.8%	45.	New York	5.9%
7.	North Dakota	.9%	44.	Washington	5.2%
8.	Arkansas	1.3%	43.	Rhode Island	5.0%
9.	Montana	1.4%	42.	Kentucky	5.0%
10.	Utah	1.4%	41.	Illinois	4.7%

unfunded liability for state pensions systems exceeded $1.26 trillion in 2009.[10] Economists Joshua Rauh and Robert Novy-Marx[11] have put the value over $3 trillion. Nebraska, North Dakota and Tennessee not only have some of the lowest debt levels among the states, they are also among the states with the least amount of unfunded pension liability. This can be seen in Table 18.6.

Many of the most indebted states also have the highest levels of unfunded pension liability. Hawaii, Kentucky, Illinois, Mississippi, and Rhode Island are all among the ten most indebted states and the ten most underfunded pension systems. Their failure to live within their means will put tremendous strain on their future ability to provide public services to their state constituents over time. Both people and capital are fairly mobile between states. Thus, it is difficult for states to dramatically raise taxes to fund debt without motivating income earners to move to other states. Because people are more likely to move across states than across countries, the federal government has more power to increase tax rates than do individual states.

[9] Source: Forbes Magazine January 20, 2010.

[10] "The Trillion Dollar Gap Grows Wider" The Pew Center on the States. April 25, 2011. http://www.pewcenteronthestates.org/initiatives_detail.aspx?initiativeID=85899358839

[11] "The Liabilities and Risks of State-Sponsored Pension Plans" *Journal of Economic Perspectives* Vol. 23, No. 4, Fall 2009.

Table 18.6 **2010 TOP TEN MOST AND LEAST UNFUNDED STATE PENSIONS AS A PERCENTAGE OF GROSS STATE PRODUCT**[12]

Rank	State	Unfunded/ GSP Liability	Rank	State	Unfunded/ GSP Liability
1.	Delaware	12.4%	50.	Rhode Island	58.7%
2.	Nebraska	13.5%	49.	Ohio	57.9%
3.	North Dakota	16.4%	48.	Mississippi	53.3%
4.	Tennessee	16.5%	47.	Wisconsin	47.1%
5.	New York	17.4%	46.	Alaska	43.9%
6.	North Carolina	17.7%	45.	Illinois	43.5%
7.	Virginia	18.4%	44.	Kentucky	42.8%
8.	Massachusetts	19.3%	43.	Alabama	41.9%
9.	New Hampshire	19.6%	42.	Hawaii	40.8%
10.	Florida	19.6%	41.	Oklahoma	39.1%

Unfunded Liabilities and National Governments

With the US national debt over $14.3 trillion, the current unfunded liability in Medicare and Social Security is roughly $104 trillion.[13] That amounts to $330,000 per person. Ninety percent of the US unfunded liability comes from Medicare. Left unchecked, the US federal government is on a collision course with fiscal disaster. Piling on more current consumption without paying for it simply is not possible without seriously jeopardizing the future standard of living for all Americans.

The US federal government is not the only developed country with unfunded liabilities. Even in 2003, Europe's unfunded pension liabilities were already beginning to pile up, as Table 18.7 illustrates. Yesterday's unfunded liabilities add to tomorrow's debt. Greece, Spain, Portugal, and Italy were among the countries where the European debt crisis intensified in 2010 and 2011. Their unfunded pension liabilities of 2003 transformed into high levels of debt in a very short time frame. In contrast, countries such as Japan, Norway, Netherlands, and Canada lead the way in funding their pension liabilities with fully funded public systems.

In summary, debt is not always harmful to the debtor. If the debt is used to finance investments that increase future earnings by more than the interest

[12] Source: Forbes Magazine January 20, 2010.

[13] Fisher, Richard. February 12 2010 Dallas Federal Reserve President Richard Fisher Speaking before the World Affairs council of Dallas/Fort Worth.

Table 18.7 UNFUNDED PENSION LIABILITIES AS A PERCENTAGE OF GDP, 2003[14]

Greece	807%	Finland	379%
Spain	717%	Italy	352%
France	407%	Denmark	317%
Portugal	396%	Austria	292%
Belgium	395%	Sweden	264%

payments on that debt, then debt can be growth enhancing. If debt is used to increase current consumption, then it will be growth diminishing. An increase in a country's debt/GDP ratio over time indicates that their public debt is primarily being used to finance current consumption at the cost of future consumption. As noted in Chapter 16, the vast majority of US federal spending is on entitlement programs which are consumptive in nature. The US is borrowing in an attempt to increase current consumption at the expense of future generations. Unless the US government meaningfully addresses entitlement and tax reform, the US national debt will continue to grow and inhibit future economic growth.

[14] Source: ABN AMRO 2003.

Glossary

Crowding in—where decreased government borrowing increases private investment by driving down interest rates and increasing funds available for private investment

Crowding out—where increased government borrowing limits private investment by driving up interest rates and decreasing funds available for private investment

Debt ceiling—the amount of money the US government is legally allowed to borrow

Gross state product—the sum total of all goods and services produced within a state in a given year

Intergovernmental holdings—government debt held by government agencies such as the Social Security Administration

Questions for Review

1. How large is the US national debt? 14.3 trillion.
2. What measure of national debt is most important? Why?
3. How do US debt levels compare to other countries?
4. Where did the US national debt come from?
5. Why are high debt levels problematic for future economic growth? What role does crowding out play? Is debt always harmful to the economy? Explain.
6. Which states have the least amount of debt? The most? Nebraska, Hawaii
7. Which states have the least amount of unfunded pension liability? The most? Delaware, Rhode Island.
8. Which countries are most likely to default? Why? Greece,
9. Which countries have the lowest debt burdens? Hong Kong.
10. How is government debt redistributive in nature?

Chapter 19 Rational Expectations and Rent Seeking

The 2007–2008 recession ignited a public debate over whether stimulus spending had a significant impact on either the short term or long term health of an economy. The two most prominent, and opposing, economists involved in the debate were Paul Krugman (Princeton) and Robert Barro (Harvard). The former complained that the $787 billion stimulus package was too small.[1] The latter argued that stimulus spending is not actually stimulative.[2] Chapter 15 examined theoretical Keynesian fiscal policy (as adhered to by Mr. Krugman). Chapters 16 and 17 presented actual government spending and taxation done at the federal level. In this chapter, we examine why fiscal policy may not be as effective as Keynes suggested or as Krugman argues.

Fiscal policy does not happen in a vacuum. Unlike scientific experiments that can be run in controlled laboratories, fiscal policy experiments must be run in the real world with its myriad of economic actors. These actors each engage in daily

[1] "The Obama Gap" January 8, 2009 http://www.nytimes.com/2009/01/09/opinion/09krugman.html.

[2] "Stimulus Spending Doesn't Work" October 1, 2009 Robert J. Barro and Charles J. Redlick *The Wall Street Journal*.

decisions about what to produce, how to produce, how much to charge, what to invest in, what to buy, and what to save. Advocates of fiscal policy assume either that individual actors are not engaging in actions that maximize their own self-interest (broadly defined); that in so pursuing their own self-interest they have made systematically incorrect errors that can corrected by government intervention; or, that if everyone correctly pursues their own self-interest, they reach an equilibrium that is inferior to one that could be reached by government directed collective action. In a nutshell, fiscal policy is needed if the average citizen is either a masochist, ignorant, or unwilling to play well with others while the government is all caring, all knowing, and can use the threat of force to make people collaborate for their own good.

Rational Expectations

A typical assumption made by economists is that people act in their own enlightened self-interest. That is, most people do not purposefully or consciously make decisions to bring harm to themselves or their loved ones. Decisions made at a specific time and place impact decision makers over both time and space. A decision to purchase a home today impacts tomorrow's house payments. A decision to invest today impacts tomorrow's bottom line. **Rational expectations theory**, introduced by John Muth,[3] states that individuals make decisions based upon their expectation of the future. Consumption, saving, and investment all happen based upon current knowledge and expectations about the future.

Expectations about the future may turn out to be incorrect. Firms may over or underestimate the future demand for their product, causing them to under or over invest in new capital. Rational expectations theory does not suggest that people perfectly know the future. It does, however, suggest that firms and individuals do not make systematic or predictable errors in their expectation of future events. Robert Lucas used rational expectation theory to suggest that government intervention in the economy is ineffective.[4] Any action taken openly by the government will cause decision makers to change their future expectations and act accordingly.

If the government borrows money to engage in stimulus spending, then individuals and firms know that the resulting higher debt will require higher taxes in

[3] "Rational Expectations and the Theory of Price Movements" *Econometrica* 29, no. 6 (1961): 315-335.

[4] *Models of Business Cycles*. Oxford: Basil Blackwell, 1987.

the future. If consumers make their current consumption decisions based on their expectation of lifetime wealth (as proposed by Milton Friedman)[5], then increased government spending would not increase current consumption. In fact, current consumption would decrease so that consumers had enough money to meet their future tax burden. Likewise, businesses would curtail investment in the face of higher future taxes. The resulting decrease in consumption and investment would offset the increase in government spending.

According to the idea of **Ricardian equivalence** put forth by Robert Barro, an increase in debt has the same effect on the economy as an increase in current taxes to pay for increases in government spending. His analysis uses rational expectation theory to show that increased debt to rational observers means higher future taxes. Rather than a large public debt being seen as a sign of an intergenerational transfer of wealth, Barro assumes that private individuals will respond to higher public debt levels with an increase in their private savings for transfer to future generations. Rational expectations theory and Ricardian equivalence fall apart if people do not care about the economic fate of future generations. Likewise, if current generations assume that future generations will be wealthier than current generations, people looking to smooth consumption over generations may deliberately choose to burden future generations with debt in order to increase current consumption.

Ricardian equivalence also negates the spending multiplier. The application of a spending multiplier to a change in government spending assumes that people believe that new spending is free. The spending multiplier promises a free lunch by boosting spending beyond the original government expenditure. In reality, there is no such thing as a free lunch. Tradeoffs exist in a world of scarce resources. Increased government spending crowds out private investment and private consumption as Chapter 18 discusses.

Under rational expectation theory, the only way that an increase in govern ment spending would cause an increase in GDP is if that government spending provided for the optimal production of a **public good** that, due to **the free-rider problem** would not have occurred without collective government action. A pure public good has two qualities. The benefits of the good are non-excludable and consumption of the good is non-rival. A good is **non-excludable** if there is no way to prevent those who do not pay for the good (free-riders) from consuming it. A good is **non-rival** if one person's consumption of the good or service does not prevent or limit another person's consumption. Left to the private market, pure public goods may be under invested in because people can still benefit from them without having to help pay for them. National defense, police, and the court system are often viewed as public goods. The problem fiscal policy is that the optimal amount of public goods provided is not always countercyclical.

[5] 1957. *A Theory of the Consumption Function*. Princeton: Princeton University Press.

Rent Seeking

It is one thing to identify that people make forecasting mistakes and another to suggest that the government is able to predict and correct these mistakes in a systematic fashion. Put another way, real market failures should not be compared to theoretical government intervention by an all knowing, all caring government. They should be compared to actual government actions complete with their own mistakes. If markets were perfect, we would not need governments. If governments were perfect, we would not need markets. The relevant question, then, is one of relative competence. This analysis is the study of **public choice**.

Is the government all knowing, all caring, and all powerful? No, no, and no. The government attempts to collect aggregate economic data to get an approximation of where the economy is. With the time lags discussed in Chapter 15, governments use fiscal policy to try and take an economy from a point where we think it was months ago to where we think we want it to be months from now. Since individuals are still in charge of most of their economic decisions, governments are incapable of knowing what is in everyone's best interest. A one size fits all government policy to affect 300 million people of varying preference and time horizons is unlikely to serve as a **Pareto improvement**. A Pareto improvement is where no one is made worse off while at least someone is made better off.

In the absence of pareto improvements, governments are left picking winners and losers for their policies. This is contrary to the assertion that governments are all caring. The question becomes who do they care more about and why? The government is not a single entity, it is made up of individual decision makers each motivated by their own interests and beliefs. Fiscal policy is made by politicians who are elected to fixed terms. Members of the US House of Representatives serve two year terms and are therefore perpetually concerned with winning an upcoming election. Because their interest in getting re-elected near term may differ from the long term interests of the economy, politicians often engage in actions that benefits today's constituents (theirs) over tomorrow's (someone else's').

Capital Building in Washington DC, close up

Government spending is done through a political process rather than an economic one. No group of government economists sits and objectively determines the best spending projects with cost-benefit analysis. Government spending disproportionately goes to states and districts of Congressional committee chairpersons and ranking members of each political party's establishment. The receipt of government largess is often more a function of Congressional tenure than of economy boosting potential. Between 1995 and 2006, Senator Byrd (D-WV) brought over $1 billion in federal funds in projects to his state such as the Robert C Byrd Bridge, the Robert C Byrd

Courthouse, the Robert C. Byrd statue, and the Robert C. Byrd Biotechnology Center.[6] As a ranking member of the Senate Appropriations Committee, Senator Byrd was able to direct spending to where it benefitted his interests the most.

Congressional interest in bringing government projects to their town districts is obvious. If politicians can be seen as delivering free goods, they often viewed as successful. After all, the taxes for the spending are spread throughout the country. This concentration of benefits and dispersion of costs allows special interest groups to also hold sway over what and how much spending occurs. In his parting address as president,[7] President Eisenhower warned of the undue influence of the industrial military complex. Certain companies benefit from war and defense spending, so they will lobby leaders to spend more on the military.

Lobbying and donating to political campaigns are done in order to influence both government spending and the tax code. **Rent seeking** is engaging in costly nonproductive actions in search of profit. Money spent on lobbying and on political campaigns represents a cost to society in forgone output, as scarce resources are directed away from production and shifted towards motivating the system to reallocate resources. The more of a society's resources they devote to taking things from each other, the less they devote to making new wealth. While taking from party A to give something to party B may improve party B's life, it comes at the cost of party A and the economy.

Fiscal policy has become increasingly concerned with income redistribution over time. The extension of unemployment benefits to 99 weeks (up from 26) has nothing to do with providing public goods or building infrastructure. It is merely an income transfer from workers to non-workers or from one special interest group to another. Increased social safety net spending and income transfers made up the majority of the 2009 stimulus package.[8] Subsidizing unemployment may make some politicians and some unemployed people feel better, but it does not stimulate production.

Because government leaders give special favors to interest groups, these interest groups are forced to compete with each other to gain politicians' favor. They hire lobbyists, pay for Congressional junkets, and try to "educate" politicians about the issues. The expenses associated with lawmaker influence erode the benefit of a government perk or contract. A firm who pays a lobbyist to get a tax break will be willing to pay up to the amount they get in the tax break in order to earn the tax break.

---

[6] "West Virginia Loves Byrd and Pork" ABC News, Imaeyen Ibanga, September 17, 2008. http://abcnews.go.com/Politics/5050/story?id=5830414&page=1

[7] "Farewell Address to the Country" January 17, 1961.

[8] "Getting to $787 Billion" *Wall Street Journal* February 17, 2009. http://online.wsj.com/public/resources/documents/STIMULUS_FINAL_0217.html

Lobbying expenses and political donations are all supposed to be reported to comply with the law. As a result, individuals can see which politicians get money from special interest groups and how much. Open Secrets.org[9] provides a database for such information. For instance, the National Association of Realtors contributed over $39 million to federal politicians between 1990 and 2010. In 2010 alone, they spent an additional $17.5 million employing lobbyists. It is not uncommon to find politicians who are in charge of writing regulations for an industry to be the primary beneficiaries of political donations by firms in that industry. Senator Barney Frank (D-MA), who co-sponsored the Dodd-Frank Financial Reform Bill, received $945,771 in political donations between 1989 and 2010 from the securities and investment industry.[10] The other co-sponsor, Senator Chris Dodd (D-CT), during the same time period received $6.4 million in political donations from the securities and investment industry.[11]

By diverting resources from the production of goods and services, rent seeking retards economic growth. There are two methods that could be used to limit rent seeking. The first is to more strictly limit the amount of money people and groups can give to the political process. It also could involve restricting the access of lobbyists to politicians. The problem with this method is that it strikes against the first amendment to the US Constitution which guarantees freedom of speech and expression. The US Supreme Court in Citizens United v. Federal Election Commission (2010) limited the government's ability to limit the inflow of money into politics.

The second and more productive way to lower rent seeking is to limit the number of special favors that the government can hand out. Simplification of the tax code, the banning of earmarks, and elimination of entitlement programs would dramatically decrease rent seeking activity. People will not pay for favors if favors cannot be granted. However, as long as the government engages in taxing and spending policies, firms and individuals can gain by tilting the rules of the game in their favor.

Not only is government neither all knowing nor all caring, they are also not all powerful. Even when governments make certain transactions illegal, they still occur. From illicit drugs to gambling to prostitution, the **underground economy (black market)** operates to provide consumers with the products they desire. Government price controls generate black markets where the prices of products reflect their relative scarcity and demand. Even in the most totalitarian of states, black markets flourish.

Furthermore, individuals can and do react to changes in government policies over time. An increase in the marginal tax rate might net positive revenues in the short run, but negative revenues in the long run, as people adjust their labor and entrepreneurial activities accordingly. As long as consumers and firms are allowed

---

[9] http://www.opensecrets.org/

[10] http://www.opensecrets.org/politicians/summary.php?cid=N00000275&cycle=Career

[11] http://www.opensecrets.org/politicians/summary.php?cid=N00000581&cycle=Career

to pursue their own interests, **the law of unintended consequences** will remain in effect. This law states that for any government policy enacted, the number of unintended consequences will exceed the intended consequences. Failure to account for the unintended consequences that result from policy actions causes policy makers to overestimate the value of their policies. The true cost of government policies includes the costs of both the intended and unintended consequences.

In summary, fiscal policy is, at best, an imperfect tool used by imperfect people in an attempt to achieve political goals of short-sighted politicians. It is not a tool that can actually bring about Pareto improvements. As such, no group appreciates fiscal policy as much as elected politicians. With it, they can reward special interest groups of their choosing. Without fiscal policy, politicians would lose a lot of their influence over the economy. While a balanced budget amendment to the US Constitution would virtually outlaw countercyclical fiscal policy, the idea has never garnered the support of Congress, whose power would be limited.

Glossary

Non-excludable—describes a good or service for which there is no way to prevent those who do not pay for it (free-riders) from consuming it

Non-rival—describes a good where one person's consumption of the good or service does not prevent or limit another person's consumption

Public choice—the study of how politicians make public policy

Public goods—goods that are non-excludable and non-rival in consumption

Rational expectations theory—introduced by John Muth, states that individuals make decisions based upon their expectation of the future

Rent seeking—engaging in costly nonproductive actions in search of profit

Ricardian equivalence—the theory that in increase in public debt has the same effect as an increase in taxes on the economy

The free-rider problem—when people can benefit from a good without paying for it, they typically fail to pay according to their consumption of the good

The laws of unintended consequences—actions always have effects that are unanticipated or unintended

Underground economy (the black market)—the exchange of goods or services in violation of government law

Questions for Review

1. Is the government all-knowing? Why or why not? How does their knowledge, or lack there-of, impact the use of fiscal policy?
2. Is the government all caring? Why or why not? Who is the government supposed to care for? Why? Who do politicians generally show care for? Why?
3. Is the government all powerful? Why or why not? Where are the government's powers best directed?
4. Which industries gave the most to the 2008 presidential candidates? (Use www.opensecrets.org to answer this question). Finance, Insurance + Real estate. others // Retired, Lawyers/Lawfirms
5. Which industries gave the most to the 2008 congressional candidates? (Use www.opensecrets.org to answer this question). ① lawyers, law firms ② Retired, ③ Securities/invest
6. Where do the politicians who support your district/state get money from? (Use www.opensecrets.org to answer this question). Yarmuth, John A (Dem) ① Kindred Healthcare ② Carpenters + Joiners
7. What can be done to decrease the amount of rent-seeking in society? Why is it important?

Chapter 20

Money and Banking

"When I was young I thought that money was the most important thing in life; now that I am old I know that it is."

— *Oscar Wilde*

"I traded a video game for three beans."

Many classic fairy tales note that the accumulation of money allows people to live happily ever after. The widow and her son, Jack, in the story *Jack and the Beanstalk*[1] were very poor. Jack was sent by his mother to the market to trade their cow for food. Instead, Jack traded the cow for magic beans which meant that Jack and his mother had to go to bed hungry. Later in the story, when Jack steals gold from a giant, he and his mother are able to live happily ever after. Neither Jack, nor his mother intended to eat the gold, and yet the mere presence of gold meant that their lives would be comfortable. In a different children's story, all of Hansel and Gretel's worries were likewise over when they returned back to their father with the wicked witch's jewels.[2]

Money might not be able to buy you love, but it can buy you a flat screen TV. This chapter will examine what an economy looks like without money, describe what constitutes money, and illustrate how money has evolved over time. It will also examine the role that banks play in monetary creation and destruction.

A Barter Economy

Money is a human invention, and as such has not always existed. People existed and engaged in economic transactions long before money came into being. Economies without money are called **barter economies**. In a barter economy people engage in economic transactions by trading goods and services directly for each other. In order for a voluntary economic transaction to occur, both parties involved in the exchange need to value the other's offerings more than their own. This act of both parties wanting what the other party is offering is known as a **double coincidence of wants**.

An economics professor would likely have a hard time generating wealth in a barter economy. What she has to offer to the market is a series of lectures regarding the interworking of an economy. If she desired pizza for dinner, not only would the economics professor need to find a pizzeria, she would have to find a pizzeria that wanted to trade pizza for an economics lecture. Likewise a shepherd would have to trade with people who wanted sheep, wool, or mutton. Wealth creating economic exchanges face high transaction costs in a barter economy. These high transaction costs discourage wealth creation. As a result, barter economies have had poor records of wealth creation. Monetary economies can overcome some of these transaction costs with the use of money.

Three Functions of Money

A **monetary economy** is an economy where goods and services are exchanged for money. Money serves three major functions in an economy. Money serves as a

[1] Benjamin Tabart. *The History of Jack and the Bean-Stalk* (1807).

[2] The Brothers Grimm. *Hansel and Gretel* (1812).

medium of exchange, a store of value, and a unit of account. If everyone wants a common asset, then that asset substitutes for the double coincidence of wants. If party A likes money and party B also likes money, then exchanges can occur without barter. Put another way, bartering still occurs, but that barter is between a good or service and money. By facilitating exchange, money acts as the grease in the wheels of an economy. A shortage of money makes transactions difficult to complete. A surplus of money means than even more of it will need to be supplied for any given transaction.

©Yellowj, 2012, under license Shutterstock, Inc.

Some people produce goods or services that create temporary wealth. A farmer who grows a tomato only creates wealth if that tomato is sold, traded, or consumed before it becomes rotten. By selling the tomato for money, the farmer is able to store his wealth in order to purchase goods or services in the future. Money only serves as a good store of wealth if the quantity of money does not increase relative to the quantity of available goods and services in the economy. If the tomato farmer sells his tomato for a ruby and tomorrow a new ruby mine is discovered that increases the number of rubies in existence, then any given ruby will be less scarce, and thus, less valuable.

When people go to the store, they like to see how much each of the items cost that they are considering buying. The price of each item is presented to them in terms of that country's money. Because money is the common denominator for economic transactions, it serves as a unit of account. All products and prices become priced according to the common money. Note that this common money may be a form of commodity money which has its own intrinsic value or fiat money that has no value other than its usefulness as money.

Commodity Money

Throughout history, societies have identified certain items that most people were willing to accept in trade. Whether that product was useful or not to one owner, if everyone else wanted it, it served as commodity money. **Commodity money** is money that has an inherent or intrinsic value. Historically, people have valued shiny metals and minerals. Diamonds, rubies, and gold have value because they are scarce and people tend to find them pretty.

Gold, silver, and to a lesser extent bronze, seashells, and tobacco leaves have all served as commodity money in different economies. In truth, any commodity or asset could be called money if large numbers of people wish to own it. Still, some commodities have been more popular than others when it comes to their use as money. For instance, gold has been a much more popular commodity money over time than have cows. The most practical types of commodity money are uniform, durable, easily divisible, have a high value to weight ratio, and are difficult for the average person to reproduce.

Fourteen karat gold is fourteen karat gold. It doesn't matter if Eon or Madison mined it. It has a uniform metallic characteristic. Diamonds are not uniform. Diamonds differ by carat, color, cut, and clarity. Rather than learn the four C's of diamonds, people just had to learn how to weigh gold to determine its value. While diamonds are durable and have a high value to weight ratio, they are not easily divisible. Unlike gold, you can't melt diamonds and then cool them to create the size you want.

Due to its relative scarcity, gold is a more popular commodity money than either silver or copper. Its value to weight ratio is much higher than the other two metals. For instance, on August 16, 2011, gold sold for $1,785 an ounce compared to $39.82 for an ounce of silver or $3.99 for an ounce of copper. A person looking to buy a parcel of land with a bag of gold was much more likely to be able to carry the necessary gold than if they had to carry the equivalent value in silver or copper. Imagine trying to carry enough pennies to buy a new Corvette!

Cows can die on their way to market, gold cannot. Porcelain china can be dropped and broken on the way to market. While gold can be dropped, you can't realistically break it such that it is of no future use. Gold too does not grow on trees, making it harder to supply more of than say, apples. Because gold has to be located and mined from the ground in an arduous process, new gold is difficult to produce. Nevertheless, when the Spanish imported massive amounts of gold from South America to Spain in a relatively short period of time, there was massive inflation.

When the United States gained its independence from Great Britain, the US set a bimetallic standard. That is, it used both gold and silver as officially recognized currency with a set price for gold in terms of silver. Fifteen ounces of silver equaled one ounce of gold. Because this was an arbitrary price of gold, only gold or silver typically was used in the US. When gold was undervalued by the official rate of exchange, people sold their gold abroad in exchange for silver and only silver coins circulated. **Gresham's Law** states that bad money drives out good. When the government increased the price of gold to sixteen ounces of silver, gold became overvalued and silver fled the country as only gold coins circulated, leaving the US with a de facto gold standard. In 1900, the US government officially adopted a gold standard. Any paper money issued by the federal government had to be redeemable by gold.

In 1933, President Roosevelt declared it illegal to hoard gold or use it as money in economic transactions. All gold deposits had to be turned over to the federal government in exchange for paper currency. While the relationship between paper money and gold was linked thereafter, it was not linked at a 1 to 1 ratio. Instead, the government increased the price of gold for international exchange purposes, as they increased the domestic money supply faster than the supply of new gold. In 1971, President Nixon ended all convertibility of US currency into gold. Later, President Ford made it legal again for private individuals to own gold. Today there is no relationship at all between the amount of gold in the US and the amount of paper money in circulation. Thus, there is not currently a gold standard in the United States.

Fiat Money

While commodity money may be bulky to handle, an additional problem with commodity money is that its supply is not constant or predictable. During early American history, the colonists faced a shortage of money. They lacked the gold and silver they needed to make monetary exchanges and therefore often had to resort to barter. The gold and silver the colonists came into was quickly used to purchase goods from Great Britain. One solution to the scarcity of money is to create an artificial, or fiat money.

Fiat money has no intrinsic or inherent value. People have no use for it apart from it being used as money. The value of fiat money is derived from faith in the government that issues the money. On each US Dollar are the words, "this note is legal tender for all debts public and private." The US Dollar is worth something not because you can eat it, smoke it, or stitch it into cloth, but because the US government says it has worth. At a minimum, the federal government says that they will accept US Dollars as payment for taxes, so people will be willing to trade goods and services for dollars because tax payment in said dollars keeps the government from taking one's other, more useful, assets.

Because the dollar is also good for all private debts, the federal government has made it illegal not to accept payment in US dollars. It is illegal to demand to be paid in gold for an economic transaction offered to the public. Because the value of a fiat currency is derived from faith that the issuing government will back up its claim as legal tender, the value of a currency is only as good as its issuing government. The value of US and Confederate dollars fluctuated daily with events of the US Civil War. Confederate dollars became worthless once the South lost. What good is a Confederate Dollar without a government to accept it as payment for taxes or enforce its use as currency? Confederate dollars ceased to have worth.

As a country runs its printing presses to increase the quantity of fiat money, more of their currency is needed to buy goods and services in the economy. When Germany printed currency following World War I to make reparations

payments, the value of the German mark went from \$1 = 4.2 marks in 1916 to \$1 = 4.2 trillion marks by 1923. A more extreme example is the country of Zimbabwe, which printed money so quickly in 2008 and 2009 that it had a 98% inflation rate *per day*. This means prices almost doubled each day. Figure 20.1 shows samples of Zimbabwean currency. Once their currency notes reached \$100 Trillion, they lopped off zeros, went back to \$100 and kept printing. Apparently they thought that a quadrillion dollar bill would have been ridiculous. Zimbabwean currency also has became worthless, except as a souvenir of a country that experienced record-breaking inflation. The willingness to hold fiat money is dependent upon peoples' faith that the issuing country will not dramatically increase the supply of the currency.

The Money Supply

The money supply is the amount of money in circulation. If a government prints more fiat currency, the money supply will go up. If it shreds currency without replacing it, the money supply will go down. Other than physically changing the amount of money in circulation, the other way to increase the money supply is to make multiple people believe they have access to the same physical dollar. Two people each having a dollar in their pocket has the same effect as each believing they have a dollar in their checking account, even if only one dollar actually exists.

Before fiat money was commonly used in the US, gold was the commodity money of choice. Many people felt unsafe storing their gold on their person or in their house, as robbers and thieves would routinely relieve people of their gold. Goldsmiths, people who turned raw gold into jewelry and golden objects, dealt with large sums of gold. As a result, they commonly owned safes and hired watchmen to protect their gold stores. People often turned to goldsmiths to store their gold for them. In return, these depositors would receive gold certificates indicating that they could redeem their certificate at the goldsmith in return for their gold. As such, goldsmiths became bankers.

Goldsmiths quickly learned that it was unlikely that everyone who paid them to store their gold would demand their gold be returned to them on the same day. Therefore, they could loan out some of the gold to other people and charge them interest. By not holding one hundred percent of deposits in their vault, goldsmiths initiated the **fractional reserve banking system**. This system allowed them to lend out part of their deposits in order to earn interest payments. Inadvertently, goldsmiths created money in the process.

The gold that goldsmiths loaned out circulated as money. So too did the gold certificates handed to gold depositors. Shopkeepers were willing to sell their wares for gold certificates because the certificates were redeemable for gold and easier to carry. Therefore, multiple people began believing they had access to the same gold, and the money supply increased. Over time banks began to make so much money charging interest on loans that they often didn't charge depositors for watching their money. Some banks even paid depositors interest to attract deposits. Still, some people still pay banks to watch valuables in safe deposit boxes.

While there are many modern definitions of the money supply, the most common is **M1**. M1 = Cash + checkable deposits. Deposits in checking accounts are counted as money because people have ready access to the money. When they look up their checking account balance online and see $1,000, they know they can purchase a good or service with a check if it costs less than that $1,000. Still, it is unlikely that their $1,000 is really in the bank. The bank loans out a majority of its deposits to earn interest, knowing that not everyone will want their money back at once. If everyone does want their money back at once, it is known as a bank run. If during a bank run a bank is unable to meet the demand for cash by depositors, it is legally forced to close. Popular representations of bank runs can be found in such movies as *Mary Poppins* and *It's a Wonderful Life*.

Bank runs and the subsequent banking panics they caused plagued the US banking system until the **Federal Deposit Insurance Corporation (FDIC)** was created in 1935. The FDIC insures peoples' bank deposits up to $250,000. That is, even if a bank makes bad loans, if it is FDIC insured, depositors are guaranteed to get their money back. This insurance put an end to bank runs. Now if everyone else withdraws their money at once, a person still will get theirs. As a result, there are no more bank runs. Savings and loan banks can also purchase insurance from the **Federal Savings and Loan Insurance Corporation (FSLIC)**. It is unwise for depositors to place large sums of money in financial institutions which do not purchase deposit insurance.

Because banks can change the money supply simply by lending out money and creating the belief among people that multiple people have access to the same physical dollar, any attempt to manipulate the money supply must also include power over banks. Chapters 22 and 23 will examine how monetary policy is conducted in the United States. The remainder of this chapter is dedicated to examining how a change in a bank's balance sheet can create or destroy money.

Table 20.1 represents a typical bank's balance sheet. **Assets** are things a bank owns. **Liabilities** are that which a bank owes. At any given time, a bank's assets must equal their liabilities. **Deposits** represent money placed in the bank by savers. This money is owed back to the depositors. **Stock holder equity** is the money a bank's owners' initially placed in the bank in order to gain a banking charter, along with any bank profit that has not been distributed to bank share holders. **Reserves** are money the bank has in its vault or on deposit with another bank. Loans are money lent to others that a bank has the legal right to reclaim. These loans include federal government bonds, since in order to gain a national charter, banks must loan some of their deposits to the federal government.

Table 20.1 **THE FIRST BANK OF TUCKER**

Assets		Liabilities	
Reserves	$ 500	Deposits	$4,000
Loans	$3,200	Stock Holder Equity	$1000
Bonds	$1,300		

Banks must hold on to a minimum amount of their deposits as reserves at all times. The reserve requirement is a function of the **required reserve ratio**, or the percentage of deposits that banks must legally hold in required reserves. If the required reserve ratio is .1, then banks must hold at least 10% of their deposits as **required reserves** at the close of every business day. Failure to do so will force a bank to close.

REQUIRED RESERVES = TOTAL DEPOSITS * REQUIRED RESERVE RATIO

Banks can choose to hold onto **excess reserves** in addition to their required reserves. In Table 20.1, assume that Tucker deposits $4,000 in The First Bank of Tucker. If the reserve requirement was .1, then the bank's required reserves are $400 (10% of deposits). Since the bank has $500 in actual deposits, they are holding $100 in excess reserves.

ACTUAL RESERVES – REQUIRED RESERVES = EXCESS RESERVES

Now assume that The First Bank of Tucker has decided to loan out all of its excess reserves. It does so by lending $100 to Colette. As it does so, now two people believe they have access to the same $100, both Colette, who has the money in her pocket, and Tucker who thinks his entire deposit is in his checking account.

Table 20.2

The First Bank of Colette		The First Bank of Oliver		The First Bank of Thatcher	
Assets	**Liabilities**	**Assets**	**Liabilities**	**Assets**	**Liabilities**
Reserves + $10	Deposits + $100	Reserves + $9	Deposits +$90	Reserves + $8.1	Deposits +$81
Loans + $90	Stock Holder	Loans + $81	Stock Holder	Loans + $72.9	Stock Holder
Bonds	Equity	Bonds	Equity		Equity

If Colette deposits the money in her checking account before she spends it, then her bank's balance sheet will change. Deposits will increase by $100. If the First Bank of Colette wants to make money and loan out 90% of its checkable deposits, then it will loan out $90 while keeping $10 in reserve.

If that $90 loan is made to Oliver, then he will have $90 in his pocket that both Colette and Tucker believe is in their checking accounts. Now three people believe they have access to the same $90. If Oliver deposits the $90 into his bank and his bank again loans out 90% ($81) to Thatcher, then yet another person will believe they have access to the same money. As long as new borrowers place their loans in their checking accounts and hold no cash while no banks hold onto excess reserves, then the resulting increase in the money supply will equal the initial increase in loans multiplied by the **money multiplier**.

THE MONEY MULTIPLIER = 1/RR.

The money multiplier represents the infinite series of changing the money supply by ever smaller incremental amounts. The money multiplier is oversimplified, because some borrowers do hold onto cash, and banks are rarely fully loaned out. However, if banks did fully loan out their excess reserves and individuals kept their money deposited in their banking institutions, then

CHANGE IN MONEY SUPPLY = CHANGE IN EXCESS RESERVES*MONEY MULTIPLIER.

In the above example, by loaning out $100, The First Bank of Tucker set in motion a chain of events that resulted in a an increase in the money supply of ($100 *(1/.1)) = $1,000.

While banks are not legally allowed to destroy legal tender, they can reduce the money supply by reducing the amount of money loaned out, thereby reducing the number of people who believe they have access to the same dollar. If The First Bank of Tucker decides that it cannot find good credits risks to loan money to, then it may decide to loan out less money. If it makes $200 in fewer loans, this sets in motion a contraction of the money supply that is greater than $200. Again, the change in the money supply will equal the initial change in loans times the money multiplier. An initial decrease in loans by $200 where the reserve requirement is .1 and all banks are fully loaned out and no one holds cash, would cause a decrease in the money supply by ($200 * (1/.1)) = $2,000.

All of a bank's loans are not immediately callable. When a borrower signs a thirty year mortgage on their house, they cannot be forced to repay the entirety of their loan at a bank's whim. However, some businesses do engage in callable loans in order to get a reduction on the interest rate they are charged. A certain percentage of all banks' loans are callable so that they can react to changing market conditions. Table 20.3 illustrates the chain of events that occurs as The First Bank of Tucker calls in $200 in loans. Colette is forced to withdraw $200 from her checking account. This causes her bank to have to call in a loan from Oliver in the amount of $180. Oliver's Bank will then have to call in $162 worth of loans from Thatcher. Thatcher's bank will have to call in $145.80 in loans, and so forth and so on until the money supply falls by $2,000.

Table 20.3

The First Bank of Colette		The First Bank of Oliver		The First Bank of Thatcher	
Assets	Liabilities	Assets	Liabilities	Assets	Liabilities
Reserves – $20	Deposits – $200	Reserves – $18	Deposits – $180	Reserves – $16.2	Deposits – $162
Loans – $180	Stock Holder	Loans – $162	Stock Holder	Loans – $145.8	Stock Holder
Bonds	Equity	Bonds	Equity		Equity

When the economy is growing and banks are making more loans, the money supply naturally increases. As banks make fewer loans due to a sluggish economy, the money supply naturally decreases. The causal relationship between the change in the money supply and the growth of the economy is a subject of debate, as previously mentioned in this text, between Milton Friedman and Friedrich Hayek. Friedman believes that a decrease in the money supply will cause a decrease in output, as fewer loans are made available to businesses. Hayek believes that the decrease in the money supply is caused by a lack of loans made by profit maximizing banks. There is no doubt that the money supply and short term Real GDP are correlated. The debate over monetary policy revolves around whether changes in the money supply will affect short term economic growth, long term economic growth, both short and long term economic growth, or neither short nor long term economic growth. Monetary policy, and its problems, are examined in Chapters 22 and 23, while Chapter 21 examines the Federal Reserve Bank of the US.

Glossary

Assets—things that are owned

Bank run—when a bank's depositors demand for the immediate return of their deposits exceeds a bank's ability to provide the cash due to the lack of liquidity in a bank's assets

Barter economy—an economy where people engage in economic transactions by trading goods and services directly for each other

Commodity money—money that has an inherent or intrinsic value derived from its use as something other than as money

Deposits—money placed in a bank by savers

Double coincidence of wants—a state where both parties engaged in a trade want what the other has to offer

Excess reserves—cash a bank holds in excess of its required reserves

Fiat money—money whose value is derived from faith in its issuing government and that has no other use than serving as money

Fractional reserve banking system—a system where banks only hold onto a portion of all bank deposits in order to loan the remainder to others

Gresham's Law—bad money drives out good

Liabilities—that which an entity owes to another

M1—a common measure of money supply measured as cash + checkable deposits.

Monetary economy—an economy that uses money as the chief medium of exchange

Money multiplier—1/rr, it represents the multiplicative power of an initial change in loans on the money supply

Required reserves—the minimum amount of cash held in a bank's vaults, defined as the amount of deposits times the required reserve ratio

Reserves—cash held in a bank's vault or in a bank's account at another bank

Required reserve ratio (rrr)—the minimum percentage of a bank's deposits a bank must hold in reserves in order to stay open

Stock holder equity—the principle put forward by a bank's owners used to open a bank plus any undistributed (possibly negative) bank profit

Questions for Review

1. What are the three functions of money?
2. What characteristics would an ideal commodity money have?
3. How does fiat money differ from commodity money?
4. Is the US dollar fiat or commodity money? Why?
5. What is M1? Why is the money supply more than currency in circulation?
6. What is a bank run? Why did they come to an end in the US?
7. How can private banks create or destroy money?
8. Why do barter economies find it difficult to grow?
9. How does changing the supply of commodity differ from changing the supply of fiat money? Under which type of money is hyper-inflation more likely? Why?
10. Use the following T account to answer:
    a. if the reserve requirement is .2, how many required reserves does the Bank of Kent have?
    b. by how much will the money supply increase if the Bank of Kent loans out all of its excess reserves (assuming no one holds cash and banks are fully loaned out)?

The Bank of Kent			
Assets		**Liabilities**	
Reserves	$ 1,500	Deposits	$6,000
Loans	$4,500	Stock Holder Equity	$1,000
Bonds	$1,000		

Chapter 21 The Federal Reserve

"Most Americans have no real understanding of the operation of the international money lenders. The accounts of the Federal Reserve System have never been audited. It operates outside the control of Congress and through its Board of Governors manipulates the credit of the United States"

— *Senator Barry Goldwater*[1]

"He who has the gold, makes the rules."

— *Alternative Golden Rule*

[1] With No Apologies (1979).

The words at the top of every US Dollar proclaim "Federal Reserve Note." The **Federal Reserve**, the **central bank** of the United States, is one of the most powerful institutions in the world. Its decisions have ramifications on inflation, unemployment, interest rates, economic growth, the value of the US Dollar, financial sector regulation and liquidity, the ability of the federal government to borrow money, and the stability of the global financial system. Unlike the US Congress which has 535 representatives, policies of The Federal Reserve are controlled by a committee of twelve people in a single board room. In other words, The Federal Reserve has "Phenomenal cosmic powers! Itty bitty living space." [2]

The Federal Reserve is not the only significant central bank in the world. Nor is The Federal Reserve the oldest central bank in the world. In fact, it is not even the United States' first attempt at a central bank. It represents the US' third attempt at central banking. Perhaps the third time is the charm? This chapter will focus on the primary functions of a central bank, the history of central banking, the structure of The Federal Reserve, and the power The Federal Reserve has to manipulate the economy.

Functions of a Central Bank

Every developed country in the world has a central bank. All central banks serve as a bank for their respective governments. When governments collect tax revenues, they must store that money somewhere. There is no mattress big enough to hold the trillions of dollars of tax revenues the US federal government brings in annually. When the government needs to engage in government spending or wishes to send people transfer payments, it writes checks out of its account at the central bank. By virtue of acting as the sole bank for a central government, a central bank needs to be larger than other banks in the country to handle the volume of transactions needed to accommodate government activity.

A central bank also serves as a source of loanable funds for a central government. The Bank of England was formed in 1694 in part to help the English government pay for war. A central bank holds deposits of other banks and therefore has reserves it can lend to the federal government. A central bank also typically can print money to loan to the government if need be. **Seignoiorage** is revenue generated by a government from printing currency that is valued more than the cost of creating it. Rather than directly raising taxes, a government can print

[2] The Genie. *Aladdin* (1992).

money for itself. However, doing so would certainly lead to inflation, thereby lowering the value of the currency held by everyone else.

Most central banks, then, also control the money supply. The fact that the US Dollar is merely a Federal Reserve note indicates that The Federal Reserve controls the money supply in the United States. While the Department of the Treasury's Bureau of Engraving and Printing physically prints US Dollars, it is the Federal Reserve that determines the amount of money that gets printed or destroyed. Paper currency routinely wears out. The average life expectancy of a US dollar is just eighteen months. By increasing or decreasing the money supply, a central bank is said to engage in **monetary policy**. Monetary policy can be used to influence inflation, unemployment, interest rates, the value of a currency, and the ability of a country to carry debt. China's Song Dynasty (960-1279) was the first central bank to use paper money to control monetary policy. Monetary policy will be examined in depth in the following chapter.

In addition to serving as a bank to the central government and directing monetary policy, many central banks, including The Federal Reserve, serve as a bank for banks. That is, it serves as a place for banks to hold deposits, it provides banks services such as serving as a clearinghouse for checks, and it serves as a lender of last resort for banks during a banking crisis. Many central banks also serve as the principle regulator of private banks in the economy. Banks are regulated to ensure that depositor's assets are not embezzled or invested in risky activities. Of course different central banks have different amounts and effectiveness of bank regulations. Some central banks, such as that in Canada, helped their country to prevent a housing bubble like that experienced in the United States by enforcing more stringent home loan practices. Alternatively, allowing banks to fail when they make "bad" loan choices would have the same effect of long run prevention of market bubbles.

History of Central Banking in the US

When America gained its independence from Great Britain, it faced the question of whether or not to create a central bank. American colonists had lived previously under the rule of the Bank of England. Dutch colonists had lived under The Netherlands's central bank, which was started in 1609. France created their central bank in 1800. Alexander Hamilton, America's first Secretary of the Treasury and a member of The Federalist Party, advocated for the creation of a central bank in the United States modeled after the Bank of England. The purpose of the bank was to help the US government to service its war debts and issue currency for the new country.

Congress charted the first central bank in the US by creating **The First Bank of the United States** in 1791. It was given a twenty year charter, which had to come before Congress to be renewed at twenty year intervals. The bank was based in Philadelphia, the nation's first capitol, with eight branches in other major US cities. Eighty percent of the $10 million in bank stock was owned by private individuals while the other twenty percent was owned by the federal government. In this way, The First Bank of the United States was a private bank. It could loan out taxpayer money, even for commercial loans, charge interest, and make profit for the private owners of the bank. Its notes could be used to pay taxes to the federal government.

When the US house voted on the charter's renewal, it was voted down by one vote. The US Senate was evenly split as to whether or not to renew the charter. Vice President George Clinton cast the deciding vote to kill the bank. Critics of the bank feared foreign influence over US monetary policy. While three-fourths of the bank's privately held shares were owned by foreigners, foreigners could not directly elect bank directors. As tensions were rising between the US and Great Britain leading up to the War of 1812, the American public was suspicious of British control of the bank. Critics also complained that the bank consolidated too much power in the hands of Philadelphia bankers. While people connected to these bankers could get loans, capital was scarce in most of country. So, the United States went without a central bank from 1811 to 1816.

Without a central bank, state banks began issuing an ever larger number of bank notes. Yet, many banks began refusing to provide specie (gold or silver) for their notes. In order to create a national currency, keep state banks in check, and help to pay down war debt, Congress chartered the United States' second attempt at a central bank in 1816.

The Second Bank of the United States, like its predecessor, was given a twenty year renewable charter. Again it was based in Philadelphia, albeit with 29 offices in other major US cities. Once again, eighty percent of the banks' shares were privately owned. With $35 million in capital, The Second Bank of the United States was a very large bank. There was less than $70 million worth of currency in the entire US at the time.

President Andrew Jackson disliked The Second Bank of the United States. He saw it as a concentration of private power that was difficult for the government to control. He made ending the bank's charter the signature theme of his re-election campaign of 1832. President Jackson started pulling federal deposits out of the bank in 1832 and worked to ensure their charter was not renewed. As a result, President Jackson had to put federal revenues elsewhere. He hand-selected what became called his "pet banks" to hold onto the federal government's money. In this way the federal government had multiple bank accounts spread throughout the country. In theory, this was done to make capital more accessible to the rural population.

Consequently, the US had no central bank from 1836 until 1913. The era between 1837 and 1863 became known as the **free banking era**. States were allowed to charter their own banks, but no national banks existed. Therefore, no banks could operate across state lines, and each state was in charge of writing their own banking regulations. Each state bank issued their own bank notes, and these notes circulated as currency within a geographical range of their bank. The further the notes circulated, the more of a discount people demanded since they must travel further to redeem the bank notes for gold or silver. By the 1960's there were over nine thousand bank notes circulating in the United States. Private banks, such as the Suffolk Bank in Boston, served as clearinghouses for state bank notes, a function once handled by The Second Bank of the United States.

In 1863 the federal government began chartering national banks. These banks could operate between states. In order to get a national bank charter, banks had to use a portion of their capital to purchase government debt. National banks only began to thrive once the federal government began to tax state bank notes. Once state banks abandoned bank notes in exchange for personal checks, their numbers began to rise. State and national banks coexisted in a dual banking system until the creation of The Federal Reserve in 1913.

During the time when there was no central bank in the US, there existed a very public political debate over monetary policy. In the absence of a central bank, the money supply changed frequently. As banks issued more or less notes and as silver flowed in from Mexico or gold from France, the money supply was anything but constant. Populist pressure to mint silver coins was brought by indebted farmers who wanted to prevent deflation and encourage inflation at the end of the nineteenth century. The book *The Wizard of Oz* is a parody of a prominent turn of the century Democratic politician named William Jennings Bryan (the cowardly lion) who wanted to expand the money supply through the printing of silver coins.

As there was no lender of last resort, bank panics, such as the ones in 1873, 1893, and 1907 put strain on the nation's banking system and on the economy. Fear that a bank could not meet the demand for specie by its depositors could cause a run on a bank. As people all at once pull their money from a bank, few banks, even those engaged in solid lending practices, have the liquidity to give everyone their money back at once. Many sound banks were forced to close due to bank runs. Bank failures decreased people's willingness to hold bank notes or store their money in financial institutions. As a result, capital became scarcer for businesses to borrow for investment. The bank panic of 1907 made many people desire a central bank to serve as a lender of last resort. In 1913, Congress chartered the third attempt at a central bank, The Federal Reserve. This time the charter was not up for renewal, though any subsequent Congress could abolish it.

The Structure of the Federal Reserve

The first two attempts at a central bank in the US were criticized for placing too much power in the hands of unelected, private eastern establishment bankers with foreign ties. In an attempt to address this criticism, The Federal Reserve Act of 1913 established twelve central banks rather than one central bank. The US was broken up into twelve districts with one Federal Reserve Bank serving as the central bank for each region. The location of the twelve banks were chosen by Congress based upon population statistics of the early 1900's and political influence of senators from particular states. The twelve cities that contain a Federal Reserve Bank are: Atlanta, Boston, Chicago, Cleveland, Dallas, Kansas City, Minneapolis, New York Philadelphia, Richmond, San Francisco, and St. Louis. Each Federal Reserve note (dollar) has written on it the name of the Federal Reserve Bank which issued it. Figure 21.1[3] illustrates the twelve districts. Each bank also has branches in other cities in their district.

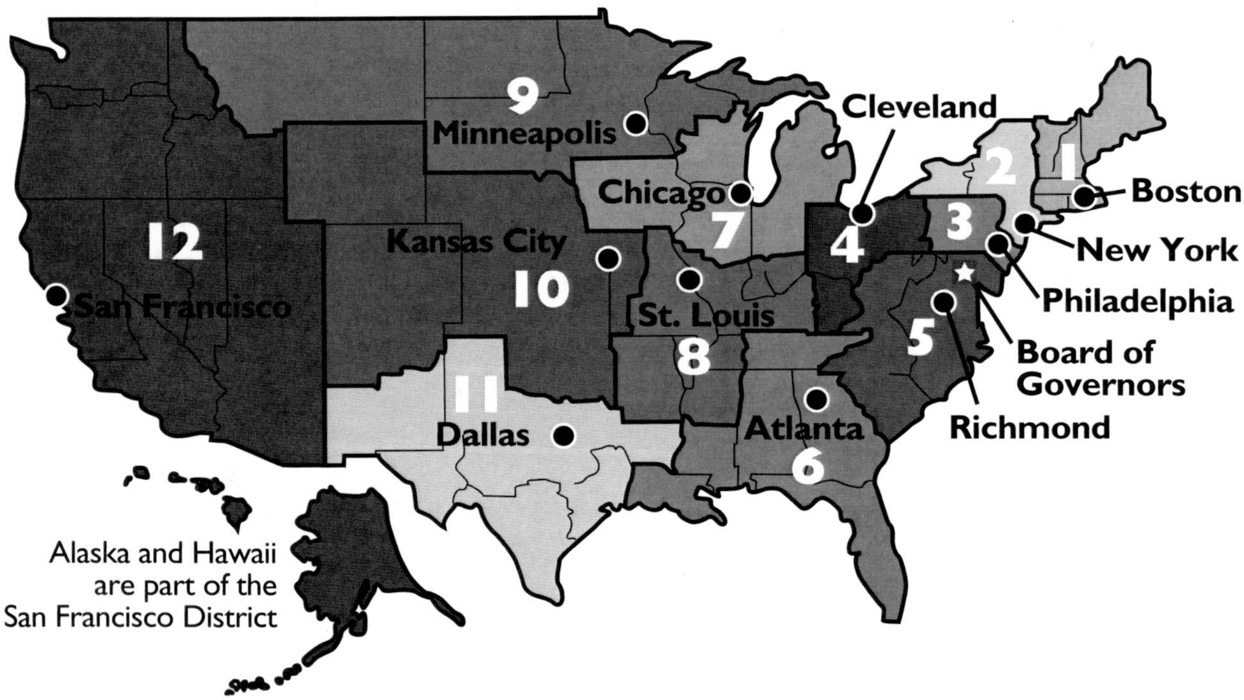

Figure 21.1

Each bank is a private corporation whose shares are owned by member banks in their district. Six of the nine bank directors are elected by the private shareholders of the bank while the other three are government appointees. The president of each Federal Reserve Bank is elected by the board of directors of each bank and is a private sector employee. Each bank serves as a lender of last resort, a check clearinghouse, and a regulator for the member banks in its district. Unlike the first two central US banks, each Federal Reserve Bank's profits are capped at a 6% annual rate of return on their assets. Profit earned above these rates must be returned to the US Treasury.

[3] http://www.federalreserveonline.org/

Originally, each Federal Reserve Bank was charged with conducting monetary policy for their district. This resulted in banks engaging in different contradictory monetary policies during the Great Depression. The New York Fed was busy increasing the money supply as the Chicago Fed was busy letting it decrease. As a result, Congress formed the **Federal Open Market Committee** in 1935 to set a single monetary policy for the United States.

The Federal Open Market Committee has 12 members. It is made up of seven presidential appointees, known as the **Board of Governors**, and five Federal Reserve Bank presidents. Members of the Board of Governors are appointed by the US president and confirmed by the US Senate to serve fourteen year terms. They are located in Washington D.C. Their terms are staggered so that one position on the Board of Governors comes open every two years. Federal Reserve Governors are limited to serving a single term, though they can fill the end of someone else's unexpired term and then serve a full term of their own. It is often the case that Fed Governors leave before their term expires because they are able to make more money in the private sector. As of August 2011, only one member of the Board of Governors had not been appointed, or reappointed, by President Obama.

Historically, members of the Board of Governors have been formally trained monetary economists, most of whom have a Ph.D. in economics. Since the beginning of the twenty-first century, this trend has changed. President Bush and President Obama often appointed governors without a Ph.D. in economics. As of August 2011, there were two longstanding vacancies on the board and only two governors with a Ph.D. in economics. President Bush whose highest degree was an MBA, appointed an MBA to the Board of Governors along with a lawyer (and son of a large campaign donor). President Obama, himself a lawyer, appointed two lawyers. Table 21.1 indicates the 2011 membership of the Board of Governors.

While all twelve Federal Reserve presidents attend the Federal Open Market Committee meetings, only five get to vote on monetary policy. The President of the New York Federal Reserve always gets to vote, as it represents the district with the largest amount of bank transaction volume. The four other spots are rotated

Table 21.1 AUGUST 2011 BOARD OF GOVERNORS

Name	Education	School	Position
Ben Bernanke	Ph.D. Economics	MIT	Chairman
Janet Yellen	Ph.D. Economics	Yale	Vice-Chairman
Elizabeth Duke	MBA	Old Dominion	
Daniel Tarullo	J.D.	University of Michigan Law School	
Sarah Raskin	J.D.	Harvard Law School	
2 Vacant Seats			

between the other eleven bank presidents. The presidents of the Chicago and Cleveland Federal Reserve Banks alternate voting membership every other year. The presidents of the other nine banks rotate voting members such that each gets to vote on monetary policy every third year.

The Federal Open Market Committee meets every six weeks to determine monetary policy, though emergency meetings can be called. The meetings are run by the Federal Reserve Chairman. The Federal Reserve Chairman is one of the Governors appointed by the President to a four year term. Current Federal Reserve Chairman, Ben Bernanke, was originally appointed to the position by President George W. Bush, and was reappointed by President Barack Obama. He was preceded by Alan Greenspan, who by virtue of filling another's expired term, was appointed or reappointed, Chairman by Presidents Ronald Reagan, George H. W. Bush, Bill Clinton, and George W. Bush. The Federal Reserve Chairman acts as the face of the Federal Reserve and testifies at least twice a year before Congress to answer questions about monetary policy. Still, they have but one of twelve votes on the F.O.M.C. and can be outvoted. Nevertheless, monetary policy is commonly assumed to be directed by the Fed Chairman. For instance, Fed Chairman Paul Volker was credited with bringing inflation under control in the early 1980's.

The 2008-2009 financial crisis brought heightened criticism to The Federal Reserve. The Federal Reserve made trillions of dollars of loans to US and foreign banks alike while working to keep the details of these loans from being made public.[4] Much like the public criticism that felled the first two central banks in the US, current criticism focuses on the secretive nature in which private banks are able to use public money to benefit private interests of their choosing.[5] The following two chapters will examine how, why, and to what end the Federal Open Market Committee conducts monetary policy.

[4] "Foreign Banks Tapped Fed's Secret Lifeline Most at Crisis Peak" *Bloomberg*, April 1, 2011

[5] "Wall Street Aristocracy Got $1.2 Trillion from the Fed" *Bloomberg*. August 22, 2011.

Glossary

Board of Governors—a 7-member board appointed by the US president and confirmed by the US Senate, based in Washington D.C. designed to provide public input into monetary policy

Central bank—a bank that serves as a bank to a central government and may serve as a lender of last resort, regulator of private banks, and a conductor of monetary policy

Federal Open Market Committee—a 12 member committee that determines monetary policy and is made up of the Board of Governors and five rotating Federal Reserve Bank presidents

Free banking era—the period of time, 1837-1863, between the end of The Second Bank of the United States and the beginning of national banks

Monetary policy—An increase or decrease in the money supply by a central bank

Seignoiorage—revenue generated by a government derived from the value of the currency being created being higher than the cost of creating the currency

The Federal Reserve—The United State's central bank consisting of 12 privately owned and operated regional banks

The First Bank of the United States—The United States' first attempt at a central bank that lasted from 1791-1811

The Second Bank of the United States—The United State's second attempt at a central which that lasted from 1816 - 1836

Questions for Review

1. What are the major functions of a central bank?
2. Who first advocated a central bank in the US? Why?
3. Why did the first two attempts at a central bank in the US fail?
4. Did the US economy cease to grow between 1837 and 1913 without a central bank?
5. What was the Federal Reserve created?
6. How does the structure of The Federal Reserve differ from the first two central banks in the US?
7. Who determines monetary policy in the US? What is the structure of the Federal Open Market Committee?
8. Why has The Federal Reserve fallen under public scrutiny in recent years?

Chapter 22 Keynesian Monetary Policy

As the previous chapter discusses, private banks trigger a change in the money supply as they increase or decrease the number of loans and consequently the amount of checkable deposits. Without outside intervention, a fractional reserve banking system can cause violent swings in the supply of money. Such swings in the money supply can affect inflation and output in an economy, both in the short run and the long run. In order to prevent large swings in the money supply, economists have advocated either eliminating fractional reserve banking or constructing a monetary authority charged with overseeing the money supply. This chapter explains what monetary policy is, describes how the Federal Reserve conducts it, outlines why many economists advocate for monetary policy, and discusses how the economy would operate in its absence.

An Economy without Monetary Policy

The United States operated between 1836 and 1913 without a central bank or monetary policy for the economy. During this time, banks engaged in fractional reserve banking, and deposits were not insured by the FDIC. While this period of time is associated with rapid economic growth and development in the US, it also contained banking panics (1837, 1857, 1873, 1884, 1890, 1893, and 1907[1]) and prolonged periods of deflation. Between 1867 and 1899 there were two years of inflation, ten years with neither inflation nor deflation, and twenty-two years of deflation.[2]

Fractional reserve banking without deposit insurance is prone to bank runs, increased failure rates of banks, and unnecessary stress on financial institutions. If fractional reserve banking was prohibited such that banks were restricted from loaning out funds in excess of those deposited, drastic swings in the money supply would be reduced dramatically. This would be the case even in the absence of a central bank. It would also work to restrict the access to credit when the economy is booming. As firms and consumers seek to borrow more for investment or consumption, they could only do so if others saved more money. This would help eliminate overconsumption and a cycle of booms and busts that result from the increases in credit access that occur with fractional banking.

The end of fractional reserve banking would also incentivize saving (through higher interest rates) and discourage credit driven consumption. The presence of private or governmentally supported bank insurance could eliminate bank runs. By ending fractional reserve banking and continuing bank insurance, the instability characteristic of the nineteenth century banking sectors could be reduced.

In a world with technological advance and economic growth, the natural state of the economy is one of mild gradual deflation. As products are produced more efficiently, the cost decreases are passed onto consumers. Recall the Quantity Theory of Money (MV=PY). If the money supply and the velocity of money are held constant over time, then an increase in RGDP (Y) will cause there to be the same amount of money chasing more goods. This will cause average prices to decline. Deflation works to discourage debt financed economic expansion. Those who take out loans must repay them with ever more expensive dollars. Advocates of a centrally controlled monetary policy often desire, and benefit from, inflation. Yet, as outlined earlier, inflation can be costly to the vast majority of society.

---

[1] Wicker, Elmus. "Banking Panics in the US: 1873-1933". EH.Net Encyclopedia, edited by Robert Whaples. September 4, 2001. URL http://eh.net/encyclopedia/article/wicker.banking.panics.us

[2] Samuel H. Williamson, "Seven Ways to Compute the Relative Value of a U.S. Dollar Amount, 1774 to present," MeasuringWorth, April 2011.

What is Monetary Policy and Why is it Often Advocated?

Monetary policy is the purposeful increase or decrease of the money supply by a central monetary authority. The Federal Reserve Act states that the purpose of monetary policy is to "promote effectively the goals of maximum employment, stable prices, and moderate long-term interest rates."[3] The goal of maximum employment was added to the act in 1977 and is referred to as the **dual mandate**. Before 1977, the Federal Reserve's stated mission was one of maintaining price stability. Unemployment and inflation are inversely correlated when aggregate demand changes. They are directly correlated when aggregate supply changes. Therefore, the only policies consistent with the dual mandate are policies that promote an expansion of aggregate supply.

Sadly, Keynesian monetary policy works to alter aggregate demand in the economy. This means that members of the FOMC must use their own discretion as to whether they are currently more concerned about unemployment or inflation. Because inflation is generally caused by central bankers, they can affect inflation much easier than they can employment. Long run inflation is solely the result of a central monetary authority increasing the money supply at a faster rate than the economy is growing.

The strategy of Keynesian monetary policy, much like fiscal policy, is to manipulate aggregate demand to get it to return to full employment. If the economy is experiencing a recessionary gap, then the goal of monetary policy is to make investment cheaper by lowering interest rates in the economy. A monetary authority can do this by expanding the money supply. This is called **expansionary monetary policy**. As the money supply increases, loanable funds increase. This means that the price of taking out a loan (the interest rate) will fall. This lowers the opportunity cost of investment. Because investment is a component in aggregate demand, as investment increases, so, too, does aggregate demand.

EXPANSIONARY MONETARY POLICY: ↑ MONEY SUPPLY => ↑ LOANABLE FUNDS => ↓ INTEREST RATES => ↑ CONSUMPTION AND ↑ INVESTMENT => ↑ AD

---

[3] Federal Reserve Act Section 2A. Monetary Policy Objectives.

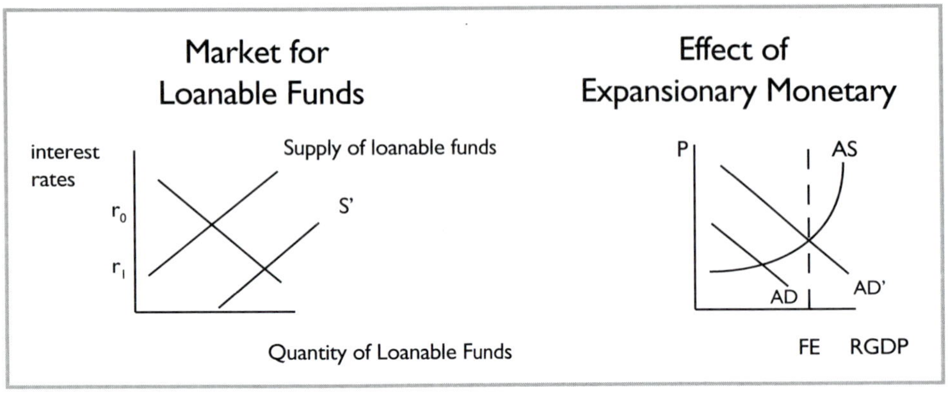

Figure 22.1 **EXPANSIONARY MONETARY POLICY USED IN A RECESSIONARY GAP**

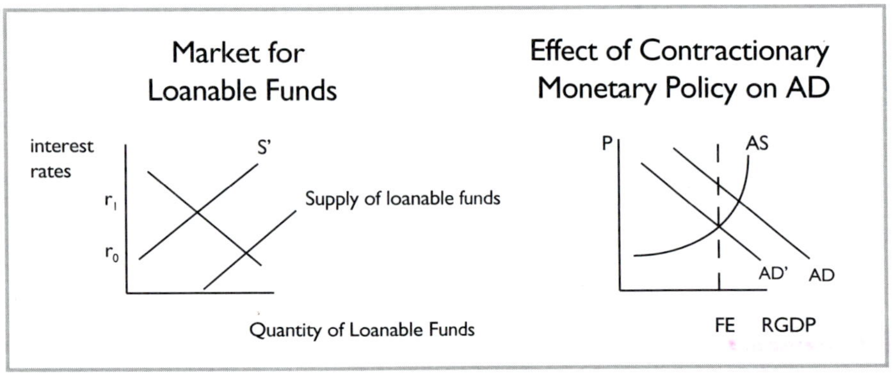

Figure 22.2 **CONTRACTIONARY MONETARY POLICY USED IN AN INFLATIONARY GAP**

If the economy is experiencing an inflationary gap, then the goal of monetary policy is to make investment more expensive by increasing interest rates in the economy. A monetary authority can do this by contracting the money supply. This is called **contractionary monetary policy.** As the money supply decreases, loanable funds decrease. This means that the price of taking out a loan (the interest rate) will increase. This increases the opportunity cost of investment. Because investment is a component in aggregate demand, as investment decreases, so, too, does aggregate demand.

CONTRACTIONARY MONETARY POLICY: ↓ MONEY SUPPLY => ↓ LOANABLE FUNDS => ↑ INTEREST RATES => ↓ CONSUMPTION AND ↓ INVESTMENT => ↓ AD

Rather than manipulating aggregate demand through changes in taxes or government spending, monetary policy's target is investment. Like fiscal policy, the use of monetary policy is complicated during stagflation. As policy makers face both high inflation and high unemployment they can choose to do expansionary monetary policy (as they did in the 1970's) to tackle high unemployment, or do contractionary monetary policy (as they did in the early 1980's) to tackle high inflation. A central bank with the sole mandate of stable prices would use contractionary monetary policy during stagflation.

Increases in aggregate supply place downward pressure on prices. If the increase in long term economic growth is slow and steady, the economy will experience low, steady deflation. Between 1940 and 2010, the US experienced only two years of deflation and no years of price stability. Throughout the other fifty-nine years the US experienced inflation. This inflationary trend is a product of the inflationary bias of the FOMC. In the summer of 2011, the FOMC debated setting an inflation target. Many members revealed that they wished to formally set an inflation target between 1.5% and 2%.[4] Over twenty central banks use inflation targeting to determine monetary policy. In so doing, central banks commit themselves to conducting both expansionary and contractionary monetary policy in such a way as to prevent both high inflation and deflation, potentially at the cost of ignoring the dual mandate of full employment.

How Does the Federal Reserve Conduct Monetary Policy?

When the FOMC meets to discuss monetary policy, their public announcement mainly consists of a specific interest rate targeted for the federal funds rate. **The federal funds rate** is the interest rate that banks charge each other to borrow money overnight. Each day some banks desire to increase their reserves in order to meet their reserve requirement or increase their excess reserves. Other banks wish to loan out some of their excess reserves. While each loan is a separate transaction, the federal funds rate is the average overnight interest rate charged by private banks. When the FOMC sets an interest rate target, it is implicitly indicating that it will increase or decrease the money supply in order to have the federal funds rate hit their target.

The FOMC cannot set interest rates by decree. They must use indirect tools to influence the federal funds rate. As a result, the actual federal funds rate often varies from the Fed's target. The New York Federal Reserve reports the daily federal funds rate history.[5] The Federal Reserve also provides a history of federal fund targeted interest rates.[6] Table 22.1 provides the federal funds rate target from July 1990 through 2011. It reveals that US monetary policy in the twenty first century has focused on keeping interest rates at historical lows. Given that the federal funds rate target cannot be negative, the FOMC reduced the federal funds rate to its lowest possible level in 2008 and has kept it there since (as of the publishing of this text). Never before in US history has the federal funds rate been so low for so long. In August, 2011, the FOMC stated it intent to keep the federal funds rate target at "exceptionally low levels…at least through mid-2013."[7]

---

[4] "Fed Officials Said to Discuss Adopting Inflation Target backed by Bernanke" *Bloomberg* June 15, 2011. http://www.bloomberg.com/news/2011-06-15/fed-officials-said-to-discuss-adopting-explicit-inflation-target.html

[5] http://www.newyorkfed.org/markets/omo/dmm/fedfundsdata.cfm

[6] http://www.federalreserve.gov/monetarypolicy/openmarket.htm

[7] http://www.federalreserve.gov/newsevents/press/monetary/20110809a.htm

Table 22.1 SAMPLE OF FEDERAL FUNDS RATE TARGETS 1990–2011

July	1990	8.00%	May	2000	6.50%
September	1992	3.00%	June	2003	1.00%
February	1995	6.00%	June	2006	5.25%
November	1998	4.75%	December	2008	0-0.25%

3 Tools of Monetary Policy

The primary tool the FOMC employs to conduct monetary policy is engaging in open market operations. **Open market operations** refers to the purchase or sale of government bonds. Recall that banks which belong to the Federal Reserve System must hold some of their assets in government bonds. When the Fed buys bonds, it gives cash to banks in exchange for government bonds. Since the banks had earned interest on their government bonds, the presumption is that they will then lend out this new cash from the sale of bonds in order to still earn interest. The Fed can't force banks to loan out the money, but if banks do increase loans, then the money multiplier can cause the money supply to increase by more than the initial purchase of government bonds. The money supply is increased both by increasing the amount of cash in circulation and through the issuance of more loans via the fractional reserve banking system.

© Zlatko Guzmic , 2012, under license Shutterstock, Inc.

When the Fed wishes to decrease the money supply, they can sell government bonds that they own to other banks. If these banks are fully loaned out, then they will have to call in loans in order to buy the government bonds at auction. This decrease in loans in conjunction with the fractional reserve banking system causes a contraction in the money supply greater than the initial sale of government bonds. Federal open market operations can only take place if a government has issued bonds. Governments with no debt cannot use a central bank to engage in open market transactions. In reality, the FOMC buys and sells government bonds on a daily basis in order to ensure that their federal funds target is being hit.

OPEN MARKET OPERATIONS FOR EXPANSIONARY MONETARY POLICY: FOMC BUYS BONDS => INCREASED MONEY SUPPLY

OPEN MARKET OPERATIONS FOR CONTRACTIONARY MONETARY POLICY: FOMC SELLS BONDS => DECREASED MONEY SUPPLY

The FOMC could employ other, less common, tools to manipulate the money supply. Serving as the lender of last resort, the Fed can loan money to member banks. The interest rate the Federal Reserve charges to these banks for overnight loans is called the **discount rate.** The discount rate serves as a penalty to banks for over-lending. If a bank cannot meet its reserve requirement they will need either to borrow money from another bank or from the Federal Reserve Bank. The higher the discount rate, the bigger the penalty banks must pay when borrowing money overnight. As the Federal Reserve raises the discount rate, banks may choose to hold onto more excess reserves to avoid having to pay the higher interest rate to the Fed. Therefore, an increase in the discount rate works to lower the money supply by discouraging loans. Likewise, a reduction in the discount rate encourages banks to lend more by reducing the penalty for over-lending, thereby causing the money supply to increase. However, because borrowing money from the Fed carries a stigma, few banks choose to borrow money directly from the Federal Reserve in normal times making changes to the discount rate largely symbolic. In other words, this tool of altering the discount rate is relatively ineffective at changing the money supply because the Federal Reserve is a lender of last resort.

ALTERING THE DISCOUNT RATE FOR EXPANSIONARY MONETARY POLICY: FOMC DECREASES THE DISCOUNT RATE => INCREASED MONEY SUPPLY

ALTERING THE DISCOUNT RATE FOR CONTRACTIONARY MONETARY POLICY: FOMC INCREASES THE DISCOUNT RATE => DECREASED MONEY SUPPLY

The Federal Reserve also controls the reserve requirement for member banks. By increasing the reserve requirement, the Fed could force banks to make fewer loans. This would cause the money supply to decrease. By lowering the required reserve ratio, the Fed would allow banks to offer more loans and increase the money supply. The Fed cannot force banks to make more loans, but they can encourage it by removing lending restrictions. In reality, the Fed rarely changes the reserve requirement because even small changes in the reserve requirement can cause large swings in the money supply. Thus, this tool is extremely powerful, but in reality rarely used for monetary policy.

ALTERING THE REQUIRED RESERVE RATIO FOR EXPANSIONARY MONETARY POLICY: FOMC DECREASES THE RATIO => INCREASED MONEY SUPPLY

ALTERING THE REQUIRED RESERVE RATIO FOR CONTRACTIONARY MONETARY POLICY: FOMC INCREASES THE RATIO => DECREASED MONEY SUPPLY

During the 2007-2008 financial crisis, the Fed created new tools to provide liquidity to the market and they began making loans to domestic and foreign commercial and investment banks. This unprecedented access to the Fed as the lender of the last resort raised many questions regarding the transparency of the Federal Reserve's business operations. These new tools include the term asset backed securities loan facility, the term deposit facility, and the decision to pay interest on bank reserves it holds. The former tool was created to provide liquidity

Table 22.2

Expansionary Monetary Policy Tools (Used to increase the money supply)	Contractionary Monetary Policy Tools (Used to decrease the money supply)
open market operations: buy bonds	open market operations: sell bonds
↓ discount rate	↑ discount rate
↓ required reserve ratio	↑ required reserve ratio

to banks that make loans to consumers and businesses. The latter two tools were designed to help the Fed lower the money supply when the time came to curtail its monetary easing.

Monetary, or quantitative, easing is the process of a central bank creating large amounts of new money and using that money to purchase government bonds. Once the F.O.M.C. had reduced the federal funds rate as much as they could, they resorted to quantitative easing to increase the money supply. Fears that such an increase in the supply of money would translate into long run inflation caused the Fed to set up tools to ensure that they could withdraw money quickly from the economy if need be. By paying interest on reserves held by the Fed, the Fed could increase their interest rates. Doing so would discourage banks from loaning out funds, as they now could instead earn higher interest rates by depositing these funds with the fed.

As the fed intervenes in the loanable funds market to meet their federal funds target, they act as a price-fixer for interest rates. Whether an institution tries to set prices for corn, apartments, prescription drugs, or for money itself, problems arise. Chapter 23 examines problems with the use of Keynesian monetary policy.

Glossary

Contractionary monetary policy—a decrease in the money supply caused by the central bank

Discount rate—the interest rate that the Federal Reserve charges to loan money to banks

Dual mandate—the Congressional law intended to force the Federal Reserve to enact monetary policy to pursue both the goals of price stability and low unemployment

Expansionary monetary policy—an increase in the money supply caused by the central bank

Federal funds rate—the interest rate banks charge each other to borrow money overnight (prime)

Monetary policy—the purposeful increase or decrease of the money supply by a central monetary authority

Open market operations—the purchase or sale of government bonds by a central bank

Quantitative easing—the creation of money by a central bank in order to purchase government bonds

Questions for Review

1. What is monetary policy? Who is it controlled by?
2. What is the primary monetary policy tool used by the Federal Reserve?
3. Under which economic situation would a central bank undertake expansionary monetary policy?
4. Under which economic situation would a central bank undertake contractionary monetary policy?
5. What happens to loans, the money supply, interest rates, and investment if the Fed buys bonds?
6. What happens to loans, the money supply, interest rates, and investment if the Fed sells bonds?
7. What are the three possible Keynesian monetary policy tools used in a recessionary gap?
8. What are the three possible Keynesian monetary policy tools used in an inflationary gap?
9. What are the three possible Keynesian monetary policy tools used during stagflation? What does your answer to this question depend upon?
10. Why has deflation virtually disappeared in the US? Is this a natural phenomenon? Why or why not?

Chapter 23

Problems with Monetary Policy

"There's an old saying in Tennessee – I know it's in Texas, probably in Tennessee – that says, fool me once, shame on – shame on you. Fool me – you can't get fooled again."

— *President George W. Bush*[1]

[1] Speech September 17, 2002. Nashville, Tennessee.

Monetary policy, by its nature, attempts to fool people into believing that they are richer or poorer than they actually are. If wealth were actually created by printing fiat currency, Zimbabwe would be the richest country in the world and post WWI Germany would have had a thriving economy. The simple fact is that if a central bank increases the money supply, there are more dollars chasing the same number of goods. There are more dollars, but each dollar is worth less. Likewise, if a government burns fiat currency, no wealth is lost. It is just redistributed from the owners of the burned currency to the owners of the remaining fiat currency. This chapter examines the theoretical and practical problems associated with Keynesian monetary policy.

Time lags

Monetary policy faces the same three time lags as fiscal policy: the recognition lag, the policy lag, and the implementation lag. Policy makers at the Federal Reserve are not clairvoyant. They make their monetary policy decisions based on data gathered from the past. Unemployment and inflation data are reported monthly, but recognizing trends in unemployment and inflation requires months of data. While the recognition lag for monetary policy is the same as that of fiscal policy, the policy lag tends to be shorter for monetary policy. Rather than engage in partisan brinksmanship, members of the FOMC meet over a two day period every six weeks to discuss and vote on monetary policy.

The implementation lag, however, can be longer for monetary policy than for fiscal policy. While the FOMC immediately can target a new federal funds rate following a meeting, the effects of this policy are often not felt in the economy for eight months or so. Firms cannot instantaneously invest in new plants and equipment. Once interest rates are changed, boards of directors of firms have to take time to decide how the new interest rate environment affects their short and long term investment strategy. If the change causes them to invest more or less, this too takes time to implement. To build a new factory, a firm will have to hire an architect, hire a construction manager, send construction specs out for bids, and physically engage in construction. The act of paying construction workers and paying for supplies could only have a multiplicative effect on the economy over time, as construction workers buy more as a result of their employment. If the construction workers believe that today's investment comes at the cost of future investment, they might spend and save according to what they believe is their permanent income.

Slowed Long Term Growth

Just as in the case of fiscal policy, the monetary policy works by making people feel more or less wealthy, even if real wealth hasn't changed. If the Federal Reserve can increase the money supply without people realizing it, then people may temporarily feel wealthier. However, as more dollars start chasing after the same number of goods, sellers will increase their prices accordingly. Recall the Quantity Theory of Money, MV=PY. An unexpected increase in the money supply could temporarily boost RGDP, but will not increase long run RGDP. Instead, it will cause inflation. If people know that the Fed is increasing the money supply, they will rationally adapt their behavior by quickly raising prices. This will reduce any possible impact of monetary policy on short run RGDP. Since monetary policy goals, (such as the targeted federal funds rate or amount of quantitative easing), are publicly announced, effective monetary policy relies on the hope that people are not paying attention to or do not understand the long run consequences of these actions.

The lower interest rates accompanying expansionary monetary policy are meant to encourage current investment. While current investment is cheaper than it would otherwise be, it comes at a cost. Low interest rates discourage savings. Long term economic growth is a function of a country's ability to save and invest. While foreign savings can be turned into domestic investment, the profits of that investment will flow abroad to the savers. Since investment in new capital is a long run consideration due to the long lifespan of new capital, the decision to move investment forward often comes at the cost of less investment later.

Inefficiencies Created when Targeting Price Stability

Further, if monetary policy is accompanied by laws and regulations that prohibit changes in prices, economic chaos ensues. During the Great Depression, The Federal Reserve allowed the money supply to fall 33%. Such a dramatic and unexpected decrease in the money supply, accompanied by unions and minimum wage laws preventing nominal wage reductions, worked to slow the market's ability to quickly lower prices in response to the lower money supply. Artificially higher wages worked to keep the unemployment rate abnormally high for years.

In the 1970's, Presidents Nixon and Carter enacted price controls in an attempt to offset inflation caused by expansionary monetary policy. These price controls led to shortages, rationing of goods, an increase in black market economic activity, and market distortion as resources flowed from price controlled industries to those industries which were unaffected by the price controls. Any attempt to fix prices not only misallocates resources, it slows long term economic growth.

Prices, even average ones, are signals. Should price stability be a legitimate goal for the Federal Reserve (or any central bank)? Consider this: should the government be in charge of creating price stability for automobiles? When the price of autos increase, should the government increase the supply of autos? When the price of autos falls, should the government buy up automobiles on the open market? After all, the government (i.e. taxpayers) owns a car company (GM) and could manipulate the equilibrium price of automobiles.

Why might the government like price stability in cars? You could argue that producers could better plan production if they knew in advance what their cars would sell for. Consumers might be able to better plan their car purchases as well. So what is the problem? By masking real prices, the government covers up information from market actors. Prices aren't arbitrary or meaningless. The price of every product is a little piece of information telling the market how to efficiently allocate resources.

Does the government know better than the market how to allocate resources in the car (or for that matter any other) industry? History tells us that centrally planned economies fail in part because planners lack information. Hayek's "man on the street"[2] is the guy with information, and he uses this information he sees from prices to make decisions to maximize his own self-interest. An ill-informed central planner setting prices will cause surpluses and shortages of products they misprice.

If the government cannot set the prices of individual goods any better than markets, then why should we believe that a central bank can set average prices better than the market? There is an aggregation problem here. Setting one price is bad; setting two prices is bad; setting three prices is bad; setting all prices is good?

What could possibly go wrong if a central bank used activist monetary policy to achieve price stability at the cost of ignoring market signals? During the 1990's and into the 2000's, many developing economies increased their ability to export cheap consumer goods to the US and other industrialized markets. All things being equal, this placed deflationary pressure on consumer prices in the US. In absence of activist monetary policy, the US would have experienced deflation as measured by the consumer price index. What the US experienced instead was a Federal Reserve increasing the money supply to prevent deflation.

There are three major questions to examine from this experience. Firstly, what signals were deflation trying to give the US economy? Secondly, what signs did the Fed give the economy instead? Thirdly, what were the consequences of getting our signals crossed?

Pretend that the US money supply was held constant while cheap consumer goods flooded the US market. The US would have the same amount of money chasing more goods, i.e. deflation in the short term and a reduction in real GDP in the long term. In the short term, deflation causes consumers to cut back on consumption. Why buy today if stuff is cheaper tomorrow? Thus, the market's natural response to an increased trade deficit would have been an increase in domestic savings and a reduction in said trade deficit.

---

[2] F.A. Hayek "The Use of Knowledge is Society" *American Economic Review* XXXV, No. 4.519-30

Being overly scared of deflation, the Fed kept their foot pressed down on increasing the money supply to generate a positive rate of inflation. In so doing they took interest rates to historically low levels. These low interest rates acted as signals to consumers, businesses, and the government that borrowing was unusually cheap. The result was an unprecedented increase in consumer, business, and government borrowing. This borrowing increased the current demand for foreign goods, driving up the US trade deficit, and destabilizing the international economic system.

When the proper response was to increase savings rates, the Fed put up street signs that said borrow as fast as you can. In so doing the Federal Reserve aided the creation of asset bubbles and sowed the seeds of the global financial meltdown. Had the Fed allowed the market to naturally read the deflationary signs, the financial crisis could have potentially been avoided.

The moral of the story is that average prices are just as much signals to the macro economy as individual prices are to the micro economy. To think that the government or a central bank has more information than the economy on what the "right" prices are is a stretch. Capitalism works best when prices are set by markets, not central planners.

The FOMC's control over the federal funds rate serves as a de facto price control for loanable funds. Like other price controls, it misallocates resources from one industry to the next and from one year to the next. If loans are made artificially cheap, then businesses and consumers are enticed to engage in an above normal amount of new investment and consumption. A period of prolonged artificially low interest rates, as seen in the early 2000's, can lead to a glut of investment in new homes or capital. Overinvestment is followed by a reduction in investment spending in later years, as consumers work to pay off higher levels of debt and businesses try to sell their unsold inventories. Similarly, artificially high interest rates, such as those put in place by the Bank of England in the 1920's, can cause new net investment to come to a virtual halt.

Liquidity Trap and Increased Volatility

Monetary policy which seeks to centrally direct investment through time often works to increase the volatility of investment from one year to the next, thereby creating business cycles. Monetary policy makers often attempt to fight fire (business cycles) with fire (creating investment cycles). Their hope is that they can correctly predict the appropriate amount of aggregate investment that is needed in the economy at any given time. Still, individual investment decisions are only profitable if their marginal benefits exceed their marginal costs. If the Fed thinks that the economy should have more aggregate investment and this causes condo builders to build condos they will not be able to sell in Las Vegas, then the resources used in that investment are not only wasted, they become unavailable for other productive uses in the economy.

The FOMC, by selling government bonds, can readily get banks to call in loans and lower the money supply. Paul Volker, Fed Chairman in the early 1980's, was able to quickly reduce the money supply and subsequent inflation. When the Fed pays more for government bonds, banks are able to increase their rate of return for risk free assets. The Fed cannot force banks to make more new loans regardless of how many bonds it buys. Banks may choose to increase their excess reserves in response to expansionary monetary policy. The Federal Reserve's inability to get banks to issue new loans during an economic slowdown has often been described as the Fed "pushing on a string." John Maynard Keynes referred to monetary policy's inability to force banks to make more loans during a recession as a **liquidity trap**.

Because the Federal Reserve cannot force private banks to make more loans, it becomes difficult for the FOMC to correctly estimate the amount of monetary policy they wish to engage in. The FOMC has drawn criticism for causing business cycles by rapidly changing the federal funds rate, or keeping it artificially low or artificially high for long periods of time. The inflationary gap of 2000 quickly became the recession of 2001, as the FOMC raised the federal funds rate up to 6.5% in May of 2000. To counteract the recession, the FOMC lowered the federal funds rate down to 1.75% by December, 2001 and kept it below 2% until November 2004. The housing asset bubble ensued.

Biases of Central Bankers

Central banks face choices. Do they engage in inflation targeting, interest rate targeting, or money supply targeting? Inflation targets ensure that a central bank will increase the money supply to prevent natural deflation, but hopefully not so much as to be above their target inflation range. The bias of central bankers to avoid deflation often means that inflation targeters are more likely to miss their inflation targets to the upside rather than the downside. John Taylor developed the **Taylor Rule** as an attempt to direct monetary policy based upon changes in inflation rates.[3]

Interest rate targets require the central bank to know what the "appropriate" interest rate is. Price fixing requires an almost infinite amount of information, unless policy makers are content to cause shortages or surpluses in the loanable funds market. Monetarists prefer to focus on money supply targets. Over time, by increasing the money supply by a fixed amount each year, they aim to control long run inflation which could occur from interest rate targeting. Strict adherence to a monetarist rule could cause swings in inflation, deflation, and interest rates in the short run. Those who advocate a gold standard reduce swings in prices, interest rates, and the money supply to the chance increase in the supply of gold. But

[3] Taylor, John. (1993). "Discretion versus Policy rules in Practice." *Carnegie-Rochester Conference Series on Public Policy,* 39. 195-214

even this can have devastating effects, as Spain saw when it suffered large inflation rates with the influx of gold from the Western Hemisphere.

The FOMC, like all other economic actors, faces tradeoffs. Its dual mandate to fight both unemployment and inflation can cause conflict between the two goals. The members of the FOMC decide which problem they wish to attempt to solve. When a single President, due to resignations by members of the Board of Governors, ends up selecting the majority of Fed governors, monetary policy becomes less independent of the political system. Historically, politically influenced banks have tended to prefer pro-inflationary policy in an attempt to lower short term unemployment. The result has been high inflation rates in many developing and under developed countries in South America, Central America, and Africa. Independent central banks have fared much better at maintaining price stability over time.

Independent central banks can be restrained in their use of monetary policy by politicians who issue public debt denominated in their fiat currency. Excessive amounts of public debt can slow down economic growth as a greater number of productive resources are tasked with making interest payments on existing debt. This economic slowdown would likely reduce employment and/or cause deflation. A central bank which is concerned with unemployment and deflation may feel the need to engage in expansionary monetary policy in an attempt to stabilize output, employment, and prices. Deflation increases the burden of existing debt. The central bank of a heavily indebted country has an incentive to **monetize** the debt by expanding the money supply, thereby making public debt easier to repay.

Bank independency and transparency to the public can be opposing goals. Serving as a lender of last resort allows The Fed to provide liquidity to banks when they are in need of it. However, public disclosure that a bank needs help from the Fed can reduce the confidence the public has in the bank and thereby exacerbate its liquidity problem. On the other hand, the lack of transparency can allow The Fed to make loans to foreign banks despite opposition by the general public. Bank independence helps to keep politicians from inflating the currency, but also allows the bank to secretly engage in actions that politicians, and the public, may find objectionable without being held to account for their actions. If the actions of a central bank become known to be at odds with the will of the public, a central bank may be forced to submit to political, and often inflation causing, oversight. In the end, central bank independence is a double-edged sword.

Because countries have different fiat currencies, their relative values are affected by the respective monetary and fiscal policies adopted by central banks and governments. Central banks may make their choice of monetary policy based upon a target exchange rate with other currencies. By so doing, central banks can face tradeoffs between domestic monetary policy and stated international monetary policy goals. As long as the US remained on an international gold standard, domestic monetary policy was constrained. Chapter 24 examines how currencies' values can change relative to each other. Chapter 25 explains how monetary and fiscal policies effect and are affected by the presence of the international sector.

Glossary

Debt Monetization—an increase in the money supply used to decrease the relative burden of existing public debt

Liquidity Trap—when during a deep recession, expansionary monetary policy is unable to force banks to make more loans due to their lack of business confidence

Taylor Rule—a monetary policy rule designed to have monetary policy respond to changes in inflation and output

Questions for Review

1. How might monetary policy increase the size of business cycles?
2. Why might an economy face a liquidity trap?
3. Why does contractionary monetary policy often work more quickly than expansionary monetary policy?
4. How are interest rate targets similar to price floors and price ceilings?
5. Why might independent central banks have better records of low inflation than politically controlled central banks?
6. How can fiscal policy constrain a central bank's use of monetary policy?
7. Is the Federal Reserve completely independent of political influence? Why or why not?
8. In what ways does central bank transparency help/hinder their role in the economy?

Chapter 24

Exchange Rates

© kentoh, 2012, under license Shutterstock, Inc.

How Much is a Dollar Worth?

That may seem like a silly question. A dollar is worth a \$1, four quarters, ten dimes, twenty nickels, or one hundred pennies. However, the purchasing power of the dollar can, and does, change over time. Products once sold at the dime store are now sold at the dollar store. The previous chapters have examined how monetary policy can increase or decrease the purchasing power of a dollar relative to domestically produced goods and services.

Still, the US economy is an integrated part of the world economy. Consumers buy products made in other countries. They also vacation abroad. Producers sell products abroad that are produced domestically and purchase inputs from abroad to be used in domestic production. While the dollar serves as a medium of exchange, a store of value, and unit of account for goods and services within the US, other countries have different currencies that do the same for goods and services exchanged in their borders. Just as the value of the dollar can change relative to domestic goods and services, it can also change relative to the value of other currencies. This chapter examines the causes and effects of international exchange using multiple currencies. It also examines the European Union's transition to a common currency.

Floating Exchange Rates

An **exchange rate** is the price of one currency in terms of another. A **floating exchange rate** is where the value of a currency is determined by the supply and demand of that currency on the international money market. Most major world currencies have floating exchange rates. The value of the US dollar fluctuates on a daily basis against other major world currencies such as the Yen (Japan's currency) and the Euro (The European Union's currency) as people voluntarily trade once currency for another. Table 24.1 illustrates how the value of the US dollar changed over a one year period of time.

A currency **appreciates** (becomes stronger) when it can buy more of another currency. Between August 2010 and August 2011, the US dollar appreciated vs. the Argentine Peso. A dollar could buy more pesos in 2011, than it could in 2010. That means that goods and services denominated in Argentine Pesos became cheaper for American consumers and producers to purchase. It also meant that goods and services denominated in US dollars became more expensive for people in Argentina to buy.

In a floating exchange rate regime, as one currency appreciates against another, the second currency is said to depreciate against the first. A currency **depreciates** (becomes weaker) when it can buy less of another currency. Between August 2010 and August 2011, the US Dollar depreciated vs. the Japanese Yen, The Euro, the Chinese Renminbi, the British Pound, the Canadian Dollar, the Australian Dollar, the Swiss Franc, and the Mexican Peso. As a result, it became more expensive for people holding US Dollars to buy goods and services from these countries, while it became cheaper for people holding these currencies to buy goods and services denominated in US Dollars.

Table 24.1 **CURRENCY UNITS PER $**[1]

Country	August 10, 2011	August 10, 2010
Japan	76.5	85.3
China	6.42	6.78
Britain	.62	.64
Canada	.99	1.05 (1.28 in March 2009)
Euro area	.71	.78
Switzerland	.73	1.06
Australia	.98	1.11
Argentina	4.16	3.93
Saudi Arabia	3.75	3.75
Mexico	12.2	12.8

Which is better, a stronger or a weaker dollar? It depends. A strong dollar is good for people who are net importers or people who own assets denominated in US Dollars. If a person holds the majority of their wealth in their home in the US, or in the US stock and bond markets, then a stronger dollar increases their wealth relative to people in other countries around the world. People who store all of their wealth in a single currency open themselves up to major swings in their wealth over time. Businesses that purchase inputs from abroad face a decreased cost of production when the value of the dollar increases.

A weak dollar is good for people who are net exporters or who store their wealth in assets denominated in foreign currency. US farmers and manufactures looking to sell their products abroad find that foreign consumers can more readily afford their products when the value of the US declines. This, in turn, drives up the demand for their products. People who store their wealth in foreign currencies can, when the value of the dollar falls, convert their savings back into dollars. By so doing, they can purchase more dollar denominated assets than they could do when the value of the dollar was stronger.

The relative supply and demand of the dollar to the international money market determines the value of a dollar on any given day. In reality, the dollar can appreciate vs. one currency while it depreciates vs. another on the very same

[1] Source: *The Economist* http://www.economist.com/node/21525955

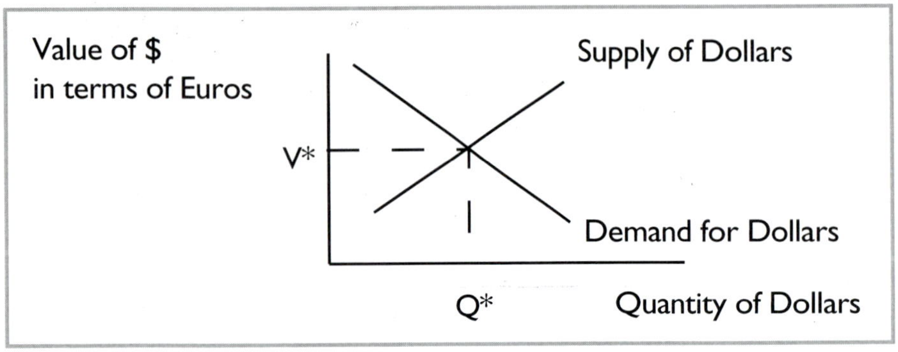

Figure 24.1 **DOLLAR TO EURO EXCHANGE MARKET**

day. This is because there is not just one currency market but many. The US Dollar is traded against each floating currency in its own market, just as each foreign currency is traded one on one with all other floating currencies. Figure 24.1 illustrates the demand and supply of the US Dollar vs. the Euro. The value of the US Dollar fluctuates against the Euro based on changes in the supply or demand of the US Dollar in the Dollar/Euro market.

Things that Cause the Demand for the Dollar to Change

Why would people suddenly, or over time, want to buy more or fewer US Dollars on the international market? To begin with, there could be a change in the demand for US goods and services. If foreigners decide that they want to buy more American made jeans or American grown wheat, they first must buy US Dollars and then they can use dollars to purchase those products. Farmer Ron growing wheat in Minnesota is not looking to get paid in Euros for his wheat. He wants to get paid in US dollars. An increase in the demand for US made goods and services abroad, including foreigners vacationing in the US, will cause the demand for the US dollar to increase, thereby causing the dollar to appreciate. A decrease in the demand for US made goods and services abroad will cause the demand for the US dollar to decrease, thereby causing the dollar to depreciate.

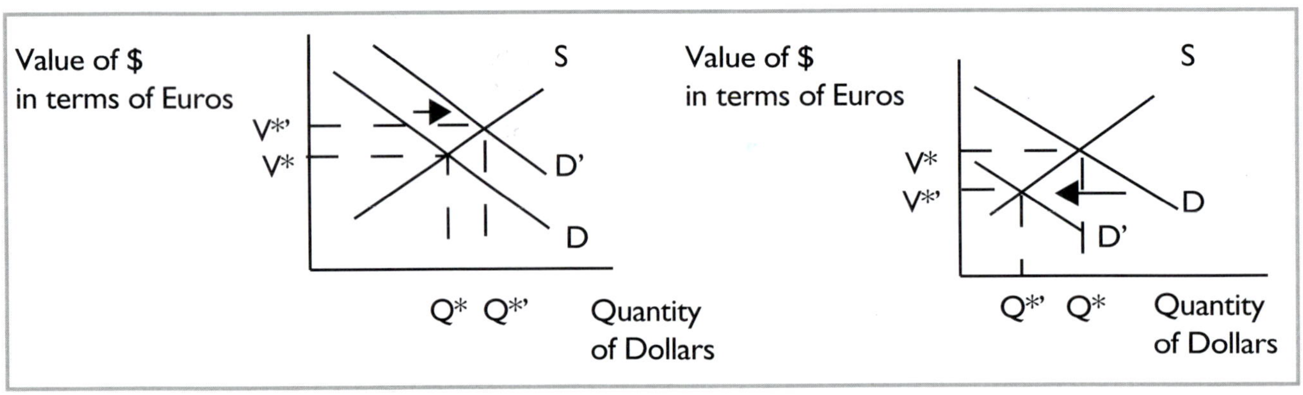

Figure 24.2 **DOLLAR – EURO EXCHANGE MARKET WITH INCREASED AND DECREASED DEMAND FOR THE DOLLAR**[2]

[2] D represents the initial demand for US Dollars, while D' represents the new demand for US dollars. S represents the supply of US Dollars to the Dollar/Euro exchange market.

A change in demand for US financial assets, such as stocks listed on the New York Stock Exchange (NYSE) or US government bonds, will cause the demand for the US Dollar to change. If people who hold foreign currencies decide that they wish to buy a share of General Electric (GE) on the NYSE, they must first buy US dollars and then purchase stock with those dollars. US stocks are not sold in exchange for Euros. When the US government runs a budget deficit and needs to borrow money, they need to borrow dollars, not Euros. Therefore, foreigners who buy US government bonds must first buy US dollars. This increases the demand for US dollars.

A change in demand for US hard assets will cause the demand for the US dollar to change. If foreign persons or businesses start buying US real estate, they must pay for their purchases in US dollars. The same thing is true for any dollar denominated asset such as a business or patent. An increase in the demand for Florida vacation homes by foreigners will cause the demand for the dollar to increase, thereby causing the dollar to appreciate. A decrease in the demand by foreigners for US real estate will lower the demand for the dollar, thereby causing the dollar to depreciate.

Finally, people in other countries may prefer to use US Dollars to engage in economic transactions between themselves. They may choose to do so if they lack confidence that their domestic currency will serve as a good store of value. Citizens of countries with high inflation rates in their domestic currency may seek to engage in transactions using a more stable currency. Two-thirds of all US Dollars in circulation are in circulation outside of the US. This is a sign that many people around the world value the US Dollar as a medium of exchange, a store of value, and a unit of account. When confidence in foreign currencies fall, the demand for the US Dollar increases. This causes the US dollar to appreciate. When foreign currencies gain people's confidence, then the demand for US Dollars falls, causing the dollar to depreciate. Taken together, these four factors work to change the demand for the dollar on a daily basis.

Chart 24.1 FACTORS WHICH ALTER THE DEMAND FOR AND SUPPLY OF US$
1. Changes in the demand for exports/imports
2. Changes in the demand for US financial assets and financial assets abroad
3. Changes in the demand for US hard assets and hard assets abroad
4. Changes in confidence in the US$ as a store of value

Things that Cause the Supply of the Dollar to Change

In order to buy more of one currency, one must, by definition, supply more of another currency to the market. Therefore, the things that cause the demand for a currency to change also affect the supply of a foreign currency. Conversely, the things that cause the supply of the US dollar to change are the same as those that cause the demand for foreign currencies to change.

The supply of dollars to the international money markets will change as there are changes in the demand for foreign goods and services, the demand for foreign financial assets, the demand for foreign hard assets, and the confidence in the US dollar. If people who hold dollars want to travel abroad more, consume more imports, invest more in foreign stock markets, bond markets, or real estate, or if they lose confidence in the US Dollar as a safe store of wealth, they will supply more dollars to the international money market. This will cause the value of dollar to depreciate.

If however, US consumers decrease their desire to travel abroad, begin to consume fewer imports, want to invest less in foreign stock markets, bond markets, or real estate, or gain confidence in the US dollar as safe store of wealth, they will supply fewer dollars to the international money market. This will cause the value of the dollar to appreciate. Figure 24.3 Illustrates an increase and a decrease in the supply of dollars to the Dollar/Euro exchange market.

Changes to the Value of a Currency Over Time

A number of actions could cause the supply or demand for a currency to change on a daily basis. In the short run, the single largest factor affecting exchange rates are relative interest rate changes between two countries' currencies. Billions of

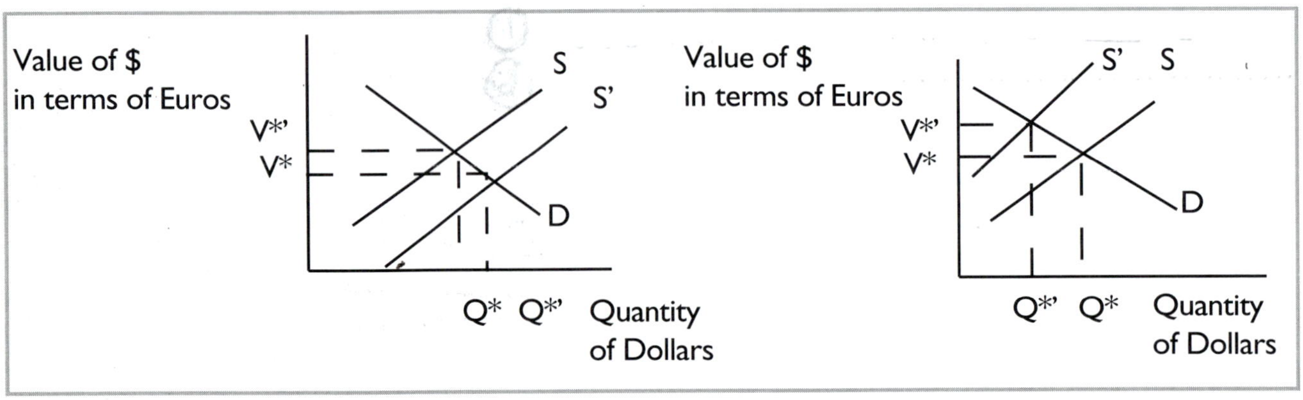

Figure 24.3 **DOLLAR – EURO EXCHANGE MARKET WITH INCREASED AND DECREASED SUPPLY OF THE DOLLAR** [3]

[3] S represents the initial supply of US Dollars, while S' represents the new supply of US dollars. D represents the demand of US Dollars to the Dollar/Euro exchange market.

dollars worth of currencies change hands on any given day. People who hold on to cash would like to earn a positive rate of return on their cash holdings. In this way, money tends to flow to currencies with higher interest rates. If country A is paying a 3% interest rate on savings accounts while country B is paying only 1%, then, all things being equal, savers will prefer to save their cash in a currency that yields them a higher interest rate. In this case it would be country A. If the central bankers in one country lower interest rates, then the value of their currency is expected to fall. That currency serves as a less good store of wealth with a lower interest rate. Conversely, if the central bank raises interest rates, then the value of their currency is expected to increase. The decline in the value of the US dollar observed in Table 24.1 was in part due to the divergence of interest rates in the US and the rest of the world. The Federal Reserve sought to keep interest rates at near zero during this time. In the short run, a strong dollar is a sign of higher than average interest rates.

In the medium run (one to three years), changes in the relative demand for domestic vs. foreign goods and services tend to explain changes in exchange rates. As Japanese automobile sales to the US have increased over time, the value of the Japanese Yuan has also increased. As Americans demanded more foreign products, they supplied more dollars to the international market and demanded more Yen. This caused the value of the dollar to fall vs. the Yen. In the medium run, a strong dollar is a sign of strong demand for US goods and services.

In the long run (more than three years), purchasing power parity is the best explanation of which direction an exchange rate is headed. **Purchasing power parity** is the concept that all goods should cost the same in every country in the long run. If a good costs more in one country than the next, and goods are allowed to move between countries at low cost with little to no trade barriers, then arbitrage will reduce or eliminate price differences. **Arbitrage** is taking advantage of price differences for profit. If a product is cheaper in Canada than in the US, then people will buy the good in Canada, transport it to the US and resell it for a profit. This action will continue until the price of all products is the same (minus transportation or tariff costs). As this international trade happens, currencies are supplied and demanded until the exchange rate is such that prices in each country are the same.

The Economist magazine for years has published an index of purchasing power parity known as the Big Mac Index.[4] It looks at the price of McDonald's Big Macs in different countries and tries to predict whether currencies are currently undervalued or overvalued relative to the US dollar. If a currency is undervalued, it means that the currency is expected to appreciate over time vs. the dollar. If a currency is overvalued it means that the currency is expected to depreciate over time vs. the dollar.

[4] Source: *The Economist*. http://www.economist.com/node/21524811

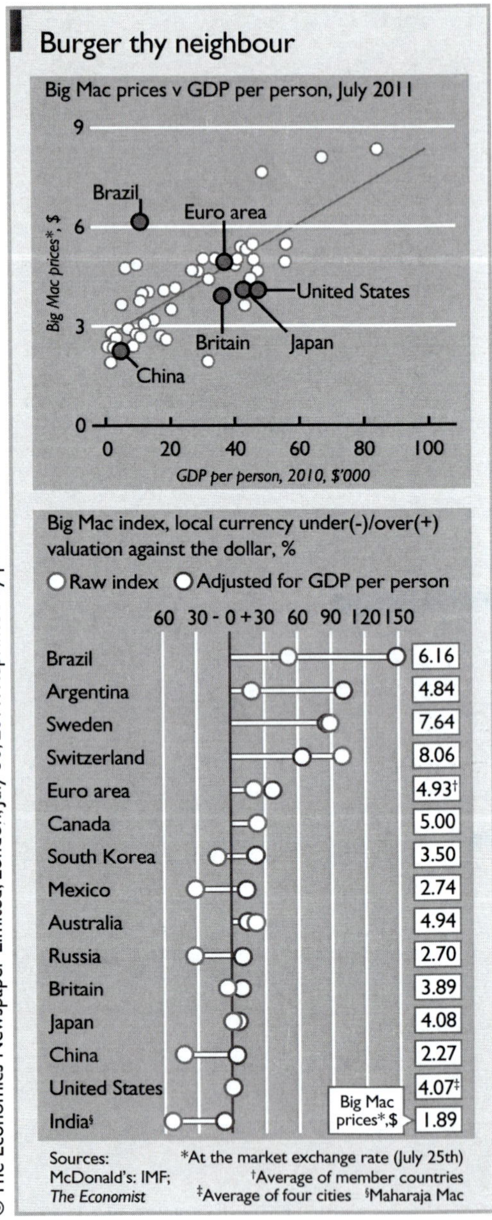

Figure 24.4

If the current price of a Big Mac is $3 in the US and 2 Euros in France, while the current exchange rate is $1 = .75 Euros, then the Big Mac Index can be used to determine whether the Euro is under or overvalued vs. the dollar. If instead of spending $3 on the Big Mac in the US, one were to convert the currency to Euros, one could purchase 2.25 Euros (3 times the exchange rate). That is more than enough Euros to buy a Big Mac in France – only two were needed. In this case the US Dollar is buying too many Euros. The US dollar, in this case, should depreciate vs. the Euro over time until the exchange rate falls to $1 = .67 Euros – the relative price difference between the Big Mac in each country.

Figure 24.4 reports *The Economist* Big Mac Index for July, 2011. Once GDP per person is controlled for, the Big Mac Index suggests that the US dollar was undervalued vs. virtually every other major world currency. It was most undervalued against the Brazilian Real. Brazil's head of their central bank went on the record to complain that the Federal Reserve's policy of quantitative easing and low interest rates was artificially causing the Dollar to depreciate vs. the Real.[5]

Fixed Exchange Rates

Rather than letting the international currency market determine the value of a currency, a government could set by government edict the exchange rate between their currency and another. A **fixed exchange rate** is where a government artificially determines the value of its currency in terms of another currency. Until 1971, the US Dollar was part of an international fixed exchange rate regime where each country's currency was pegged to the price of gold. The advantages of a fixed exchange rate include certainty, a reduction in transaction costs between trading partners, and the ability of a government to manipulate their currency to favor either importers or exporters.

Countries that engage in a lot of trade with each other may wish to provide a greater level of certainty to traders regarding the relative value of the countries' currencies. If a country has a long history of inflation, then a fixed exchange rate can work to insure international investors that their investment in a country will be protected from inflation by guaranteeing the exchange rate. Saudi Arabia sells a lot of oil to the US and fixes the value of its currency to the US Dollar. Countries like El Salvador and Panama, rather than peg their currency to the dollar, have adopted the US dollar itself as their national currency.

[5] 'Brazil's Meirelles: Fed's Latest move on G20 agenda' Thursday November 4, 2010. Reuters. http://www.reuters.com/article/2010/11/05/brazil-meirelles-idUSN0424672620101105

The downside of having a fixed exchange rate is that an artificial price of a currency is arbitrarily set by a government. This price, by definition, will vary from the true market price of the currency. Anytime a government sets prices, one of two outcomes will occur: a surplus or a shortage. Governments, then, are forced to take further actions to solve the surplus of shortage of currency in the international market. These actions may prove to be so painful to an economy that the costs imposed by them exceed the benefits of a fixed exchange rate. The following are two examples of countries that used to have fixed exchange rate with the US Dollar but no longer do.

In the early 1990's, the Mexican government supported a fixed exchange rate between the US Dollar and the Mexican Peso at four pesos per dollar. Extensive Mexican budget deficits and the resulting increase in the money supply to finance them caused the Mexican Peso to be overvalued relative to the US Dollar. The artificially high value of the Peso meant that more people wanted to trade their Pesos for US Dollars (which the market said were worth more) than wanted to trade Dollars for Pesos. The only way the Mexican government could support the artificially high value of their Peso was to intervene in the international money market by buying up Pesos with US Dollars.

Governments who wish to support a fixed exchange rate must hold onto **foreign reserves** in order to use them when they need to increase the value of their currency. A foreign reserve is foreign currency held by a government. As the Mexican government used up their US Dollar reserves to prop up the Mexican Peso, the Mexican government ran out of US Dollars. As they could not print more US Dollars, Mexico was forced to devalue the Peso. A currency **devaluation** occurs when a country officially lowers the value of its currency. While the Mexican government devalued their peso by 15%, it was still overvalued. As investors feared further currency devaluation, everyone holding Pesos became nervous about their use as a store of wealth. As people began to dump their Pesos on the international market, the market price of Pesos fell even further, making the Peso even more overvalued vs. the US Dollar.

Panic ensued as investors began pulling their wealth out of assets denominated in Mexican Pesos. The Mexican government asked the United States to intervene. The US used US Dollars to buy Mexican Pesos so as to prop up the value of the Peso. The Peso was allowed to float to ensure some stability to the Peso. This action where the US government loaned dollars to the Mexican government in 1994 was known as

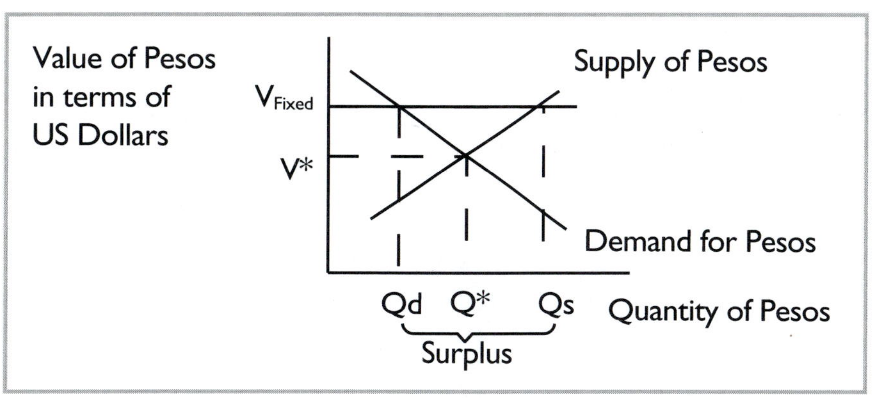

Figure 24.5 **PESO–DOLLAR EXCHANGE MARKET**

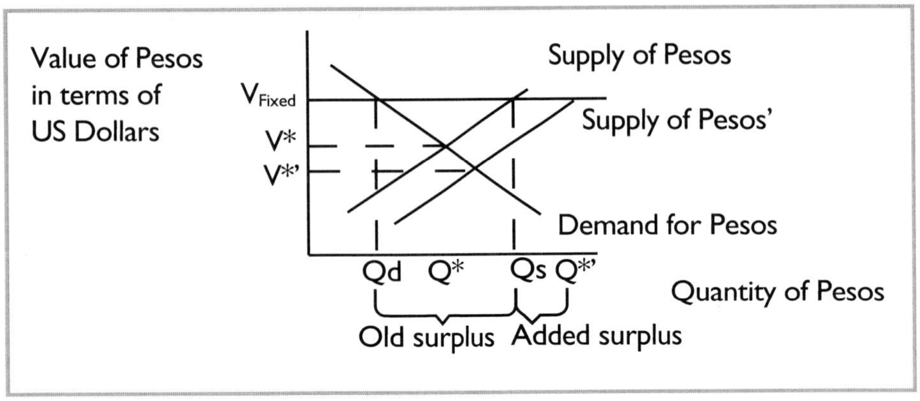

Figure 24.6 **PESO–DOLLAR EXCHANGE MARKET**

The Mexican Bailout. By preventing the Mexican economy from imploding, the bailout helped to stabilize the Mexican economy. Mexico was able to repay their loans to the US with interest ahead of schedule. Since then, the Mexican Peso has been allowed to float to prevent currency devaluation from causing further panic in the Mexican economy.

Between the mid 1990's and 2005, China had a fixed exchange rate of 8.28 Yuan per US Dollar. Over time, the Chinese currency became undervalued relative to the US Dollar, as more people wanted to buy the Yuan at that price than wanted to sell it. The Chinese government purposefully undervalued their currency in order to make their exports to the US look even cheaper. A country with an undervalued currency can either raise the official value of their currency (engage in **revaluation**) or keep it undervalued indefinitely.

A country can keep its currency undervalued by printing more currency and selling it on the world market to overcome the shortage of their currency. The downside is that expansion of the domestic money supply leads to inflation. Unlike an overvalued currency which must be devalued when a country runs out of foreign reserves, a country can keep a currency undervalued as long as it is willing to endure the ensuing domestic inflation. Yielding to pressure from Chinese citizens suffering from inflation, the Chinese government eventually somewhat abandoned their fixed exchange rate with the US Dollar. While the Chinese now claim that their currency floats with respect to the dollar, ample evidence exists to indicate that they still intervene in the currency markets to keep their currency from appreciating more strongly relative to the US dollar. While most countries have now abandoned fixed exchange rates with the US Dollar, countries like Saudi Arabia still actively maintain one.

The International Monetary Fund (IMF) is an international institution with 187 member countries (including the US) that was set up following World War II to help facilitate the fixed exchange rate regime of the day. Even as fixed exchange rate regimes have largely disappeared, the IMF still works to "foster global monetary cooperation, secure financial stability, facilitate international trade, promote high employment and sustainable economic growth, and reduce poverty around the world."[6]

[6] http://www.imf.org/external/about.htm

The IMF tries to serve these functions by monitoring the economic health of its members, while offering loans and technical assistance to countries in need. In this way the IMF was designed to be the lender of last resort for countries around the world. Loans from the IMF come with financial strings attached. Like any other creditor, they impose restrictions on debtor government finances to ensure that said countries are able to pay back their loans. The last section of this textbook examines how the use of domestic fiscal and monetary policy is complicated by the presence of the international sector.

Glossary

Arbitrage—is taking advantage of price differences for profit

Currency appreciation—when a currency can buy more of another currency (the currency becomes stronger)

Currency depreciation—when it can buy less of another currency (the currency becomes weaker)

Devaluation—a decrease in a government's official value of their currency

Exchange rate—the price of one currency in terms of another

Fixed exchange rate—a governmentally determined value of a currency in terms of another

Floating exchange rate—where the value of a currency relative to another is determined by the supply and demand of the two currencies in the international money market

Foreign reserve—a foreign currency held by a government

Purchasing power parity—is the concept that all goods should cost the same in every country in the long run

Revaluation—an increase in a government's official value of their currency

The International Monetary Fund (IMF)—an international organization intended to serve as a lender of last resort for national governments

Questions for Review

1. How does a floating exchange rate differ from a fixed exchange rate?
2. What are the pros and cons of a fixed exchange rate?
3. What causes the value of the dollar to change the most in the short run? Why?
4. What causes the value of the dollar to change the most in the medium run? Why?
5. What causes the value of the dollar to change the most in the long run? Why?
6. In what way is the IMF like a central bank for the world?
7. Why did the US dollar depreciate so much between 2010 and 2011?
8. If the current exchange rate is $1 = 100 Yen and the price of a Big Mac is $4 in the US and 300 Yen in Japan, what will happen to the value of the US Dollar vs. the Japanese Yen, over time? Why?
9. What happens to the value of a currency if fewer people around the globe want to buy goods and services produced within a country?
10. Who benefits from a strong dollar? Who benefits from a weak dollar? Why?

Chapter 25

Public Policy in a Global Economy

Domestic fiscal and monetary policies do not take place in a vacuum. This chapter explores the impact of the international sector and floating exchange rates on the use of fiscal and monetary policy. It also examines how foreign fiscal and monetary policy choices can influence the domestic economy. Three graphs that have been introduced earlier in this text: the AD/AS graph, the domestic money market, and the international money market, are used in this chapter to illustrate the interconnectedness of public policies. Fiscal policy, as presented in Chapter 15, is combined with monetary policy, as it was presented in Chapter 22, and the international economy, as presented in Chapter 24. Political barriers that interrupt the international economy are also discussed.

Fiscal Policy

Expansionary Fiscal Policy

Expansionary fiscal policy entails increasing government spending, reducing taxes, or a combination thereof. The purpose of any expansionary policy is to increase aggregate demand in the economy. Successful fiscal policy (ignoring its problems presented in Chapters 18 and 19) will increase aggregate demand (to AD' in Figure 25.1a) thereby causing more people to buy goods and services at higher prices. In order to buy more goods and services at higher prices, people will need more money. As a result, the domestic demand for money will increase. This increase in the demand for money causes interest rates to increase (from r0 to r1 in Figure 25.1b). As noted earlier in the text, an increase in interest rates will cause the international demand for the dollar to increase, as money saved in dollars now yields a higher rate of return. It will also cause fewer holders of dollars to want to dump their dollars on the international market. Combined, these factors cause the value of the dollar to increase (from vo to v1 in Figure 25.1c).

As the dollar becomes stronger, imports become cheaper and exports become harder to sell abroad. The stronger dollar yields a decrease in net exports and therefore also in aggregate demand. Aggregate demand falls (to AD" in Figure 25.1a) to account for the decrease in net exports put in place by expansionary fiscal policy. Thus, the expansionary power of fiscal policy is reduced by the international market. Note that an increase in the budget deficit used to finance fiscal expansion caused the trade deficit to increase. The trade and budget deficits are known as the **twin deficits** because larger budget deficits lead to larger trade deficits.

It is worth noting that the size of the shift in aggregate demand from AD' to AD" is dependent upon how engaged an economy is in the international sector. The more dependent a country is on trade, the larger this shift will be. That is, as an economy becomes more internationally oriented, fiscal policy's power weakens. In a world where the domestic economy is small relative to the world

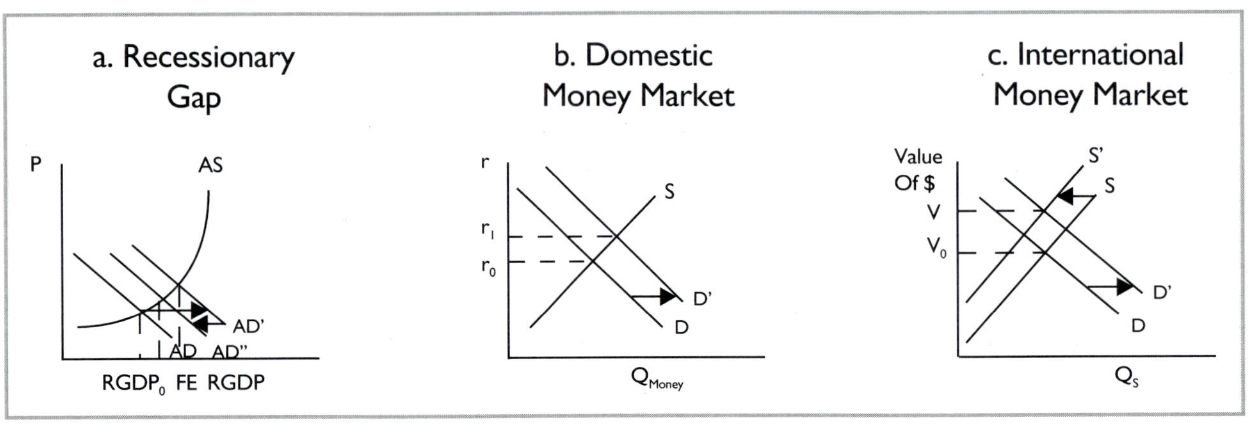

Figure 25.1 **FISCAL POLICY DURING A RECESSIONARY GAP**

economy and fully open to it, domestic stimulus will be dissipated throughout the world while the debt derived thereof will be solely born by the country engaging in fiscal policy. If the US government lowers taxes and US consumers respond by buying Chinese imports, then production in China gets stimulated at the cost of US government debt.

Also note that as aggregate demand moves from AD' to AD", this causes an additional change in the demand for money both domestically and abroad. In truth, the policy feedback mechanism of the economy is never ending. If fiscal policy makers are able to (and they are not) correctly estimate both the impact to the economy of the initial change in aggregate demand and the resulting international effects, then they could design fiscal policy such that AD" ended at full employment.

Contractionary Fiscal Policy

Contractionary fiscal policy entails decreasing government spending, increasing taxes, or a combination thereof in order to decrease aggregate demand in the economy. Successful fiscal policy will decrease aggregate demand (to AD' in Figure 25.2a) thereby causing fewer people to buy goods and services at lower prices. As people buy fewer goods and services at lower prices, people will need less money. Therefore, the domestic demand for money will decrease as seen in Figure 25.2b. This decrease in the demand for money causes interest rates to decrease (to r1). A decrease in interest rates will cause the international demand for the dollar to decrease as money saved in dollars now yields a lower rate of return. It will also cause more holders of dollars to want to dump their dollars on the international market. Combined, these factors cause the value of the dollar to decrease (to v1).

As the dollar becomes weaker, imports become more expensive and exports become easier to sell abroad. The weaker dollar yields an increase in net exports and therefore also in aggregate demand (to AD" in Figure 25.2a). Note that a decrease in the budget deficit causes the trade deficit to decrease. Once again, as an economy becomes more internationally oriented, the impact of fiscal policy weakens. In this way, fiscal policy today has become a far less powerful tool than it

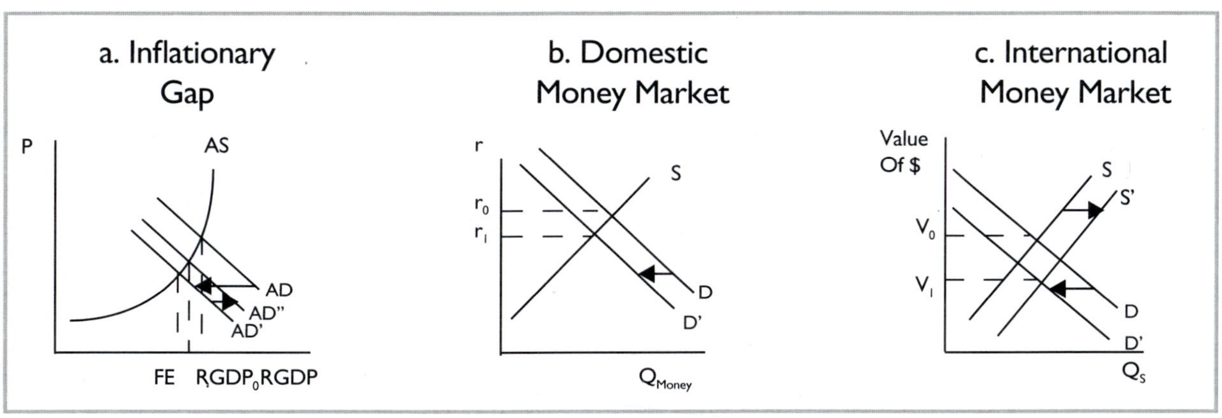

Figure 25.2 **FISCAL POLICY DURING AN INFLATIONARY GAP**

once was. In 1950, imports and exports made up less than 5% of the US economy. Today imports and exports make up more than a fifth of the US economy.

Fiscal Policy in Stagflation

In the event of stagflation, policy makers can fight either inflation or unemployment, but not both. If they choose to fight inflation, the use of contractionary fiscal policy is similar to that of the inflationary gap. If they choose to fight unemployment, the use of expansionary fiscal policy is similar to that of the recessionary gap. In this way, the above graphs can be applied to stagflation, with the reminder that any attempt to solve either inflation or unemployment during stagflation will result in making the other problem significantly worse. As such, fiscal policy makers may not wish to be seen as actively making one of these problems worse.

Monetary Policy

Expansionary Monetary Policy

Monetary policy begins in the domestic money market. Expansionary monetary policy often begins when the FOMC buys government bonds. This causes banks' excess reserves to increase. If they loan out these excess reserves, the money supply will increase, as shown in Figure 25.3b. The purpose of the expansionary money supply is to get businesses to engage in investment. Successful monetary policy (forgetting about the problems addressed in Chapter 23) would cause an increase in investment, and therefore, an increase in aggregate demand as well (from AD to AD' 25.3a). In order to buy more goods and services at higher prices, people will need more money. Therefore, the domestic demand for money will increase (from D to D' 25.3b). This increase in the demand for money will not be as large as was the increase in the supply of money caused by the central bank (from S to S'). As a result, interest rates, on net, fall from r0 to r2, as shown in Figure 25.3b. A decrease in interest rates will cause the international demand for the dollar to decrease (from D to D') as money saved in dollars now yields a lower rate of return. It will also cause more holders of dollars to want to dump their dollars on

Figure 25.3
MONETARY POLICY DURING A RECESSIONARY GAP

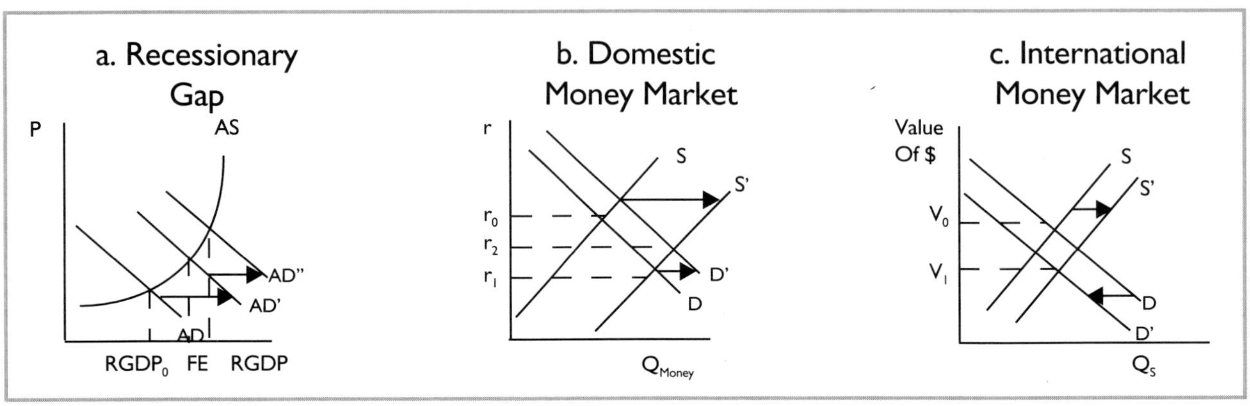

the international market (from S to S'). Combined, these factors cause the value of the dollar to decrease (from v0 to v1 in 25.3c).

As the dollar becomes weaker, imports become more expensive and exports become easier to sell abroad. The weaker dollar yields an increase in net exports and therefore also an increase in aggregate demand (to AD" in Figure 25.3a). As an economy becomes more internationally oriented, monetary policy becomes a stronger tool. In this way, monetary policy has become more powerful than it was at the end of WWII when the percentage of US GDP involved in the international economy was much less than is today. If monetary policy makers are able to (and they are not) correctly estimate both the impact to the economy of the initial change in aggregate demand and the resulting international effects, then they could design monetary policy such that AD" ended at full employment.

One side effect of expansionary monetary policy is a weakening of the dollar value. As the money supply grows, more dollars are required to exchange dollars for a foreign currency. Monetary policy makers expect to boost net exports by weakening their own currency. In 2010, Secretary of the Treasury Tim Geithner publicly denied that a purpose of quantitative easing was to boost net exports in response to accusations to the contrary from emerging markets.[1] The Treasury Secretary's claim made even less sense in the face of his boss, President Obama's, stated 2010 goal of doubling exports by 2015.[2]

Contractionary Monetary Policy

Contractionary monetary policy often begins when the FOMC sells government bonds. This causes banks' excess reserves to decrease. If, as a result, they loan out fewer reserves, the money supply will decrease, as shown in Figure 25.4b. The purpose of the contractionary money supply is to get businesses to engage in less investment. Successful monetary policy would cause a decrease in investment, and

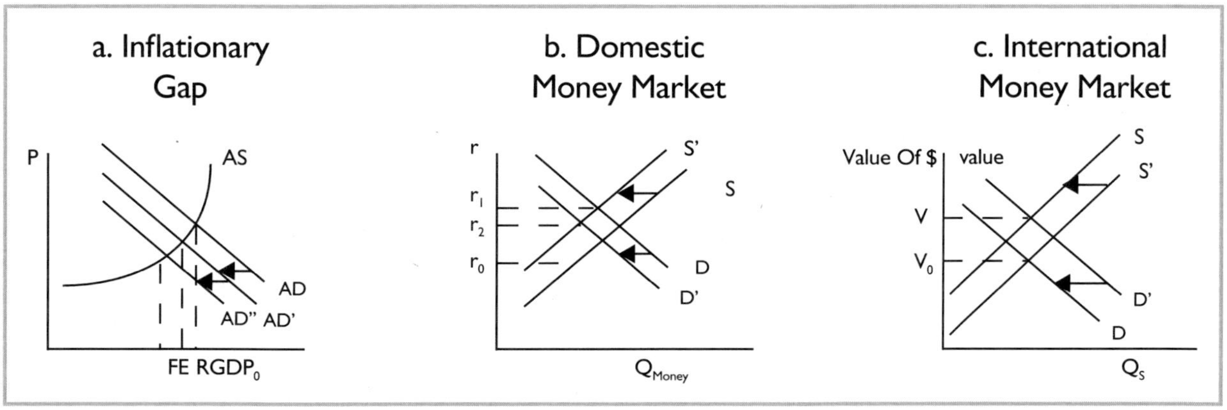

Figure 25.4 **MONETARY POLICY DURING AN INFLATIONARY GAP**

[1] Alan Beattie and Jonathan Wheatley. FT.com Geithner denies US bid to weaken dollar October 19, 2010. http://www.ft.com/intl/cms/s/0/1c62c304-db0c-11df-a870-00144feabdc0.html#axzz1X6tloQdx

[2] Helene Cooper. "Obama Sets Ambitious Export Goal" January 28, 2010. http://www.nytimes.com/2010/01/29/business/29trade.html

therefore decreases aggregate demand as well (25.4a). As consumers buy fewer goods and services at lower prices, they will need less money. Therefore, the domestic demand for money will decrease (from D to D' 25.4b). This decrease in the demand for money will not be as large as was the decrease in the supply of money caused by the central bank. As a result, interest rates, on net, increase from r_0 to r_2. An increase in interest rates will cause the international demand for the dollar to increase as money saved in dollars now yields a higher rate of return. It will also cause fewer holders of dollars to want to dump their dollars on the international market. Combined, these factors cause the value of the dollar to increase (from v0 to v 25.4c).

As the dollar becomes stronger, imports become cheaper and exports become harder to sell abroad. The stronger dollar yields a decrease in net exports and therefore also decreases aggregate demand. Aggregate demand falls to AD" in Figure 25.4a to account for the decrease in net exports put in place by expansionary fiscal policy. Once again, as an economy becomes more internationally oriented, the stronger a tool monetary policy will become. Any attempt to use monetary policy to solve stagflation runs into the same problems as noted above for fiscal policy. Nevertheless, the above graphs can be used to examine the effects of both expansionary and contractionary monetary policy during stagflation.

Self-Correction

If an economy is allowed to self-correct out of a recessionary gap, as stated in Chapter 14, then aggregate supply will shift rightward as real wages are bid down. Consumers will buy more goods and services at lower prices. The increase in consumption would lead to an increase in the demand for money while the lower prices would cause a decrease in the demand for money. The resulting demand for money would need to be an empirical matter. Theory is unable to state whether an increase or decrease in the demand for money would occur. Since the demand for money does not obviously change, interest rates, and therefore exchange rates, do not change either. Therefore, the presence of the international economy has little impact on an economy's ability to self-correct. Figure 25.5 represents both what happens as the economy self-corrects from a recessionary gap or from stagflation.

Figure 25.5
SELF-CORRECTION DURING A RECESSIONARY GAP/STAGFLATION

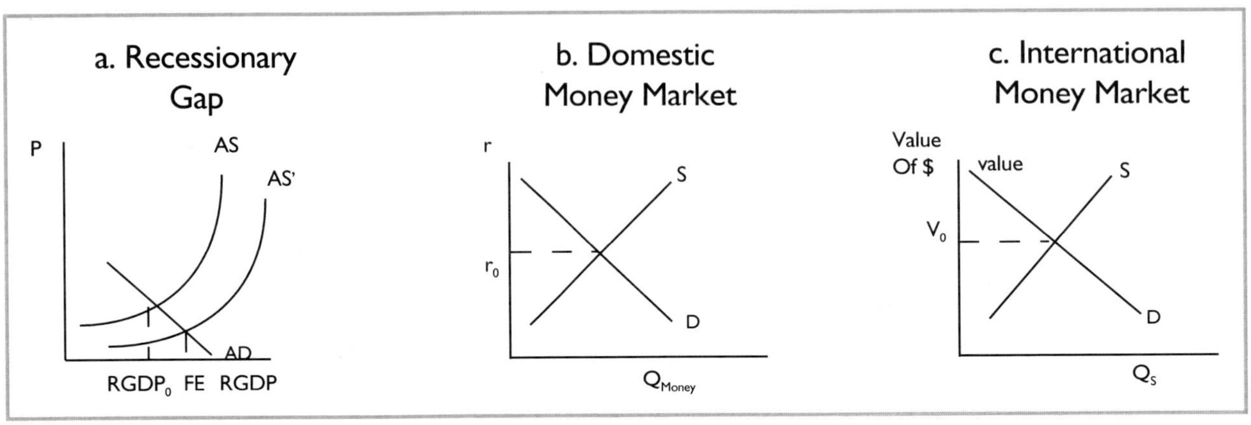

If an economy is allowed to self-correct out of an inflationary gap, then aggregate supply will shift leftward as real wages are bid up. Consumers will buy fewer goods and services at higher prices. The decreased consumption would cause a decrease in the demand for money, while the increased prices would cause an increase in the demand for money. The resulting demand for money would need to be an empirical matter. Theory is unable to state whether an increase or decrease in the demand for money would occur. Since the demand for money does not obviously change, interest rates, and therefore exchange rates, do not change either. Therefore, the presence of the international economy has little impact on an economy's ability to self-correct from an inflationary gap.

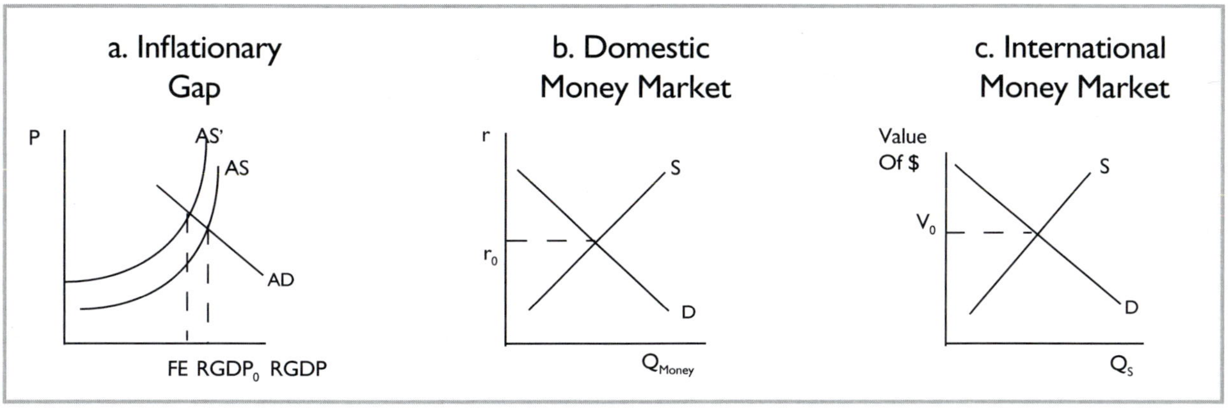

Figure 25.6 **SELF-CORRECTION DURING AN INFLATIONARY GAP**

Foreign Economies' Impact on the Domestic Economy

Economic expansions and contractions are contagious across borders. All things being equal, an increase in aggregate demand in Canada will cause the value of the Canadian Dollar to increase. This will decrease the relative value of the US Dollar, and US exports to Canada will be cheaper for Canadians to purchase. As a result, an increase in economic growth in Canada can translate into faster economic growth in the US. The world economy is not a zero sum game. If Canada's economy grows, it does not have to come at the expense of the US economy. As people become wealthier around the world, they will be able to afford more US made products. Their purchase of US made goods and services will cause economic growth in the US.

Similarly, if a foreign country goes into recession, their consumers will have less money to purchase US goods and services. The resulting increase in the value of the dollar relative to the foreign country's currency will cause US net exports to that country to decline. In this way, a stagnant European economy can slow down US economic growth as European consumers are less able and willing to buy US made products. This is why information regarding the health of other countries' economies causes movement in US stock and bond markets. It does not take an altruist to root for a growing world economy. People who want the US economy to grow should be pleased when foreign policy makers implement long term pro-growth strategies for their own countries, as this will translate into increased economic growth in the US. With China and the European Union representing two of the top three economies in the world, the health of their economies is critically important to US economic growth.

Barriers in the International Economy

In a world without government erected economic barriers, goods, services, capital, labor, and natural resources will flow to where they are most in demand. However, the world economy is not free to self-correct. Governments erect trade barriers to prevent the free flow of goods and services over national boundaries. They erect barriers to immigration to prevent people from crossing national borders to take advantage of job opportunities. They erect investment controls which stifle foreign ownership of domestic resources. Some governments also choose to fix the value of their currency to that of another country to prevent currency appreciation and depreciation.

The world does not engage in completely free trade. The US prevents free trade in numerous products such as sugar and timber. The US government also actively prevents progress in lowering worldwide trade barriers by continuing to subsidize American agriculture. Bilateral and multilateral trade deals with their many rates and exceptions often reroute trade rather than increase world trade. And, the US has slowed its approval of free trade deals with new trading partners. The existence of large and continuing trade barriers means that exports from a country may not increase as much as possible when their currency depreciates. Still, the reduction in trade barriers since WWII, largely led by the WTO, has increased the flow of goods and services across borders, thereby decreasing the power of fiscal policy while increasing the power of monetary policy.

Immigration is largely an economic phenomenon. When an economy is experiencing an inflationary gap a shortage of workers leads to inflation. If people are allowed to cross national borders freely in search of jobs, then countries whose economies are booming will benefit from an influx of workers. The influx of workers will help keep production costs lower, consumer prices down, and help people in need of money find work. When an economy enters recession, the flow of immigration into an economy slows down. Almost all countries have erected barriers to immigration, and these barriers serve to prevent the world economy from reaching equilibrium in the global labor market. The barriers also give people an economic incentive to illegally immigrate in search of jobs.

In this way, the global labor market did a much more efficient job of reaching global equilibrium in the 1800's, as people could freely immigrate to places like the US and Canada. The fact that Cubans are willing to risk their lives in rafts to move from Cuba to the US or the fact that immigrants are willing to pay human smugglers to sneak them into the US is an indication that US immigration barriers actively work to prevent the US labor market from reaching equilibrium. Still, the easing of immigration restrictions within the European Union and in countries such as Australia has increased the labor mobility of millions of laborers in Europe and Southeast Asia.

Capital is a more mobile resource. Capital can be employed anywhere in the world. Some governments, often for xenophobic reasons, prohibit the free inflow and outflow of capital into and out of their country. These restrictions prevent capital from being employed in its most efficient use. Investment controls prevent the global economy from reaching equilibrium in capital dispersement. Labor is made more productive when combined with capital and vice versa. Regulations that prevent labor and capital reaching equilibrium reduce both short term economic adjustment and long term world wealth creation.

Fixed exchange rates, in the short run, prevent the effects of domestic fiscal and monetary policy from being transferred to the global economy. By not allowing their currency to change in value, countries on fixed exchange rates increase the relative power of fiscal policy over monetary policy. In the long run, changes in fiscal and monetary policies that cause a fixed currency to be undervalued will lead to domestic inflation. An overvalued currency will lead to a reduction in foreign reserves until they run out, thereby forcing devaluation. Currently, many countries with fixed exchange rates only fix them relative to a single foreign currency. In so doing, their currencies still float against all other world currencies, but do so based upon the fiscal and monetary policies put in place by the government to which they peg their currency. Once again, the global move to floating exchange rates away from fixed exchange rates since the early 1970's has helped to strengthen monetary policy while weakening fiscal policy.

The relative strength of fiscal and monetary policy over time is but one more item of concern when determining the proper policy response to periods of unemployment, inflation, and stagflation. The following, and final, chapter of this text will summarize the arguments in favor of and against the use of fiscal and monetary policy to direct an economy back to full employment. It will also examine the relative merits of using fiscal or monetary rules rather than the discretion of policy makers to direct economic policy.

Glossary

Twin Deficits—the budget deficit and the trade deficit

Questions for Review

1. In a world with floating exchange rates and few trade barriers, expansionary fiscal policy will do what to the value of the dollar? To net exports?
2. In a world with floating exchange rates and few trade barriers, expansionary monetary policy will do what to the value of the dollar? To net exports?
3. In a world with floating exchange rates and few trade barriers, contractionary fiscal policy will do what to the value of the dollar? To net exports?
4. In a world with floating exchange rates and few trade barriers, contractionary monetary policy will do what to the value of the dollar? To net exports?
5. How are economic expansions and contractions contagious across borders?
6. What barriers exist to prohibit the international economy from reaching equilibrium? How have these barriers changed over time?
7. Should US citizens be concerned about the economic growth rate in China? Why or why not?

Chapter 26 Public Policy Debates

As nothing in life is ever free, there are advantages and disadvantages to using policy to smooth business cycles. This chapter summaries the pros and cons of using discretionary fiscal and monetary policy to smooth business cycles rather than adopting fiscal and monetary rules designed to let the economy self-correct. It also examines how the European Union was designed to consolidate fiscal, monetary, exchange rate, trade, and immigration policy decisions to an international body and discusses the pros and cons of such a move.

Fiscal Policy Rules vs. Discretion

The use of fiscal and monetary policy depends upon the ability and willingness of policymakers to use their discretion as they attempt to influence economic outcomes. In the US, Congress and the President collectively have a large amount of discretion over decisions regarding taxes and government spending. Given the bicameral nature of Congress, along with the checks and balances imposed by the executive and judicial branches, any one chamber of Congress does not have unlimited fiscal discretion. Fiscal policy is much easier to implement in countries where a single body of parliament is able to enact fiscal policies.

Even when Congress and the President agree on fiscal policy, the US Supreme Court could rule a fiscal policy to be unconstitutional, as it routinely did in the 1930's. In 1935, the US Supreme Court ruled that the National Recovery Administration overstepped constitutionally enumerated powers. In 1936, it also ruled that the Agricultural Adjustment Act was unconstitutional. President Obama's Affordable Care Act brought constitutional battles over the legality of the individual mandate to buy health insurance.

While a government can set tax rates on things like income, sales, and property, it does not mandate a specific tax/GDP ratio. People can change their behavior in response to changed tax incentives. Often, increases in tax rates are intended to raise more tax revenue than they actually yield as people change their behavior. Increasing marginal income tax rates to 90% might seem like it would yield more tax revenue for a government, but it likely will result in more people dropping out of the workforce or not accurately reporting their income to the government.

When an economy goes into recession, taxes derived from income naturally decrease, even without active fiscal policy. Likewise, during an inflationary gap, tax revenues increase without active fiscal policy. Policy makers who want to hold tax revenues constant are often forced to raise tax rates during a recession and lower them during an inflationary gap. Both actions tend to exacerbate the existing economic problems.

Keynes advocated that fiscal policy discretion be used to stimulate aggregate demand during a recession and depress aggregate demand during an inflationary gap. The former policy proved to be politically popular. The opposite was true of the latter. Many politicians' desires to get re-elected in the short run cause them to prefer polices that lower current unemployment. Liberal politicians like to campaign on the promise of more government programs designed to help this group or that. Conservative politicians like to campaign on decreasing their constituents' tax burdens.

In May of 2000, the economy was experiencing an inflationary gap. Federal Reserve Chairman Alan Greenspan made multiple speeches advocating contractionary fiscal policy. The two presidential candidates, George W. Bush and Al Gore, campaigned on lowering taxes and increasing government spending respectively. These were opposite of what Keynes' policies called for. Contractionary fiscal policy was not used and the Federal Reserve implemented contractionary monetary policy.

Between the early 1960's and the late 1990's the US Federal government ran over 30 years of consecutive budget deficits. Rather than use fiscal policy to smooth business cycles, it was used by politicians to reward current constituents at the expense of future taxpayers. Concern over the resulting national debt caused billionaire businessman Ross Perot to mount an independent campaign for President in 1992. In 1995, a balanced budget amendment passed the US House of Representatives but failed to reach a two-thirds majority in the US Senate by a single vote.

A **balanced budget amendment** is an example of a fiscal rule. **Fiscal rules** are laws that limit the use of discretion regarding levels of taxes and spending. A rule that forces tax revenue to equal government expenditures in every given year restricts the ability of the government to run budget deficits or budget surpluses. It effectively outlaws countercyclical fiscal policy. Changes in taxes can occur but only when accompanied by offsetting changes in government spending. The main advantage of such a rule is that it prohibits short sighted politicians from indebting future generations.

The main disadvantage of a balanced budget amendment is that it requires contractionary fiscal policy during recessionary gaps and expansionary fiscal policy during inflationary gaps. As tax revenues naturally fall during a recession while income assistance spending naturally increases, tax rates would either have to be increased or other government spending would have to be reduced. A strict balanced budget rule would impose tough political choices for politicians during times of national disasters, wars, or severe economic contractions.

Other possible fiscal rules include rules put in place regulating a maximum debt/GDP ratio, a maximum deficit/GDP ratio, a maximum government spending/GDP ratio or a maximum taxes/GDP ratio. A maximum debt/GDP rule allows budget surpluses, but limits the size of budget deficits. Germany passed a fiscal rule in 2009 that sets post 2016 budgets with a maximum budget deficit at .35% of GDP but forbids state governments from running any budget deficits. It does contain exceptions for natural disasters or severe economic crises. Since 2003, Switzerland has been forced by constitutional rule to never run a **structural budget deficit**. A structural budget deficit occurs when a government would be running a budget deficit even if their economy was operating a full employment (had no cyclical unemployment).

Monetary Policy Rules vs. Discretion

The Federal Reserve has a large amount of discretion in its use of monetary policy in the US. While the Chairman of the Federal Reserve is required to testify before Congress on a regular basis, Congress does not have control over discretionary monetary policy. To the extent that Congress can influence monetary policy it has to amend the Fed's charter or eliminate the Fed altogether. These actions do not lend to a daily micromanagement of monetary policy. Congress has given the Federal Reserve the broad direction to provide price stability and low unemployment. The latter mandate was only added in the late 1970's.

Monetary discretion allows an independent central bank to conduct monetary policy as it sees fit. This discretion allows central banks the freedom to conduct politically unpopular monetary policy. The chief benefit of monetary policy discretion is that it lets the monetary authority use its full range of tools to encourage investment during recessions and discourage investment during inflationary gaps and operate as a nonpolitical lender of last resort.

"Inflation is always and everywhere a monetary phenomenon."[1] The chief argument for the use of monetary rules is the tendency of central banks to cause unacceptably high rates of inflation over time by expanding the money supply faster than the economy grows. Like with fiscal policy, there is also an issue of competence. If the monetary authority lacks the knowledge of the "appropriate" money supply, then there is little reason to believe that their intervention in the money supply will aid long run growth.

Moneterists advocate a **monetary rule** that increases the money supply at a set rate each year to ensure long run price stability. If an economy is expected to grow at an average annualized rate of 3% per year, then the rule would be to increase the money supply by 3% each year. By informing every one of the expected change in the money supply, economic actors ought not be surprised by wild swings in inflation.

A major downside of monetarism is that monetary policy would be effectively outlawed. With monetarism, the monetary authority is not allowed to intervene to provide extra liquidity during a financial crisis. While prices may remain stable over time, inflation or deflation could increase or decrease in any given year, so short term price stability may be sacrificed for long term price stability. Because the central bank in a fractional reserve banking system cannot force banks to make new loans, a central bank may be limited in their ability to precisely hit their monetary rule target any given year. The missing of a stated target serves to increase uncertainty regarding monetary policy.

Other monetary rules such as **The Taylor Rule** provide guidance to monetary authorities on how to target interest rates based on current levels of inflation and unemployment. Such a rule seeks to direct monetary policy rather than eliminate it. The same can be said for inflation targeting, which could be an expressed goal serving to guide monetary policy.

While monetarists attempt to eliminate discretion for monetary policy, an end of fiat currency would accomplish the same task. Monetary policy discretion only arises when fiat money is introduced to the economic system. When the

---

[1] Milton Friedman 1970 The Counter Revolution in Monetary Theory.

world used gold as the chief medium of exchange, no country could merely print more gold during recessions. The problem with the gold standard is that the supply of gold is subject to the earth's endowment of gold relative to man's ability to find it and mine it. Changes in mining technology could lead to rapid changes in the money supply.

Advocates of fiscal and monetary rules share a distrust of and distaste for discretionary policy makers. They fear that policy makers are either incompetent or corrupt. They cite years of inflation and budget deficits as evidence that discretion is not used to provide price stability or smooth business cycles. Rather, they claim that fiscal policy is used to serve the short sighted goals of current politicians and that central bankers conduct monetary policy to aid their banking friends at large national and international banks. Both sets of policy makers, by using their discretion, make the claim that they have superior knowledge regarding what an economy needs more than do the individual economic actors whose independent knowledge is aggregated through the market process.

Pros and Cons of Fiscal and Monetary Policy during a Recessionary Gap

When an economy faces a recessionary gap unemployment is higher than normal while output and inflation are lower than normal. The three options for returning the economy back to full employment are fiscal policy, monetary policy, and letting the economy self-correct. Expansionary fiscal policy consists of increasing government spending or reducing taxes. Expansionary monetary policy entails the purchase of government bonds by the Federal Reserve to increase the money supply in an effort to boost investment. Self-correction relies on letting real wages fall, which lowers the cost of production and clears the surplus of labor in the economy. The first two policies seek to increase aggregate demand, while the latter increases aggregate supply. See Chapter 25 for the graphs that accompany the use of expansionary fiscal and monetary policy.

The purpose of listing the pros and cons of fiscal policy vs. monetary policy vs. self-correction is to allow readers to make a determination, based on their own values, which policy is most appropriate. While the choice of letting the economy self-correct can be achieved through fiscal or monetary policy rules, it is theoretically, if not practically, possible for policy makers to use their discretion to not intervene in the economy. Table 26.1 lists the pros and cons of using expansionary policy versus letting the economy self-correct.

One's policy preference depends on which economic goal or goals he or she determines are most important. For instance, if a person dislikes or is hurt by unexpected inflation, they would not advocate expansionary monetary policy; whereas if they are helped by unexpected inflation, they may wish to advocate it. Politicians may like to use expansionary fiscal policy because it allows them to use their power to pick economic winners and losers. The politically connected may advocate fiscal policy if they believe they will be the primary beneficiaries of said policy. Those who believe that policy makers are incompetent, corrupt, or acting primarily in other people's interests will tend to advocate letting the economy self-correct.

The choice of recessionary policy may depend on one's time horizon. Short sighted politicians often want to be seen as solving people's problems immediately even if by so doing they slow down long run economic growth. If increased long run economic growth is one's biggest concern then one would want to avoid increasing the national debt or transferring resources out of the private sector via expanded government spending. Temporary tax cuts that don't increase production slow down long term growth by increasing debt, while permanent reductions in marginal tax rates could incentivize more intensive resource utilization and promote long term growth. Those interested in long term economic growth would also want to avoid increasing short and long run inflation caused by implementing monetary policy. Pricing bubbles caused by inflation work to slow down long term economic growth by distorting the efficient use of resources. Letting the economy self-correct is the only policy that makes production cheaper. The chief downside is that it does so by reducing workers' real wages.

Table 26.1 PROS AND CONS OF FISCAL AND MONETARY POLICY DURING A RECESSIONARY GAP

Fiscal Policy

Pros	Cons
1. May serve as a quick boost to aggregate demand	1. Increases the national debt
2. May lowers unemployment	2. Increases interest rates which hurts long run economic growth
3. May Increase RGDP	3. Causes inflation
4. Elected politician get to exercise their ideology (which is a con if you don't like their ideology)	4. Congress and the President could screw up fiscal policy
5. Net importers are helped by a stronger dollar	5. Time lags could slow down impact on the economy
6. Net debtors may gain from unexpected inflation	6. Net exporters are hurt by a stronger dollar
7. Does not cause long run inflation	7. Net creditors may be hurt by unexpected inflation
8. The Fed cannot screw it up	8. Fiscal policy is becoming weaker over time
9. Lower taxes gives people the incentive to work more	9. Rational expectations predicts fiscal policy will be useless
	10. Greater government spending transfers resources away from the private sector which is bad for long run economic growth

Table 26.1 PROS AND CONS OF FISCAL AND MONETARY POLICY DURING A RECESSIONARY GAP *(continued)*

Monetary Policy	
Pros	**Cons**
1. Does not increase the national debt	1. Increases inflation
2. Lowers unemployment	2. Increases long run inflation
3. May increases RGDP	3. The Fed can screw up monetary policy
4. Monetary policy is becoming a stronger tool	4. Net importers are hurt by a weaker dollar
5. Net exporters are helped by a weaker dollar	5. Time lags could slow down impact on the economy
6. Net debtors may gain from unexpected inflation	6. Net creditors may be hurt by unexpected inflation
7. Congress and the President cannot screw it up	7. The Fed cannot force banks to lend money
8. Politicians cannot pick economic winners and losers	8. Rational expectations predicts monetary policy will be useless
9. Makes the national debt easier to pay off	

Self-Correction	
Pros	**Cons**
1. Decreases unemployment	1. The economy may take time to self-correct as real wages may be sticky downwards
2. Increases RGDP	2. Unexpected deflation hurts net debtors
3. Lowers inflation	3. Workers' real wages fall potentially increasing income inequality
4. Congress and the President cannot screw it up	
5. The Fed cannot screw it up	
6. Prevents long run inflation	
7. Does not increase the national debt	
8. Politicians cannot pick economic winners and losers	
9. Unexpected deflation helps net creditors	
10. There are no time lags	

Pros and Cons of Fiscal and Monetary Policy During an inflationary Gap

Policy makers again face tradeoffs when choosing their preferred policy in an inflationary gap. Contractionary fiscal policy involves increasing taxes or lowering government spending. Contractionary monetary policy involves decreasing the money supply to raise interest rates and lower investment. Table 26.2 lists the pros and cons of each policy.

Each policy will increase unemployment, since the economy is operating above full employment in an inflationary gap. The policy that most ardently attacks inflation is contractionary monetary policy. It lowers inflation in both the short run and the long run by decreasing the money supply whereas doing nothing will actually cause inflation to increase in the short run as real wages increase. By increasing interest rates, monetary policy slows down the economy as it stifles investment in new capital and consequently hurts long term economic growth.

Table 26.2 **PROS AND CONS OF FISCAL AND MONETARY POLICY DURING AN INFLATIONARY GAP**

Fiscal Policy	
Pros	**Cons**
1. Decreases inflation	1. May increase unemployment
2. Pays down the national debt	2. May decreases RGDP
3. Reduces interest rates, which is good for capital creation	3. Does not decrease long run inflation
4. The Fed cannot screw up	4. Congress and the President could screw up
5. Net exporters are helped by a weaker dollar	5. Time lags could slow down its impact
6. Net creditors may gain from unexpected deflation	6. Requires politically unpopular actions
7. Lower government spending transfers resources away from the public sector which is good for long run economic growth	7. Higher income taxes discourage work
	8. Fiscal policy is becoming a weaker tool
	9. Rational expectations predicts that fiscal policy will be useless
	10. Net debtors may lose from unexpected deflation
	11. Net importers are hurt by a weaker dollar

Table 26.2 **PROS AND CONS OF FISCAL AND MONETARY POLICY DURING AN INFLATIONARY GAP *(continued)***

Monetary Policy

Pros	Cons
1. Lowers inflation	1. May increases unemployment
2. Lowers long run inflation	2. May decrease RGDP
3. Is becoming a stronger tool over time	3. The Fed could screw up
4. Net importers are helped by a stronger dollar	4. Time lags could slow down its impact
5. Net creditors may be helped by unexpected deflation	5. Raises interest rates which slows capital accumulation
6. Congress and the President cannot screw it up	6. Doesn't pay down the national debt
7. Politicians cannot pick economic winners and losers	7. Net debtors may be hurt by unexpected deflation
8. Does not discourage work	8. Net exporters are hurt by a stronger dollar
	9. Rational expectations predicts that monetary policy will be useless
	10. Does not move resources from the government to the private sector
	11. Makes the national debt harder to pay off

Self-Correction

Pros	Cons
1. Congress and the President cannot screw up	1. Does not move resources from the government to the private sector
2. The Fed cannot screw up	2. Allows inflation to Increase in the short run
3. There are no time lags	3. Decreases RGDP
4. Politicians cannot pick economic winners and losers	4. Increases unemployment
5. Does not discourage work	5. Does not pay down the national debt
6. Workers' real wages increase, potentially decreasing Income inequality	6. Does not decrease long run inflation

Contractionary fiscal policy is the only policy that uses a booming economy to pay down the national debt. If the policy entails cutting government spending, then resources are directed from the government to the private sector enhancing long run economic growth. If fiscal policy entails increasing income tax rates, then current and future workers may choose to provide less labor thereby slowing long term economic growth. If income inequality is one's major concern, then letting the economy self-correct will allow real wages to increase, thereby reducing income inequality. This is why presidential candidate Ralph Nader advocated avoiding fiscal and monetary policy during the inflationary gap of 2000. Self-correction is again often preferred by people who believe that policy makers are either incompetent or corrupt.

The pros and cons of using fiscal or monetary policy during stagflation depend upon whether policy makers target inflation or unemployment as their primary concern. Focusing on inflation reduction will generate pros and cons similar to the inflationary gap. Focusing on unemployment reduction will generate pros and cons similar to the recessionary gap. The only policy that will simultaneously fight unemployment and inflation is letting the economy self-correct. As real wages fall, both unemployment and inflation decrease. The major problem with either monetary or fiscal policy during stagflation is that it attempts to make one problem better while making another existing problem much worse.

Advocating one policy or another may depend upon the current state of the economy. If an economy is suffering from hyper-inflation, then policies designed to bring inflation under control, such as contractionary monetary policy, may be the best catalyst for long run economic growth. If an economy is struggling with a large national debt burden, then contractionary fiscal policy may be the best catalyst for long run economic growth. Adopters of fiscal or monetary rules may wish to leave room for discretion in extreme cases. For instance, a country with a large national debt burden may find it unwise to legislate a strict balanced budget rule that outlaws budget surpluses.

The European Union

Fiscal and monetary rules work best when barriers to economic self-correction are removed. The European Union is an example of a supranational organization that employs fiscal and monetary rules on its member countries. Members of the European Monetary Union ceded monetary policy authority to the **European Central Bank** in Frankfort, Germany which issues **Euros**. Originally in order to join the EU, countries were supposed to keep budget deficits lower than 3% of their GDP. The EU augments policy rules with the free trade and free movement of people and capital between member states. In addition, it has common foreign trade, capital, immigration, and regulation policies that allow the markets in goods, services, and labor to self-correct more quickly.

Table 26.3 THE EUROPEAN UNION

"Original" 15 members of the EU		
Austria	Germany	Netherlands
Belgium	Greece	Portugal
Denmark*[2]	Ireland	Spain
Finland	Italy	Sweden*
France	Luxemburg	UK*

"New" members of the EU	
Czech Republic	Malta
Cyprus	Poland
Estonia	Slovakia
Hungary	Slovenia
Latvia	Bulgaria
Lithuania	Romania

Applicant countries to the EU:
Croatia, Iceland, Macedonia, Montenegro, and Turkey

If Spain experiences high levels of unemployment while German unemployment is low, then laborers are legally allowed to immigrate to Germany from Spain. French students can go to school in Italy. Greek chefs can go to work in Belgium. Polish plumbers can work in the UK. Just as the US has a common fiscal and monetary policy for all fifty states, the European Monetary Union has a common monetary policy for its member countries. In light of debt problems plaguing the economies of Greece, Italy, Ireland, Portugal, and Spain, the EU is considering tighter fiscal rules for its member countries.

A common currency requires a common monetary policy. The benefits of a single currency in the European Monetary Union include reducing the costs of engaging in trade and travel between countries. It also prevents member countries from inflating their own currencies. This gives European investors increased confidence in the long term benefit of the Euro as a store of value. The biggest drawback of monetary union is that countries lose sovereignty over their own monetary policy. If a country believes it is their best interest to have expansionary or contractionary monetary policy that differs from that of the European Central Bank, they are not allowed to engage in it. If the Spanish economy is struggling while the German economy is thriving, should monetary policy be made to keep inflation low in Germany or unemployment low in Spain?

[2] * indicates that the country did not adopt the Euro as its official currency.

Loss of monetary control prevents heavily indebted countries, such as Greece, from printing their way out of debt. Therefore a supranational currency serves as a check to keep countries from getting too far in debt. This imposed fiscal discipline helps long term economic growth. Still, if domestic leaders ignore fiscal discipline, as they did in Greece, they quickly discover that they have brought fiscal calamity to their country with no easy option for debt repayment. Lack of fiscal discipline among some Euro countries has placed stress on both the European and global economies. The Greek debt crisis has served as a good example of why monetary union needs to be accompanied by fiscal rules or concentration of fiscal discretion to the same level where monetary policy is controlled.

Should North America have a common currency? Canada and Mexico are two of the US' top five trading partners. Trade and travel would be easier between countries if they shared a common currency. International monetary union would also serve to help check the excessive buildup of North American governmental debt. Still, a monetary union will only work well if it is accompanied by fiscal discipline by its member countries and the free movement of goods, services, capital, and labor between member countries. Political opposition to the loss of US sovereignty over its fiscal or monetary policy has prevented much discussion of a North American monetary union, though the **Amero** was once proposed by Canadian economists as a possible North American currency. The US government does not mind a single currency as long as all monetary authority rests in the hands of the US. In other words, if Canada and Mexico wish to adopt the US Dollar as their official currency, the US will not stop them.

Conclusion

So why are some countries richer than others? Some countries pursue public policies that promote the use and expansion of available resources, encourage productivity enhancing human capital, technology, trade, and entrepreneurship, protect property rights, and prevent fiscal and monetary policy from causing large public debts and inflation. Other countries focus their attention on fiscal, monetary, and regulatory polices to micromanage today's output mix allowing rent-seekers to leverage their government connections for their personal benefit at the cost of long term economic growth via government favors or redistributive handouts. They fail to define and protect property rights or encourage the use and expansion of available resources, productivity enhancing human capital, technology, trade, and entrepreneurship.

Keynesian fiscal and monetary policy is inherently focused on the short run economic goals of controlling unemployment, inflation, and current economic growth. After all, Keynes noted that "In the long run, we are all dead." Use of these policies implies a level of knowledge and benevolence on the part of policy makers that is greater in theory than in practice. Obsessing with short run aggregate data can cause policy makers to sacrifice long term economic growth in an attempt to meet short run goals. F.A. Hayek claimed that, "The curious task of economics is to demonstrate to men how little they really know about what they imagine they can design."[3] The lack of effectiveness of fiscal and monetary stimulus following the 2007-2008 financial crisis casts serious doubts going forward as to the efficacy of short term discretionary fiscal and monetary policy.

In the end, US fiscal, monetary, trade, immigration, and regulatory policies will go a long way in explaining whether the US economy continues to grow in the future. Between 1973 and 2010 the US' share of global economy activity fell from 18.6% to 13.3%.[4] During this time the US moved from being a net creditor to a net debtor and from a net exporter to a net importer. The global economic hangover from excessive European and US debt guarantees that the future study of macroeconomics will be interesting.

---

[3] The Fatal Conceit.

[4] "Economic Focus" *The Economist* September 10, 2011.

Glossary

Amero—a proposed common currency for North America

Balanced budget amendment—an amendment to the US constitution that would outlaw budget deficits or budget surpluses

Euro—the common currency of the European Monetary Union

European Central Bank—based in Frankfort, Germany it conducts monetary policy for countries who have officially adopted the Euro

European Monetary Union (EMU)—an organization of countries which have adopted the Euro as their official currency

European Union (EU)—an organization of 27 European countries which set common immigration, trade, and regulatory policies

Fiscal rules—laws or constitutional rules that restrict the use of discretionary fiscal policy

Structural budget deficit—the amount by which a budget would be in deficit if the economy were operating at full employment

Monetarists—people who advocate that monetary policy be restricted to a proscribed annual increase in the money supply

Monetary rules—laws or constitutional rules that restrict the use of discretionary monetary policy

The Taylor Rule—a monetary rule that pegs target interest rates by examining unemployment, inflation, and economic growth

Questions for Review

1. What are the pros and cons of fiscal rules vs. fiscal discretion?
2. What, if any, fiscal rule would you propose? Why?
3. What are the pros and cons of monetary rules vs. monetary discretion?
4. What, if any, monetary rule would you propose? Why?
5. What are the pros and cons of using fiscal policy to solve a recessionary gap?
6. What are the pros and cons of using monetary policy to solve a recessionary gap?
7. What are the pros and cons of letting the economy self-correct to solve a recessionary gap?
8. Which option do you prefer during a recessionary gap? Why?
9. What are the pros and cons of using fiscal policy to solve an inflationary gap?
10. What are the pros and cons of using monetary policy to solve an inflationary gap?
11. What are the pros and cons of letting the economy self-correct to solve an inflationary gap?
12. Which option do you prefer during an inflationary gap? Why?
13. What have you learned during your study of macroeconomics to make you a more productive citizen? A wealthier citizen? A happier citizen?